MEINONG

The Arguments of
the Philosophers

EDITOR: TED HONDERICH
Reader in Philosophy, University College, London

The group of books of which this is one will include an essentially analytic and critical account of each of the considerable number of the great and the influential philosophers. Each book will provide an ordered exposition and an examination of the contentions and doctrines of the philosopher in question. The group of books taken together will comprise a contemporary assessment and history of the entire course of philosophical thought.

Already published in the series

Plato J. C. B. Gosling

Santayana: An Examination of his Philosophy Timothy L. S. Sprigge

MEINONG

Reinhardt Grossmann

*Department of Philosophy,
Indiana University*

Routledge & Kegan Paul
London and Boston

First published in 1974
by Routledge & Kegan Paul Ltd
Broadway House, 68–74 Carter Lane
London EC4V 5EL and
9 Park Street,
Boston, Mass. 02108, USA
Set in Monotype Garamond 11pt, 1pt leaded
and printed in Great Britain by
The Camelot Press Ltd, Southampton

ISBN 0 7100 7831 5
Library of Congress Catalog Card No. 73-92983

Contents

CONTENTS

vii

Preface

This book on Meinong is primarily concerned with his arguments for the positions for which he is famous among some philosophers and infamous among others. But philosophical contentions carry little weight when they are viewed in isolation. Matters are too complex, too difficult, to be settled in an isolated way. Every argument must be evaluated against a background which includes a philosopher's other arguments and some of his basic assumptions or – if you wish – prejudices. I therefore discuss Meinong's arguments within the context in which they appear, but with an eye on his earlier positions as well as on his later changes of mind. There are at least two further reasons for adopting this particular approach in Meinong's case.

Findlay, in his classic study of Meinong's philosophy, compares him with G. E. Moore.[1] Although this comparison is apt, there is one respect in which Meinong differs greatly from Moore. Meinong's philosophy develops over the years from a sparse ontology into an ample one. Every new idea is built upon an old one; new problems arise in the wake of earlier solutions; certain questions are raised time and again, but their answers are more and more refined. In short, there is a definite development, with a definite trend, definite stages, and a distinct final view.

I also wished to impress on the reader how misleading the prevalent view is that Meinong was a spendthrift metaphysician who delighted in multiplying entities continuously and needlessly. If one becomes aware of how Meinong's full ontology develops very slowly over many years from very austere beginnings, how he resists the temptation to solve a problem by admitting a new kind of entity, and how he gives in only after a whole series of arguments for the new kind of entity has accumulated, one will, hopefully, be less inclined in the

ix

future to think of Meinong as the 'supreme entity-multiplier in the history of philosophy'.[2]

I should like to thank my colleague Professor Paul Eisenberg. He read the manuscript and made many helpful suggestions.

Bloomington, Indiana   REINHARDT GROSSMANN

I

Individuals and Properties

The nominalism-realism issue has been discussed from so many different points of view and in so many different terminologies that it is impossible to explain Meinong's position, unless we agree first on several basic distinctions and a number of crucial terms.

In a nutshell, the issue is this: Are there attributes in the non-mental world? By an attribute I mean either a property or a relation. Colors or, more accurately, certain shades of colors, are examples of properties; so are shapes and pitches. Spatial and temporal relations are the most obvious examples of relations. A property, as understood here, may belong to many individual things. Two perceptual objects, for example, may have the same shade of color. Similarly, a (two-term) relation may hold between more than just one couple of entities. The spatial relation *to the left of*, for instance, may hold between two books as well as between two chairs. Notice that the issue of nominalism concerns the non-mental world. This qualification excludes as irrelevant a great number of considerations about the nature of mental concepts, their acquisition, and their function in perception and thought.

Nominalism is the view that there are no attributes; realism, the view that there are. Since we distinguished between properties and relations, there are several versions of realism. Full realism maintains that there are both properties and relations. Weak realism, on the other hand, asserts merely that either properties or relations exist, but not both. The first kind of weak realism, to give the flavor of this distinction, is in the Aristotelian tradition. According to this tradition, there are attributes in the form of modifications of substances; but there are no relations between substances. Relations, then, must be somehow reduced to properties. The second kind of weak realism tries to reconstruct properties out of relations among individuals.

What comes to mind are the various attempts to 'define' properties by abstraction through equivalence relations.

I believe that realism (full realism) rather than nominalism is true. There exist both properties and relations. Meinong, on the other hand, is a nominalist at the time of the *Hume Studies*.[1] However, he is a nominalist with a twist. The twist consists in the fact that he thinks of his ontology as containing properties and relations when it really does not. But there is no point in talking about his view in generalities; let us go *in medias res*.

1 *Complexes v. Individuals*

What kind of an entity is an ordinary perceptual object, say, a red billiard ball? There are, in the main, two traditional answers to this ontological question.[2] According to the Aristotelian tradition, a red ball is a *substance* or, as I shall also say, an *individual*. Such a substance *has* modifications, but it does not *consist* of them. According to what I shall call the Berkeleyan tradition, on the other hand, a red billiard ball is a bundle or *collection* of properties. Anticipating Meinong's later terminology, I shall from now on speak of *complexes* of properties. Such a complex consists quite literally of the properties that form it. The relation between a perceptual object and one of its properties is not that of *exemplification* – as in the Aristotelian tradition – but that of *whole to part*.

Meinong, like most of Brentano's students, embraces an ontology of complexes rather than substances.[3] And he seems to do so for the same reasons as Berkeley. 'The concretum,' he says at one point, 'comprises nothing but the complex of characteristics which by virtue of the nature of the object impress themselves all at once upon the senses. . . .'[4] In the second *Hume Study*, he identifies complexes of properties with substances. He claims that he need not discuss whether or not Locke and other critics of the notion of substance are right; 'for it is certain that substances offer nothing else for a comparison than their properties.'[5] In short, a so-called substance, in his view, is nothing but a complex of properties.

But even though it is clear that Meinong sides with Berkeley rather than Aristotle, it is not at all clear what reasons he has for this choice. And when we turn to his empiricist precursors, we do not find much in the way of argument either. Berkeley, for example, contends that we are not acquainted with substances (individual things), that we never actually perceive such entities.[6] But this contention is not at all obviously true. We do indeed see colors, shapes, and other properties – as Berkeley claims – but we also see the individual things which have these properties. What could be plainer than that when we see an apple, we do not just see certain colors and a certain shape, but see the apple?

Meinong, at any rate, rejects substances. An individual thing, as I said, is in his view a complex of properties. But this is not quite correct. A complex of properties really only forms a momentary *slice* of a perceptual object. It takes many of these slices to constitute the temporal individual. This makes the perceptual object a complex of slices and, hence, a complex of complexes. This type of analysis raises the well-known problem of how much an individual may change while remaining the same entity. Meinong recognizes this problem – and the further problem of how to distinguish between essential and inessential properties – but does not discuss it in the *Hume Studies*.[7] Let us therefore continue to talk as if individuals were really temporal slices of individuals, and correct this inaccuracy whenever it matters.

What is a complex (of properties)? The most immediate answer is that complexes are classes. Berkeley's use of the word 'collection' almost forces this interpretation upon us. If complexes are classes, then the red billiard ball is a certain class C of properties, and to say that this ball is red comes down to saying that the property red is a member of C. The so-called part-whole relation, which we distinguished earlier from exemplification, turns out to be class-membership.

But if this is Berkeley's view, we may ask, why would he believe that the class C is any less 'transcendental,' or any more 'knowable,' than the individual thing A? The class C is one entity, its members – the various properties of A – are quite different entities. Presumably, one knows the properties of A, that is, a certain shape, a certain color, etc. But we do not know, according to Locke's and Berkeley's line of argument, anything else. According to Locke, we may at least infer that there must be something else which supports these properties.[8] But if this inference is illegitimate, as Berkeley claims, why would it be acceptable to infer that there must be a class to which these properties belong? The class C is in the same boat with the individual A; and so, indeed, is any other type of entity whether we call it a 'bundle' of properties, a 'collection,' an 'aggregate,' a 'sum,' or what have you. If we can know nothing but properties, then we cannot know complexes, or collections, or aggregates, or sums. And if we cannot infer that there must be some support for these properties, then we cannot infer that there must be something of which these properties are elements or members.

But the view that complexes are classes is doomed at any rate; for not every such class of properties yields an individual. Since there are red billiard balls and green billiard balls, there exists the class consisting of the two properties *red* and *green*. Yet there exists no corresponding individual thing. The ontological reduction of individuals to classes of properties fails for this reason alone.

There is a second possibility. Perhaps a complex of properties is simply a *complex property*. This interpretation might also be thought to escape from the objection I just raised against Berkeley. If we hold that one can be acquainted only with properties, then we need not exclude complex properties from what we are acquainted with. The red ball would then be analyzed into the complex property: *red and round and heavy and* . . . But this interpretation does not stand up either. A property is always a property of something, while this complex property is not *of* anything. Thus even if we grant that there are complex properties, this kind of complex property does not exist.

This leaves us, as far as I can see, with only one viable interpretation.[9] Complexes cannot be classes of properties, we saw, because not every existing class of properties forms an individual. But what happens if we assume that there is a certain relation, call it *association*, such that a complex consists of all and only those properties which are associated with each other? The properties red and green do not form an individual thing, because they are not associated with each other. A complex, in short, is an entity composed of properties in the *relation of association*. This gambit, however, acknowledges a new fundamental *category*, namely the category of complex. Thus the empiricistic substitution of complexes for substances does not lead to a smaller ontology. Nor does it dissolve, as is obvious, the alleged mystery of how one can be acquainted with anything else but properties.

The most defensible view, then, which we can attribute to a philosopher in the Berkeleyan tradition is this. Perceptual objects are complex entities, consisting of properties in some sort of relation of association. In addition to the association relation, there exists also another relation which corresponds to exemplification. Let us call this relation from now on the relation of being *part of*. Red, for example, is *associated* with the property *round* in our example of the red ball; it is also *part of* the complex of properties that is identical with the ball. Thus we have two categories and two fundamental relations: the two categories of *property* and *complex*, and the two relations of *association* and of being *a part of*. Compare this with the 'Aristotelian alternative.' According to this ontological analysis of an ordinary perceptual object, we also have two categories, but we have only one relation. The two categories are those of *property* and *individual*; the single relation is *exemplification*.

2 *Instances v. Properties*

A perceptual object, in Meinong's view, is a complex of properties. A closer look, though, shows that Meinong's properties are not our properties. While it is of the very nature of our properties that they can belong to more than just one perceptual object, it is of the essence of Meinong's 'properties' that each one of them belongs to just one complex. Assume that there are two red billiard balls which have the very same (shade of) color. According to the realist's view, one and the same property is then exemplified by the two balls. On Meinong's view, however, each ball has its own color. If, for the sake of brevity, we call the respective shade of red simply 'red,' then it would not be accurate to say, according to Meinong's view, that both the ball A and also the ball B are red. Instead we should have to say, describing the ontological situation more perspicuously, that A is red_1, while B is red_2. Red_1 and red_2 are thus not properties in our sense of the term. I shall from now on call these entities *instances*.

Instances, it is clear, are particulars rather than universals. Thus Meinong has to face the problem of why, if each ball has its own redness, both balls are nevertheless red. Put differently, what is there in or about instances that makes them belong to different groups, that makes some of them instances of red, for example; others, instances of blue; still others, instances of roundness, etc.? Traditionally, there are two main answers to this question. Firstly, some philosophers hold that, in addition to instances, there are also properties of which the instances are instances.[10] In addition to red_1 and red_2, for example, there also exists the property red. The two billiard balls then contain numerically different instances of the same color. Secondly, other philosophers hold that there exists a relation of similarity (equality) between instances. Red_1 and red_2 are instances of the same color, as one usually says, because they stand in this similarity relation to each other. $Blue_5$, on the other hand, is not similar to red_1 or red_2 and, hence, is not an instance of red. Meinong opts for this second view. Yet he makes a crucial mistake. It is obvious that the second answer only works if the similarity relation is itself a genuine relation rather than an instance. Otherwise, we can ask what there is in or about two or more instances of the similarity relation that makes them all instances of this particular relation. Meinong does not realize this further step in the dialectic. He thinks of the similarity relation itself as an instance. This is his mistake and this is why I called him a nominalist. We shall return to this point in the next chapter when we discuss Meinong's analysis of relations.

No doubt, some philosophers defend the existence of instances because of a nominalistic bias. By turning properties into particular entities, they hope to avoid having to acknowledge the existence of universals. But this is not always the case. Husserl, for example, accepts both instances as well as properties. Thus we can separate the two issues, that concerning the existence of instances from the realism-nominalism controversy. Why does Meinong think that there are instances?

Meinong offers only one argument for this ontological position. Here it is:

> Suppose we have two congruent triangles, A and B. Now is the triangularity of A identical with the triangularity of B? That is, is the triangularity of A the triangularity of B? No one will deny that A can persist even if B is destroyed; just as no one will challenge that the attribute adheres to its object, persists with it, but also vanishes with it. Now, if B no longer exists, then the triangularity of B does not exist either, while A and the triangularity of A continues to exist undisturbed. But now, according to Mill, the triangularity of A is the triangularity of B. Hence, the very same triangularity both exists and does not exist which no one will be inclined to consider possible.

The crucial assertion in this argument is that an attribute adheres to an object in such a fashion that it vanishes when the object vanishes. And the crucial notion is that of adherence. Now, if properties were parts of individuals, then it would indeed be plausible to say that the properties vanish when the individuals do. For example, assume a line drawn in the middle of a triangle so that we can speak of its left side and its right side. If we erase the triangle, we destroy its (spatial) parts, its left as well as its right sides. On the other hand, if we think of properties as being exemplified by individuals, then it does not follow at all that the destruction of the individual leads to the destruction of its properties. The property of being a triangle, for example, is exemplified by the triangle A. If A is destroyed, then A no longer stands in the exemplification relation to this property, but the property itself is not at all affected by the destruction of A.

Meinong's argument appears to be sound only if we think of properties as parts of individuals.[12] What is really required, to be succinct, is the assumption that a property is an *individual* part of an individual thing; for if several individual things could share the very same part, then such a part would not be destroyed by the destruction of just one of the individual things of which it is a part. We see now how Meinong's argument begs the question. To say that the triangularity of A may persist while the triangularity of B is destroyed is to imply that we are dealing with instances rather than properties. But whether

6

we are dealing with instances rather than properties is precisely the question under discussion.

When Meinong's students in 1913 prepared a collection of his earlier papers, they added a large number of instructive footnotes to the original texts. One such footnote, prepared by Auguste Fischer, but likely to reflect Meinong's own later view, occurs at this place in the first of the *Hume Studies*. Here it is argued that the entity *triangularity of A* is different from the entity *triangularity of B*, because it has the property of *being the triangularity of A*, even though the entity *triangularity* or the property *triangular* is identical in both.[13]

If I understand this argument correctly, it claims that the triangularity of *A* cannot be identical with the triangularity of *B*, because the former has at least one property which the latter does not have. This is the property of being the triangularity of *A*. Thus while the triangularity of *A* has the property of being the triangularity of *A*, the triangularity of *B* does not, that is, it is not the triangularity of *A*.[14]

In order to see that this argument is not sound, one merely has to realize that it is of the same form as the following argument: I notice the son of John; here 'the son of John' must stand for an entity that cannot also be the son of Mary; for otherwise something other than John could have John's son; but this is in fact false. It may be replied that the relation between a property and its bearer is not like the relation between a father and his son. But this is, of course, part of the dispute. The opponent of instances claims that the two relations are at least alike in this one respect, namely, that just as a son is the son of more than one person so a property is the property of several things. When we describe a property in terms of some one individual by which it is exemplified, that description is not in the least meant to suggest that the property cannot also be exemplified by other individuals. The case is quite clear when we substitute for 'the triangularity of *A*' the phrase 'the shape of *A*.' The triangle *B* could quite obviously have the same shape as the triangle *A*. What may mislead the proponent of instances in cases like this one is the fact that we sometimes use expressions like 'the triangularity of *A*' in order to describe a kind of triangular shape, say, the shape of an equilateral triangle. If the triangle *B* is not equilateral, one could perhaps say that it does not have the same triangularity as the triangle *A*, but another triangularity. But this does not imply, of course, that each one has its own triangularity as required by the view that there are instances. But be that as it may, the argument under study is obviously not sound.

There is, in the same vein, Brentano's argument against properties.[15] He claims that the notion of property involves a contradiction. To hold that there are properties, Brentano argues, is to hold that two entities can agree in every respect. For example, to say that two

7

triangles have the same property of triangularity is to say that there are two entities, the triangularity of the triangle A and the triangularity of the triangle B, but that these two entities are nevertheless identical. This is the alleged contradiction. Brentano simply assumes that there must be two entities, two instances, when the two triangles share the same property. But this is, of course, what the opponent of instances would deny. Quite to the contrary, he would insist that only one property is involved, and that this property is exemplified by A as well as by B. Brentano, no doubt, would object that one and the same entity cannot be at two different places at once. The property of being a triangle, he would insist, cannot be at two places at once, namely, over here where the triangle A is and also over there where the triangle B is. His argument thus rests ultimately on the assumption that every entity must be localized in space and time. But this assumption is denied by the proponent of properties. According to his view, individual things are indeed localized in space and/or time, but properties are not so localized.

But is it not obvious that the property of being a triangle, if there is such a thing, would have to be localized? Would it not have to exist over here, where A is, and also over there, where B is? Can we not plainly see the 'property' of being a triangle over here as well as over there? The proponent of properties replies that what we see over here is the individual thing A which exemplifies the property of being a triangle, and what we see over there is the individual thing B which exemplifies the same property. What we see is not the same property in two different places, but – accurately speaking – the same property as exemplified by different individuals in two different places.[16]

I said earlier that all of Brentano's students believed in instances. None of them, however, defended instances as persistently and brilliantly as G. F. Stout. In four articles, spanning a period of almost twenty years, Stout presents a series of arguments for instances.[17] Let us consider one of these arguments, an argument which will lead us directly to Meinong's view of individuation.

Stout starts with the assumption that we may perceive two perceptual objects as distinct, even though we do not perceive any difference in their respective 'properties' (their shapes, sizes, colors, etc.). He assumes, secondly, that a perceptual object is a complex of 'properties.' Hence, if one perceives two perceptual objects as distinct, one perceives two complexes as different. But complexes can differ only in their parts. Hence we must in this case perceive a difference in at least one part between the two perceptual objects. We must perceive that object A contains at least one part which object B does not contain, or conversely. Now, if the parts of A and B were really properties, then we could not perceive the two objects as distinct. Therefore, the 'properties' of the two objects must really be particular. They must be instances rather than properties.[18]

Stout's argument centers around the problem of individuation. He acknowledges that there is a problem by admitting that two objects may be perceived as different, while all their 'properties' are perceived to be the same. There is a hidden assumption, namely, that a perceived difference between perceptual objects must rest on a perceived difference between their parts, if I may put it so. Since a perceptual object is assumed to be a complex of 'properties,' this means that one could not perceive two such complexes to be different without perceiving a difference in at least one of their 'properties.' Stout now maintains that if the 'properties' were properties, then one could not possibly perceive such a difference. And he concludes that the 'properties' must be instances.

This argument contains a curious tension. On the one hand, Stout starts with the assumption that the 'properties' are perceptually indistinguishable; on the other hand, he also comes to the conclusion that they must be perceptually distinguishable. One could object that the first assumption contradicts his conclusion. Assuming that he has reasoned correctly, another premise in his argument must be false. It is not hard to put one's finger on this premise. Stout's argument, by assuming that perceptual objects are complexes of 'properties,' already contains a rejection of individual things. If we insist that the two objects are two individuals which *have* properties, but do not *contain* these properties as parts, then we can accept the first assumption and yet avoid Stout's conclusion; for even though all the properties are perceived to be the same, it is also true, by Stout's own admission, that the two perceptual objects are perceived to be different. These perceptual objects are nothing but the individuals of the proponent of properties. This proponent insists that we perceive two individuals as different and their properties as the same. And that is just as it should be.

We have so far looked at four arguments for the existence of instances and found every one of them wanting. But if these arguments are faulty and, moreover, quite obviously so, there is the suspicion that the attraction of an ontology of instances does not rest on a particular argument or even a whole series of such arguments, but on certain very fundamental metaphysical dogmas. I think that there are indeed two such dogmas which demand or, at least, reinforce a belief in instances. One of these is connected with the Berkeleyan approach to perceptual objects. If perceptual objects are complexes of 'properties,' if they literally contain such 'properties' as parts, then it is plausible to assume that these 'properties' are just as particular as the perceptual objects themselves.

The second dogma is even more fundamental. I shall give it a name, too, and speak of a Kantian theme and a Kantian dogma. According to the theme, presentations (*Vorstellungen*) are divided into intuitions (*Anschauungen*) and concepts (*Begriffe*). Intuition, and this is one crucial idea, is the window onto the sensory world. Through intuition and intuition alone are we acquainted with sensible entities. If we are acquainted with other entities at all, then we are acquainted with them through mental acts other than intuitions. And if there are other kinds of mental acts, then they must acquaint us with entities which are not sensible. But now let us ask whether, according to the Kantian theme, colors, say, are sensible. The answer is that they could not possibly be sensible entities; for the second crucial idea of the Kantian theme is that all the objects of intuition are particular. According to this theme, the sensible is identified with the particular. Nothing can be both sensible and non-particular. Properties, therefore, cannot be sensible. Colors, it follows, cannot be sensible. But if not even colors turn out to be sensible, what entities could possibly be sensible? Something must surely be wrong with a view that forces us to deny that colors are sensible entities.

That intuition is the only way of being acquainted with what is sensible may pass for the moment. Not so, however, the assertion that all objects of intuition are particular. How could one possibly make this assertion in view of the fact that we are acquainted with colors through the senses and that colors are not particular? The assertion follows from the Kantian dogma that space and time are the forms of intuition. This means that all objects of intuition are localized in space and/or time. What is so localized is particular. Thus it follows that the objects of intuition must be particular, since they are always localized in space and/or time.

What is a philosopher to do, who, on the one hand, accepts the Kantian dogma of localization and, on the other, cannot shake off his conviction that colors are sensible objects? Well, he could invent color instances. The color instance, blue$_5$, for example, is particular; hence it can be an object of intuition. Yet it is not a mere 'bare' particular; it has something to do with the color blue (with a certain shade of blue), and hence helps to explain our conviction that colors are known through the senses. In this fashion, the Kantian dogma leads to the invention of the new ontological category of instances. Instances thus owe their existence, at least in part, to an irresolvable tension between the Kantian dogma of localization and the common-sense belief that such properties as colors are sensible entities. With a rejection of this dogma, there disappears much of the ontological attraction of instances.[19]

The lesson for the proponent of properties is clear. The dogma of localization is false. Space and time are not forms of sensibility or perception. Sensible entities do not have to be localized in space and/or time. They do not have to be particular. Properties, colors for example, can be perceived. Nor do we have to stop at properties, of course. If there are entities other than individuals and properties, there exists the possibility that we can perceive these entities as well.

3 *Places and Moments*

We noted a moment ago that Stout solves the problem of individuation in terms of instances. Meinong solves it by means of places and moments. The slice of a perceptual object which we have called a complex of instances contains, according to him, a place and a moment. Furthermore, no two such slices contain the same place. [20] But if there are instances, then the problem of individuation for complexes is solved. Any two complexes are distinguished by virtue of the fact that they have different parts. Thus Meinong does not have to embrace places and moments in order to solve the problem of individuation. Yet he does. Did he have other reasons for accepting them?

Places and moments may, of course, belong to that part of the furniture of the world which is so obviously presented to us in perception that one simply cannot help but admit its existence. But this is quite clearly not the case. A great many philosophers – I am one of them – hold that plain observation shows that there are no places and moments. Be that as it may, it is a fact that places and moments are not as obvious as chairs and tables. Nor does Meinong really insist that they are.

It is very likely that Meinong did not fully understand the role of instances for the problem of individuation, and that he therefore accepted places and moments as individuators. [21] He did not clearly see that two complexes are automatically individuated through the instances which they contain, since no two complexes ever share an instance. There is a revealing passage in one of his later articles which sheds some light on his earlier confusion. [22] Meinong there confesses that in earlier publications he had the wrong notion of what it means to be an individual (substance). The nature of an individual, he used to think, consists in its *independence* from other things. For example, a certain color when combined with a certain shape and certain tactile and other qualities may constitute an independent perceptual object, say, an apple. Complexes of this sort which can exist by themselves used to be his paradigms of individuals. On the other hand, a certain instance of color, since it cannot exist by itself, was thought of by him as universal. But now Meinong has realized that independence is not essential to thinghood. The difference between a property and an individual is already contained in the difference between *green*, on the one hand, and an instance of green, on the other.

What is evident from these remarks is that Meinong's earlier distinction between properties and individuals was based on the distinction between dependent and independent parts of complexes.[23] Thus, an instance of red, since it cannot exist by itself but only in connection with an instance of a certain shape as well as other instances, is conceived of as somehow being universal, that is, as a property, while an independent complex of such instances serves as the paradigm of an individual. Meinong does not realize in the *Hume Studies* that instances are individuals rather than properties, since he bases his distinction between properties and individuals on the dependence-independence dichotomy rather than on the distinction between entities that can and entities that cannot be parts of more than one complex. But if he thus thinks of instances as properties, it is easy to understand why he should also believe that complexes of instances have to be individuated by places and moments.

There is a second important reason why Meinong accepts places and moments, a reason which has nothing to do with individuation. Meinong, as we shall see in great detail in the next chapter, holds that every relation is somehow 'created' from its terms. Moreover, he holds that the terms determine the nature of the relation. Consider, for example, spatial relations. According to the view just sketched, they must have spatial terms. But what else but places could these spatial terms be? And similar considerations hold also for temporal relations. Thus Meinong's theory of relations forces him to embrace an ontology of places and moments.

Three last remarks about these special entities. Firstly, note that places and moments are very peculiar parts of complexes. They cannot really be instances among instances; for several instances of, say, midnight blue are all instances of the same color, while several places or moments are not instances of anything. There is, in the case of places and moments, neither a unifying universal nor a similarity relation that collects the places or moments into instances of the same sort. In brief, places and moments are, in all but name, individuals of the customary kind. If we take this fact into consideration, then we can describe Meinong's ontology at this point in the following way. He accepts, whether he knows it or not, at least three main categories: (1) complexes, (2) instances of properties and relations, and (3) places and moments.

Secondly, it is clear that a moving perceptual object contains successively different places. It consists, therefore, of a great number of individuated complexes. These complexes are the 'slices' we mentioned earlier. The unity of a perceptual object must be explained, on

Meinong's account, quite differently from the way in which the traditional substance philosopher explicates it. While the latter may hold that one and the same entity, a certain substance (individual), occupies successively different places, Meinong must hold that a number of individuated complexes which are spatially and temporally contiguous constitute a perceptual object.

Thirdly, places and moments do not solve the problem of individuation for mental individuals; for such things are not in space and can severally exist simultaneously. Meinong is aware of this problem, but his remarks are rather obscure.[24]

4 *Abstraction*

The nominalism-realism controversy centers in modern philosophy around the problem of abstraction. Berkeley, we recall, does not deny absolutely that there are general ideas, but only that there are abstract general ideas.[25] The problem of abstraction looms so large because it is usually taken for granted that nominalism is the correct view, and it only remains to answer the questions of how and why we nevertheless use general terms.

Meinong, in his discussion of Berkeley's view, points out that Berkeley comes very close to admitting the possibility of a kind of abstraction which would completely satisfy the conceptualist and, we may add, the realist. A perceptual object, according to Meinong, consists of dependent (inseparable) as well as independent (separable) parts. For example, the color of an object is a dependent part of it; a (spatial) piece, on the other hand, is an independent part of the object. Now Berkeley concedes that we can form ideas of independent parts of perceptual objects. In this sense, we can abstract from the rest of the perceptual object and concentrate on just one spatial part of it. But this is not the interesting case of abstraction. Can we also pay attention to a dependent part of a perceptual object, abstracting from the rest of the object? Meinong maintains that there can be no doubt that one can also abstract in this interesting sense of the term. When we abstract in this sense, we merely single out in attention a certain (dependent) part or complex of parts of a perceptual object. That this kind of mental act is possible, Meinong holds, plain experience teaches us. And Meinong points out that Berkeley concedes that even this kind of abstraction is possible in the famous passage in which Berkeley maintains that a man may consider a figure merely as a triangle without paying attention to the particular properties of the angles or relations of the sides.[26]

Abstraction, in Meinong's view, consists thus in a mental act by means of which we pay attention to a part of a complex, neglecting

13

the rest of it. [27] Thus we may abstract from all other features of a billiard ball and merely consider its color. In this fashion, we can form an abstract idea of a certain color. Consider now this particular instance of, say, a certain shade of red. Does this idea deserve to be called *general*? Obviously not, even though we shall grant that it is an abstract idea, since it is formed by a mental act of abstraction. This idea is an idea of an instance and, hence, of something particular rather than general. The nominalist must explain, by the rules of the dialectic, how we form general ideas, unless, of course, he rejects such ideas altogether, as Berkeley sometimes seems to do. Meinong's insistence that there are acts of abstraction, we see, does not by itself solve the problem of how we come by our general ideas. Yet he believes that he has defended not only abstract ideas but general abstract ideas as well. He thinks that by means of abstraction, as he explicates it, we can have ideas of general rather than particular entities. This mistake rests again on his confusion between dependence and universality. He believes that the abstracted idea of a particular instance of red is a general idea *because the instance itself is no longer particular*; and it is no longer *particular because it is no longer viewed as being connected with a place and moment*. Husserl describes Meinong's view most succinctly in the following words: [28]

Abstraction as exclusive concern eo ipso *produces generalization.*
The abstracted attribute is *de facto* an element in the appearance
of the individual complex of attributes that we call the phenomenal
object. But the 'same' attribute, i.e. one fully agreeing with it
in content, can occur in countless such complexes. What distinguishes the repetitions of this same attribute from case to case,
is uniquely and solely their individualizing association. Abstraction,
therefore, as exclusive concern, causes the distinction, the
individualization, of what is abstracted to vanish.

Husserl, then goes on to criticize this view. [29] He points out, first, that the abstracted attribute, since it is conceived of as a literal part of the complex, cannot really be the same in different complexes. In other words, he points out that the abstracted attribute must really be an instance. In this connection, he gives his own arguments for the existence of instances. He argues, secondly, that if we are really presented with a property by paying attention to a particular instance of a complex, then we can no longer explain how we can be presented with an instance as an instance rather than a property. What happens, he asks, if we expressly refer, not to the property, but to the instance? Husserl thus argues: (1) that the parts of a complex must be instances rather than properties; (2) that by abstraction we can only pay attention to an instance, not a property; and (3) that even if by paying attention to an instance we could be presented with a property, we would now have the problem of how we are presented with instances as instances.

Meinong is caught between the horns of the following dilemma. Either the parts of complexes are really instances or they are properties. If they are instances, as he seems to argue at certain times, then his theory of abstraction will not yield general ideas. If they are properties, then the theory of abstraction works, but now certain of his arguments, those dealing with the existential dependence of the parts on the complex, will no longer be sound. What leads to this dilemma, as we have said before, is the confusion of the dependent-independent with the universal-particular distinction.

There is a way out of this dilemma, and Meinong will eventually take it. A part of an existing complex cannot be changed from an instance into a property by the mental process of abstraction. This much is certain. Rather, after abstraction has taken place, a 'new' object must be before the mind, namely, a complex which consists of properties rather than instances and which does not contain a place and a moment. Thus we must distinguish between two kinds of complexes, complexes which have instances (and places and moments) as parts and complexes which have properties as parts. This, as we shall see, is Meinong's later view.

There is another problem with Meinong's view concerning abstraction. He discusses this problem in a paper published twenty-three years after the first of the *Hume Studies*.[30] Consider again a specific shade of red. How do we get from this shade, and other shades of other colors, to the 'property' color? By means of abstraction, we could be said to pay attention to a certain part of this shade, a part which it presumably shares with other shades of other colors; and it is this part which is the 'property' *color*. There is, of course, first of all the problem of whether this part is an instance or a property. But let us waive this question and assume, for the sake of the argument, that the part under discussion is indeed a property and, hence, a common part of many shades of many colors. The problem that arises for Meinong's theory of abstraction is that, in order to contain a common part *color*, shades of colors must be complex entities, while – phenomenologically speaking – nothing could be plainer than that they are simple entities. Meinong's theory of abstraction rests on the assumption that abstraction is possible only in regard to a complex. Hence, if one gets the general idea of color by abstraction from specific (shades of) colors, Meinong must hold that these shades of colors are complex. Or else he must show that abstraction is possible even for simple entities.

Meinong cannot bring himself to deny that specific shades of colors are simple. He tries, therefore, to develop a theory of abstraction that allows for abstraction in regard to simple entities. At the time of the later paper, Meinong sharply distinguishes between an idea and the intention of an idea, between the content of a mental act, as it was usually called, and the object of the act. It is this distinction which Meinong tries to utilize in order to explain how abstraction in regard to simple entities is possible.[31] Meinong identifies ideas with concepts; the intentions of ideas, with the extensions of the concepts. This identification shows at least two confusions. An idea and its intention are not related to each other as a property is related to its extension. For example, the idea of a certain shade of red, call it 'red' for short, has as its intention, not the class of red things, but the property *red*. This is the first confusion. Furthermore, a property is not the same as its extension. We must distinguish, as we shall see in the next section, between the idea (concept) of red, the property *red*, and the extension of this property. What is important for our present purpose is that the concept of red (in the sense of idea) cannot possibly intend a class of red things. The class would be intended by a concept of that class.

But let us grant, for the sake of the argument, that the idea red can intend the class of red things. The class of red things is quite a different thing from the property *color*. Meinong next claims that the idea of red can intend, not merely the class of red things, but also other things, things which are similar to the members of the class of red things in that they are colored too. In brief, the idea of red can be made to intend the class of colored things. And this is, presumably, the way in which we get an abstract idea of color.

But if the idea of red is thus 'imprecise,' intending as its 'core' the class of red things and as its 'fringe' ultimately the class of colored things, how could we possibly ever have an idea of just this shade of red? All our ideas would have to intend, not certain shades of colors, but the property *color* instead. Meinong admits that the difference between a reference to a certain shade and a reference to a shade and many similar ones cannot lie in the idea itself. He puts it, therefore, into the mental act of presentation, the act of having an idea, and makes it a matter of attention. In his words, 'changes in the precision of acts of presentation have to be taken as changes in the intensity of these acts.'[32]

Abstraction in regard to a simple entity becomes thus a matter of attention just like abstraction in regard to a complex. But it is obvious that the two cases differ radically. When we form the abstract idea of red, there occurs a mental act of presentation with this idea for its content; and this content is quite different from the one which characterizes the presentation of the complex of which red is a part. There occurs a shift from the complex idea of the complex object to the simple idea of red. In the case of color, on the other hand, the idea does presumably not change at all, only the intensity of the act of presentation changes. When we form the abstract idea of color, according to Meinong, we really have a presentation with the idea of, say, red; this presentation differs only in degree of intensity from a presentation which has the same idea, but which intends the color red. How the degree of intensity of the mental act determines whether the color red or the property of being a color is the intention of the act, remains a complete mystery.

Meinong's account of how we form such abstract ideas as that of color involves at least three fundamental confusions. First, he confuses the intention of an idea with the extension of a concept. Second, he mistakes the extension of a concept for the concept itself; the idea of the extension of the property *red*, for the idea of *red*. Third, he mistakes the class of red things and similarly colored things for the class of colored things.

The degree of this confusion is a measure of how desperately he attempts to reconcile his old view of abstraction with the fact that there are properties of properties. This fact clashes with the Berkeleyan ontology of complexes. According to Meinong, one pays attention, in abstracting, to a property of a perceptual object. But this property is not thought of as being exemplified by the perceptual object, it is conceived of as a part of that object. The exemplification relation is supplanted by the part-whole relation. But this substitution runs into trouble as soon as we turn to properties which exemplify properties; for such 'first-order' properties may be simple. To put it differently, while it may appear plausible to claim that a perceptual object literally consists of certain properties, it does not appear plausible at all to say that, e.g., a certain shade of red consists, among other entities, of the property *color*. When we think of complex properties, we simply do not count their properties among their parts. Rather, the parts of a complex property are what Frege calls *marks* of that property.[33] For example, the complex property *red and square* consists of the mark *red* and the mark *square*.

We see how the ontological view that perceptual objects are complexes of properties derives some of its plausibility from the notion of a complex property. To be sure, there are two important differences. First, a complex of properties includes a place and a moment, while a complex property does not. Second, the characteristic relation of a complex is the relation of association, while the characteristic relation of a complex property is conjunction (conceived of as holding among properties rather than states of affairs). But we also see now that the apparent similarity between complexes of properties and complex properties soon breaks down. The properties that constitute the parts of a complex are properties *of* that complex, if I may so put it, while the properties that constitute the parts of a complex property are not properties but marks of the complex property. Finally, since the relation between a property like *red* and its property *color* is neither that of association nor of conjunction, the proponent of an ontology of complexes has to acknowledge the existence of at least three basic relations, namely, the association relation, the relation of part-whole, and a third relation, call it exemplification, which holds between properties and their properties. The proponent of individuals, on the other hand, requires for the same purposes just one relation, namely, that of exemplification.

5 *Concepts and their Objects*

One of the main topics of the first *Hume Study* is a division of all concepts into general and particular concepts, on the one hand, and into abstract and concrete concepts, on the other. Meinong's discussion of these two dichotomies contains a number of confusions. But it is not our intention to point these out in detail. Rather, we merely wish to set the stage for later, more thorough, discussions of these matters.

Concepts, according to Meinong, have *contents* and *extensions*. The extension of a concept consists of the objects which fall under the concept. So far, Meinong's view is relatively clear. Before we go any further, though, we must point out some ambiguities in the term 'concept.'

First. There is a traditional distinction between concepts and intuitions. Both concepts and intuitions are called presentations. Presentations are contrasted with judgments. This distinction is usually vitiated by the lack of a clear separation of the mental act from its intention. By an 'intuition,' for example, one sometimes means the act of intuiting, at other times, the entity intuited. In the latter sense, intuitions are said to be particular, while concepts are thought of as general. I shall from now on use 'presentation,' 'intuition,' and 'conception,' to mean mental acts rather than their intentions. I shall then speak of the intention of an intuition, the intention of a presentation, and so on. What I call the intention of a mental act is often called the object of the mental act. But we shall need the term 'object' later for another purpose.

Second. There is a traditional distinction between concepts and objects which amounts to a distinction between properties and the individuals which have them. This agrees, roughly, with Frege's use of these terms.[34] A concept, in this sense, is a non-mental entity, what I have called a property. To say that an object falls under a certain concept is to say that the individual exemplifies that property. The extension of a concept is the class of all individuals which fall under the concept, that is, it is the class of all the individuals which have the property.

Third. There is, finally, a traditional distinction between concepts and what concepts are concepts of. This distinction coincides with the one between ideas and what ideas are ideas of. In this sense of the term 'concept,' concepts are the inner, mental, 'pictures' of 'outside' entities. For example, the concept *midnight blue* is a concept of a certain color. It is, as many philosophers have said, that color 'as it exists in the understanding.'

Meinong, as we shall see, eventually makes all of these important distinctions, but in the *Hume Studies* he does not. His very first pronouncement about the so-called content and the extension of a concept shows his confusion:[35]

> It is also obvious that what the logicians call the content of a
> concept coincides in the case of abstract concepts with only that
> part of the respective concrete complex presentation which is
> accentuated through attention, while one must count as belonging
> to the extension of this concept all individuals which have the
> totality of attributes which constitute the content of the concept.

Meinong is here talking about the second of three basic distinctions. His point could be expressed as follows: The content of an abstract concept, that is, the concept itself, is that part of a complex which by means of attention is separated from its individuating features of place and moment; the extension of this concept consists of all the complexes which contain the concept as a part. However, in what Meinong literally says he confounds, first, the complex which is the intention of a presentation with a complex presentation. And, second – and in the same vein – he confuses the abstract concept with the intention of this concept, that is, with a property (an instance, 'de-individuated' by abstraction). Meinong's main mistake, occurring throughout the *Hume Studies*, consists in this identification of presentations with their intentions.

Meinong sets himself the task of distinguishing between four kinds of concepts: (1) abstract concepts, (2) concrete concepts, (3) general concepts, and (4) particular concepts. The distinction between (1) and (2) corresponds to the traditional dichotomy between intentions of concept and intentions of intuitions. An abstract concept is thus a property or, more accurately if less intelligibly, an instance which is 'de-individuated' by abstraction. A concrete concept, on the other hand, is simply an instance. A general concept is a concept under which more than one individual falls. It is a property which is exemplified by more than one individual; or, in Meinong's terminology, an instance which, after it has been 'de-individuated,' can be a part of many different complexes. A particular concept, lastly, is a concept under which only one individual falls.

Abstract concepts cannot be concrete, and conversely. General concepts cannot be particular, and conversely. Furthermore, a concrete concept must be particular. But Meinong makes much of the fact that a particular concept may be abstract. He emphasizes repeatedly that there are abstract concepts under which only one individual falls; and he distinguishes between two cases of abstract concepts which are particular. In the first case, the single object is uniquely related to a concrete complex. In the second case, it is the sole member of a certain class. For example, the concept of *man who repaired my car yesterday* is abstract, because it does not contain the individuating features of place and moment. But it is nevertheless a particular concept, since there is only one individual which falls under this concept. An example of the second kind is the concept *wisest man on earth*. Abstract concepts which are particular are simply properties, relational or non-relational, which uniquely determine an individual.

Let us review the highlights of Meinong's early ontology. Perceptual objects are complexes of 'properties.' In regard to whether these 'properties' are really properties or are instances, Meinong holds an inconsistent view. He believes, in effect, that they are both, depending on whether or not one considers them as connected with certain places and certain moments. His view is inconsistent because it cannot make a difference to the ontological nature of a part of a complex whether it is abstracted or not. The problem of individuation is solved in terms of places and moments. Complexes and their parts are identified with complex presentations and their parts; in other words, a complex idea is identified with the complex of which it is an idea. Meinong is thus at this point a Berkeleyan in two important respects. First, he accepts an ontology of complexes rather than substances (individuals). Second, he identifies the parts of the complexes with presentations, that is, with mental entities. He differs from Berkeley primarily in regard to his solutions of the twin problems of individuation and qualitative sameness.

Ideal and Real Relations

In the history of philosophy, relations have fared even worse than properties. The Aristotelian tradition, for one, has not been hospitable to relations. Relations, it is obvious, would have to belong to the category of accident rather than that of substance. But a (two-term) relation, if it is conceived of as an accident, would have to involve two different substances at once – as Leibniz put it, it would have to have one leg in each one of two distinct substances – and this is simply impossible for an accident, as the Aristotelian understands it. [1] Nor does the fate of relations change with the advent of the empiricistic attack on substances. The Berkeleyan conception of a perceptual object as a complex of properties leaves relations homeless. [2] They are neither complexes nor are they parts of complexes. In order to break with the Aristotelians or the empiricistic tradition, one has to admit the existence of relations in addition to and as distinct from substances and accidents or complexes and their parts, respectively. This break, as we know, occurred only very recently. It is associated with the names of Frege, Russell, and – as we shall see – Meinong.

Now, if relations do not exist, as the tradition steadfastly maintains, then the meaning of relational statements must somehow be explained in another way. Relations, as one usually says, have to be reduced to other kinds of entities. In the main, there are two such attempts at reduction. First, there is the straightforward way. [3] It consists essentially in the claim that a sentence of the form '$R(A, B)$' is merely short for a sentence which mentions certain properties of A and B, but does not mention any relation. This approach has two characteristic features. Certain properties of A and B are singled out as the 'foundations' of the reduced relation R. It is these foundations which form the onto-logical basis for the reduction. Furthermore, one usually distinguishes between genuine relation expressions on the one hand and syncategorematic expressions purporting to represent relations on the other. The reduction sentence, it usually turns out, does contain relation expressions after all; for example, the word 'and' or the word 'entails.' But these terms are then said to be syncategorematic.

Second, there is what I shall call the conceptualistic way. According to this position, relations are not just nothing, they do indeed exist, but they exist only as products of a mental activity. They are mental creations. Relations, to be succinct, are conceived of as products of mental acts of comparison. The mind, confronted with two complexes, actively compares these complexes with each other, and, by so comparing the two, it creates a third entity, namely, a relation. The *locus classicus* of this approach is Book II, chapter xii of Locke's *Essay*. According to Locke, the mind gets its ideas of relations by 'bringing two ideas, whether simple or complex, together, and setting them by one another, so as to take a view of them at once, without uniting them into one.' [4] Berkeley, we recall, holds that relations are known, not by ideas, but by notions, since they involve an activity of the mind. The conceptualist insists on two points. The idea of a relation presupposes that the mind is active rather than passive. The activity consists in some kind of comparison.

At first, Meinong follows in the footsteps of Locke and Berkeley. [5] He argues that relations are mental, that they are the product of mental activity, and that they require acts of comparison. But later on he has second thoughts about this view. He suddenly discovers three relations which do not seem to fit into the conceptualist's mold. We find here his first hesitant steps toward a realistic view; a view which, as we shall see, is consciously accepted in his later works.

Meinong's ontology of complexes and their parts, as we saw in the last chapter, requires the explicit acknowledgment of at least three important relations. First, there is the relation of *equality* between instances which assures that instances can be grouped in the required way. [6] Thus, where the realist speaks of the *same* property of different individuals, Meinong speaks of (numerically) *different* but *equal* instances in several complexes. Second, there is the relation of *association* that assures the unity of complexes. Third, there is the *part-whole* relation which corresponds in Meinong's scheme of things to predication. We shall have to pay special attention to Meinong's treatment of these three relations.

It is impossible, however, to discuss Meinong's arguments, unless we continue to pursue a policy introduced in the last chapter. In order to make certain points, we simply must overlook two of Meinong's most pervasive confusions. We shall again pretend most of the time that he is talking about perceptual objects when ostensibly he is talking about our ideas of such objects. And we shall also have to pretend that

Meinong is talking about relations when he is really talking about instances of relations.

1 *Foundations of Relations*

Meinong begins his systematic discussion of relations with the observation that a person who makes a judgment about a relation is active in a very special way. Then he claims that the assertion of a relation is in many cases completely independent of the assertion of the existence of the things which it relates. If one thinks of two different colors or shapes, then one can call these similar or dissimilar, even if one does not know whether they exist in reality or even if one knows that they do not exist.[7] From this alleged fact, he seems to draw the conclusion that the relation so considered must be a mental entity. The complete argument, we may surmise, involves the following further steps. Since my assertion about the relation is completely independent of any knowledge about the existence of its terms, I cannot really be concerned with a relation between these terms. What exists quite independently of the existence of these terms is, of course, the respective ideas of the terms. So, what the mind can at best compare are these ideas. Hence, the mind can produce, by such a comparison, a relation only between the ideas. But a relation between ideas, since ideas are mental, must itself be mental. Therefore, the relation under discussion is a mental entity.

This kind of argument is only plausible, of course, as long as the distinction between an idea and its intention (what an idea is an idea of) is not carefully made. But we must note that Meinong's argument contains the seed for another view. If we can compare, say, two colors, irrespective of whether there are such entities as colors, and if what we compare are the colors themselves, not their ideas, then it follows that we can gain knowledge about relations between these colors which, in an important sense, is independent of experience. Such knowledge would be paradigmatic of so-called *a priori* knowledge.

There is a second argument for the conclusion that the relations produced by comparison must hold between ideas and, hence, must be mental:[8]

In so far, however, as relations are products of mental activity, it is clear that, strictly speaking, there can be no relations other than subjective ones even for the realist. Hence Locke already goes too far when he maintains that what is compared are things or ideas; only the latter is admissible, for one can only compare what one has ideas of (*was man vorstellt*).

It is clear that this argument, too, presupposes an identification of ideas with their intentions. Meinong claims that all relations must be mental (subjective), since one can compare one's ideas only with each other. That one can compare one's ideas only with each other is taken to follow from the fact that one can compare only what one first of all brings before the mind by having ideas. But, of course, this fact must be distinguished from the quite different notion that one can compare one's ideas only with each other. That Meinong confuses the former with the latter, can be seen from still another context: 'If I ascertain a difference between a meter and a foot, the relation of difference can be based on nothing other than the ideas of foot and meter.'[9] What a relation is based on, we must add to understand Meinong's point, is, in ordinary talk, the terms of the relation. Meinong is saying here that the two terms of the relation of difference between meter and foot are the two ideas of meter and of foot, respectively.

Next, Meinong argues that every relation requires (at least) two *foundations*. These foundations must not be confused with what we ordinarily call the terms of a relation. For example, when we assert that a red cube A is different (in regard to color) from a blue cube B, we seem to be asserting a relation between the two entities A and B. A and B would ordinarily be called the terms of this relation. Meinong claims, however, that the relation is established through an act of comparison which compares, not the two cubes A and B, but rather two colors.[10] More accurately, what we compare, according to him, are two color instances which are parts of the two complexes A and B. These instances are the foundations of the relation.[11] The foundations for all relations are therefore ultimately instances. I say ultimately, because Meinong maintains that relations themselves may be compared and, hence, give rise to relations. But he is very emphatic in stating that the hierarchy of relations must ultimately be built on non-relational foundations; for, as he says, 'A relation without absolute foundations would be a comparison in which nothing is compared.'[12]

This principle of the existence of absolute foundations yields Meinong's strongest argument for the existence of places and moments. Assume that the cube A is to the left of cube B. Then it follows from this principle that A and B must contain as parts certain foundations. Now, if we take a look at these parts, it is clear that such parts as (instances of) colors, shapes, etc., will not do as foundations for a spatial relation. Hence we must infer that in addition to these parts, A and B contain (non-relational) spatial parts. These spatial parts, which function as foundations for spatial relations, are called places. And a similar argument leads to the conclusion that there are moments. Meinong is fully aware that by embracing places and moments, he embraces what is traditionally called an absolute view of space and time.

He mentions Locke and Hume as proponents of the relative view, and he argues that they are wrong. But his argument simply comes down to an affirmation of the principle of the existence of absolute foundations.[13]

Of course, this principle yields Meinong's conclusion only if we combine it with his ontology of complexes. Assume that perceptual objects are individuals rather than complexes. In this case, there is no need to introduce places as absolute foundations of spatial relations in order to satisfy the principle; for the individuals themselves constitute such foundations. What colors are to color-similarity, individuals are to spatial (and temporal) relations. Individuals, and only individuals, are then the bearers of spatial and temporal relations. In other words, the category of individual is coextensive with the category of spatial and/or temporal entity. Since individuals correspond in a way to the complexes of Meinong's ontology, one may ask why he did not avoid an absolute view of space and time by holding that spatial and temporal relations hold between complexes. To raise the question is to answer it: when we produce a relation between two complexes A and B, we always compare them *in regard to certain parts of theirs,* but what would a comparison between A and B be like that is not a comparison between some of their parts? How could a comparison between a complex consisting of, say, green and round and a complex consisting of red and round lead to a spatial relation? On Meinong's analysis of perceptual objects into their colors, shapes, etc., it is indeed hard to accept the view that spatial and temporal relations hold between complexes.

2 *Equality and Similarity*

A comparison of two 'properties' can yield only one of two results, according to Meinong. Either they are *equal* or they are *unequal*. Equal 'properties' are often said to be identical, but this is, of course, a misleading expression; for equality is not identity. The 'properties' we compare are, of course, instances. Since no two complexes contain the same instance, no two instances can be identical. But they can be equal. Two cubes of exactly the same shade of blue, for example, contain equal but not identical color instances. Equality is thus the equivalence relation by means of which the different instances are grouped together to form instances of the same shade. The proponent of properties does not need this relation; he has the relation of identity. One could express the matter paradoxically by saying that equality is that relation which holds between two instances of, say, a color whenever two perceptual objects have the *same* color.

As Meinong sees it, the most important question is whether or not similarity can be reduced to equality.[14] The obvious proposal is to define similarity between two complexes as partial equality. For example, a midnight blue cube and a midnight blue billiard ball may be said to be similar, since their colors are equal. But how can one apply this proposal to the case where two shades of color are similar to each other? Meinong maintains, quite correctly, that the proposal must be judged in the light of how plausible it is to think of particular shades of color as being complex. Since there is a color continuum, Meinong reasons, such complexity may even have to be infinite.[15]

On the other hand, if we do not accept the view that, for example, a shade of color is complex – perhaps even infinitely complex – then we must admit a new principle. Meinong does not say what this new principle is, but it is clear that it will have to be incompatible with Meinong's reduction of relations to their foundations. Even if we assume that similarity is not reducible to partial equality, Meinong's problem remains: a similarity relation, like any other relation, requires foundations; hence if there are several shades of color which are *more or less similar* to each other, then these shades must be complex. Within the framework of Meinong's analysis of relations, he has a choice between two equally unacceptable views: he must either hold that the shades are not more or less similar to each other or he must hold that the shades are complex. Meinong would not and could not deny the existence of similarities among various shades of color. Nor does he, as we saw in the last chapter, deny the simplicity of particular shades of color. The principle of which he speaks, therefore, can only consist in the acceptance of irreducible relations of degrees of similarity.

The situation, then, is as follows. If Meinong tries to reduce similarity to partial equality, the shades of color must be complex; and if there are infinitely many shades, they must be infinitely complex; otherwise he cannot account for the infinite number of degrees of similarity that can occur. On the other hand, even if Meinong is willing to admit similarity as *a* relation in its own right, the fact that there are degrees of similarity between different shades requires that the shades must be complex; and if there are infinitely many of these degrees, then the shades must be infinitely complex. Meinong's only reasonable way out consists in giving up his analysis of relations.

Meinong, of course, does not draw this conclusion. He does not try to settle the thorny issue of the nature of similarity in the second *Hume Study*.[16] He merely claims that one thing remains true no matter how we try to account for degrees of similarity, namely, that similarity is always a special case of inequality; for, if two complexes were not unequal in some respect, they would be equal rather than merely similar. He maintains that his distinctions stand: relations of comparison divide into the relation of equality and the relation of inequality; the relation of inequality, furthermore, divides into the relation of similarity and the relation of dissimilarity.

Equality, we said, is Meinong's equivalence relation.[17] But this relation will group the various instances of the same shade of color only if it is a genuine relation and does not itself dissolve into a large number of instances. If no two pairs of foundations can found the same relation, then it follows that no two foundations can have anything in common. But this means that different instances of equality can have nothing in common that characterizes them as instances of *equality*.[18] From a formal point of view, the problem of qualitative sameness can only be solved if not all properties and relations dissolve into instances. Meinong does not see this at all in the *Hume Studies*. His particular brand of nominalism may therefore be thought to be defective in at least two important respects. First, there is Meinong's mistaken notion that instances of relations can be reduced to instances of properties. Second, even if Meinong had admitted instances of relations as irreducible, these instances would have to be supplemented with genuine relations in order to solve the problem of qualitative sameness.

3 *Incompatibility*

Meinong holds that there is a second kind of relation, what he calls the incompatibility relation. No individual thing can be both round and square (at the same time). In other words, *round* and *square* are incompatible with each other. *Round* and *green*, by comparison, are compatible with each other. Does this mean that there is a relation between the two properties *round* and *green,* the relation of compatibility, just as there is the relation of inequality between them? Meinong argues that the two cases are not analogous. While there is indeed the inequality relation, talk about the compatibility (or incompatibility) of two properties is merely elliptical: to say that *green* and *round* are compatible is to say that both of these properties can be associated with the same place and moment; to say that *round* and *square* are incompatible is to say that they cannot be associated with the same place and moment. This can be seen more easily when we realize that *round* and *square* are not incompatible as such or by themselves: the round table is perfectly compatible with the square box, as Meinong puts it. Their incompatibility depends on a certain condition, namely the condition mentioned above, that they be conceived of as belonging to the same place and the same time.[19]

Meinong's point is important. We can formulate it as follows. Granted that *round* and *square* cannot be properties of the same individual, is this fact of the form *No complex can contain both round and square*

27

as parts, or is it of the form *Round and square are incompatible*? In other words, is it a quantified fact concerning all complexes or is it a non-quantified fact to the effect that a certain relation holds between two properties? If it is of the first kind, then it resembles other general laws; if it is of the second kind, then it resembles such facts as *Midnight blue is darker than canary yellow*.

Now, this difference makes a profound difference because of the way in which many philosophers have explicated *synthetic a priori knowledge*. That midnight blue is darker than canary yellow, most philosophers say, is a synthetic *a priori* truth. In order to prove that it is known *a priori* rather than *a posteriori*, they usually use the following argument. First, knowledge *a priori* is explicated as *knowledge not based on experience*. Then one raises the rhetorical question: what future experiences could convince you that midnight blue is not darker than canary yellow? The expected answer is, of course, that there could be no such future experience. But if we thus admit that the statement could not be refuted by experience, we are admitting that it cannot be based on experience. Hence we are admitting that it is known *a priori*.

This argument suffers from a basic ambiguity in the expression 'future experience.' Assume that we compare a midnight blue sweater with a canary yellow shirt; more precisely, that we compare the colors of these two things. Assume that we notice on this occasion that midnight blue is darker than canary yellow. Would we try to confirm this recognition by looking at further pairs of midnight blue and canary yellow things? Would we, for example, try to make sure that the one color is darker than the other by comparing next a midnight blue ball with a canary yellow wall? Of course not. The *kind* of individual compared is completely unimportant. What we noticed was a relation between two colours, and it is a mere accident that we noticed this relation in connection with a sweater and a shirt rather than a ball and a wall. We are therefore certain that no future experience *of this nature* could change our mind about the relation between these two colors. In this sense, then, it is indeed true that our knowledge of the relation between midnight blue and canary yellow is not 'based on experience.' But it is now also clear what this sense is. Our knowledge of the relationship between the two colors, we simply admit, is not a matter of *induction*. We do not gain it by comparing more and more couples of more and more diverse midnight blue and canary yellow *things*. Nor could it be a matter of induction; for the fact known is not a quantified fact at all. It is of the form: $R(F, G)$. It is of the same form as the fact: This table is to the left of that chair; and just as this latter fact could not possibly be known by induction, so the former could not either. In brief, in one form, the argument under scrutiny says that a certain fact is known *a priori* because it is not known by induction.

In this form, it is a perfectly sound argument. Unfortunately, though, it also leads to the undesired conclusion that facts like the one about the table and the chair are known *a priori*; for upon this explication of the *a priori*, every non-quantified fact is known *a priori*. Even such paradigms of *a posteriori* known facts as that this table is brown or that this table is to the left of that chair turn out to be known *a priori*.

If 'future experience' does not mean 'further comparisons between couples of midnight blue and canary yellow things,' but includes, for example, the perception of a midnight blue thing which is not darker than a certain canary yellow thing, then the rhetorical question of the argument has not the expected answer. What future experience could show that midnight blue is not darker than canary yellow? Well, if one were to perceive that the color of a midnight blue thing is not darker than the color of a canary yellow object, one would have an experience that would tend to show that our first view was false. There is absolutely no difficulty in describing what kind of experience would disconfirm our original view. Of course, whether we expect to have such an experience is quite a different matter, a matter which depends on how firmly we believe in our original insight. Since there is thus an experience that would disconfirm our belief, there is no reason to assume that the belief itself is not based on (an) experience. Nor is it hard to say what this experience is: it is the perception of midnight blue's being darker than canary yellow. In short, upon the present interpretation of 'future experience,' the earlier argument is not sound and, hence, does not show that the fact that midnight blue is darker than canary yellow is known *a priori*.

It is apparent now why it is so important to decide whether the fact that nothing can be round and square is quantified or not. If it is quantified, then it can be known only by induction.[20] Hence the argument that it is known *a priori* breaks down even for the first of our two interpretations of the phrase 'future experience.' On the other hand, if it is of the same form as *Midnight blue is darker than canary yellow*, then we could at least argue that it is known *a priori* in the sense of not known by induction. Meinong, I said, rejects this latter possibility. In this, I think, he is correct. There simply is no such relation as that of compatibility (or incompatibility).[21]

We seem to have reached the conclusion that there is no significant difference between the way in which we know that nothing can be round and square and the way in which we know that nothing can be a whale and also a fish. And some will surely object that this conclusion proves that there is something wrong with our analysis of the issue. We all feel, it may be said, that there is a difference between these two 'laws.' Meinong is no exception. Although he denies that the fact under discussion involves a relation of incompatibility, he nevertheless insists that there is something special about it. What distinguishes an 'ordinary' law from the law under discussion, according to Meinong, is the feature of *evidence* which attaches to a judgment concerning the latter, but is not attached to a judgment about the former.[22] This evidence, as we shall see, is the mental counterpart to necessity. Thus we can put Meinong's view this way: the law that nothing can be round and square is *necessary*, while 'ordinary' laws are not. Thus there is a difference between this law and 'ordinary' laws after all.

Meinong remains convinced throughout his philosophical career that there is necessity. At the beginning, (e.g.) here in the second *Hume Study*, he thinks of it as a mental feature of judgments and calls it evidence. As soon as he overcomes this idealistic position, though, necessity acquires an objective, non-mental, status as a feature of objectives. We shall return to this topic more than once in the following pages. For the moment, what is of paramount interest, is Meinong's defense of necessity in the second *Hume Study*. We shall look into this defense in detail in the next section. Before we do, let us complete our account of incompatibility.

Up to now, I have talked as if Meinong accepts the notion that the fact that nothing is both round and square is a law as commonly understood. But this is a simplified view. We must realize that Meinong, at the time of the *Hume Studies*, was not altogether clear about the nature of laws. Nor was he clear about the nature of judgments. Meinong denies that incompatibility is a relation (between properties) like inequality. But he does not tell us, positively, what precisely it is that we assert when we say that no thing can be both round and square. Somehow, according to his view, we make a necessary judgment, but what is it that we judge?

In the *Hume Studies*, there is no answer to this question. But Meinong returns to it later in the second edition of *Über Annahmen*. He hints there that incompatibility (and compatibility) are relations between objectives, that is, states of affairs.[23] What we are judging in our case, we might infer, is the state of affairs that the two states of affairs (a) *This place and moment are associated with round and* (b) *This (same) place and (same) moment are associated with square* are incompatible. Of course, the judgment must really be about any such place and moment and, hence, must be general. It is simply not clear from what Meinong says even at this later time how he accounts for the generality. But I shall interpret him to mean that the fact that no thing can be both round and square is of the following form: It is necessary that, for all places and moments, the state of affairs (a) is incompatible with the state of affairs (b).

4 *Necessity*

I share the view of many philosophers that the (alethic) modalities do not belong to the furniture of the world. But if it is true that, say, necessity does not exist, what are we saying when we assert, for example, that the sun will necessarily rise tomorrow or that 4 is necessarily greater than 2? According to my way of thinking, we mean either one of two things.[24] To put it differently, there are two main ideas behind our ordinary talk about necessity.

The first idea, as Frege pointed out, is this.[25] Sentences like 'Necessarily *P*' or 'It is necessary that *P*' are merely short for '*P* is a law or there are laws from which *P* follows.' To say '*P* is possible' is to say either (a) 'There are no laws from which not-*P* follows' or (b) 'Not-*P* is not always the case.' Frege gives the following examples for (a) and (b): 'It is possible that the earth will at some time collide with another heavenly body' and 'A cold can result in death.' Furthermore, to say that *P* is impossible is to say, according to this explication, that there are laws which contradict *P*. What is possible, I said, is what does not contradict any laws. An actual state of affairs, of course, does not contradict any laws and is therefore possible. We must distinguish between possible states of affairs in this wider sense and *merely* possible states of affairs. The latter do not obtain.

This explication of the modalities leads to a distinction between different kinds of necessity and possibility in terms of kinds of laws. For example, we can and must distinguish between ontological modalities and logical modalities. It is a law of ontology that individuals are not exemplified. It follows from this law that the pencil on my desk is not exemplified. Hence it is ontologically necessary that this pencil is not exemplified by anything. On the other hand, the pencil is not (now) both red and not red (all over). But there is no law of ontology from which it follows that this pencil could not be both red and also not-red. It is, therefore, ontologically possible that it is both red and not-red. However, that the pencil cannot be both red and not-red follows from a law of logic. Hence it is not logically possible that the pencil is both red and not-red. Thus we see that what is ontologically possible may not be logically possible.

In addition to ontological and logical modalities, there are also arithmetic possibilities and necessities, geometric possibilities and necessities, biological possibilities and necessities, and so on. How many kinds of modalities we shall have to distinguish altogether depends on how many fields of inquiry we are able to distinguish by subject-matter.

It may be objected against this explication that, far from showing that necessity is not a part of the world, we have actually put it into the laws we talk about. Necessity, it may be said, is precisely that ingredient which distinguishes a true law from an accidental generality. The shoe is really on the other foot, as it were. Instead of explicating necessity in terms of lawfulness, one must explicate lawfulness in terms of necessity. The issue, then, is whether or not there is a common constituent that distinguishes laws from accidental generalities. If there is such a constituent, then we may call it necessity; and necessity is then undoubtedly a part of the furniture of the world. Now, I do not think that there is such a constituent. There is no ontological difference between the kind of fact we call a law and the kind of fact some philosophers call an accidental generality. What difference there is, in my opinion, is to be explained in terms of such further features as that the alleged law has instances, that there are other general facts which can be deduced from the alleged law or from which it can be deduced, etc. The general nature of my reply to the objection is so well known that I shall not spell it out here in detail. [26]

Meinong, in his first main argument for necessity, rejects this explication of the modalities. Consider the law that nothing can be both round and square. We would argue that this is a geometric necessity, because it follows from the geometric law (a) that everything that is round is not square together with the logical law (b) that nothing can be both round and not round. Meinong turns our attention to the geometric law (a). It, too, is usually said to be necessary. We would have to maintain that it is a geometric necessity, simply because it is a geometric law. Now Meinong's objection starts: [27]

> But more than that: how do I get the knowledge anyhow that something has not existed so far and does not now exist? For that I only have the argument that nobody has found it, and from this arises always a certain probability; but how far this is from certainty is shown by the simple consideration that one – of course, always without using a determination of incompatibility – cannot even assert with complete certainty about a sensibly given circle that it isn't at the same time square, since it is – though most improbable – not absolutely excluded that the squareness for some reason eludes perception. If one contrasts with this that which actually happens and of which everyone has sufficient experience, namely that under favorable circumstances (as in the case of round and square) the decision is made immediately and without the slightest resource to cumbersome data of the above sort, then one will unhesitatingly admit that at least in this fashion the relations of compatibility cannot be replaced.

Meinong, in effect, objects to our explication that it does not account for the certainty which we feel in regard to some laws and not to others.

Having watched one pot of water boil after it has been heated, we may surmise that other pots will boil under similar circumstances, but we will not be as certain that the corresponding law is true as we are about the geometric law, even after we have noticed just once that a circle is not square. Meinong, actually, presses the point further. What he claims is that while we cannot be certain that the water is actually boiling, we can be absolutely certain the circle before us is not square. But I take it that this is due to the fact that, while we cannot be certain that the law of physics holds, we can be certain that the geometric law holds.

We are back to what earlier I called a felt difference between certain laws and certain others. We seem to be impelled to admit that we know that nothing can be square and round in an entirely different way or to a different degree of certainty from that which in knowing that water always boils when heated. I think that there is indeed a difference. Meinong's first argument, in so far as it tries to establish this difference, is sound. But I also maintain that this difference can be explained without assuming the existence of necessity. This leads us to the second main idea behind necessity.

According to this notion, a necessary state of affairs is such that we cannot even *imagine* what its negation would be like. [28] We can imagine what something would have to be like in order to be a mermaid, for example, but we cannot imagine what something would have to be like to be round and square. Thus even though it may be a biological necessity – in our earlier sense – that mermaids do not exist, it is not a necessity in our present sense. On the other hand, that nothing can be both round and square is not only necessary in the first sense, but also necessary in this second sense. We must therefore distinguish between facts for which we can and facts for which we cannot imagine their negation. In the case of laws, although all laws are necessary according to our first explication, there are laws for which we can imagine exceptions, while for others, we cannot. Ontological laws are of the latter kind. I cannot imagine, for example, what it would be like for an individual to be exemplified by something. Logical laws are of the latter kind, too. One cannot imagine what it would be like for an individual, say, to be both red and also not red. Laws of arithmetic and set theory are of the second kind. Last but not least, there is a group of laws concerning time, space, and what I shall call the sense dimensions for which we cannot even imagine exceptions. It is this last mentioned group which, if I am not mistaken, has always yielded the paradigms for *synthetic a priori* truths. [29]

Let me mention a few of these laws. First, there are certain facts which constitute the sense-dimensions. Examples are: Green is a color; Round is a shape; Of any two different pitches, one is higher than the other; Only a pitch is in this sense higher than anything else. Second, there are truths about relations between two or more members of the same sense-dimension; for example: Midnight blue is darker than canary yellow; E is higher than C. Third, still other facts concern relations which hold between the properties of a single sense-dimension. Examples are: If the first of three pitches is higher than the second and the second is higher than the third, then the first is higher than the third. Fourth, certain facts concern the mutual dependence or exclusion of the members of one or more dimensions. Of this kind are the following facts: What has shape, has color; Nothing has two pitches; Nothing is both round and square.

We agree, then, with Meinong that there is a difference between 'ordinary' scientific laws ('laws of nature') on the one hand and such a law as *Nothing is both round and square* on the other. But we disagree with his explication of this difference. He thinks that necessity enters into the latter kind. We propose to account for the difference in terms of what we can and cannot imagine. Meinong's second main argument in defense of necessity is directed against our proposal. He objects, first, that human imagination can be improved, so that one person may be able to imagine what another cannot. Then he adds, second, that there are in fact complications which transcend all human ability to imagine and to which, nevertheless, nobody takes exception – this holds even for our ordinary numbers, since surely nobody can be found who can imagine one hundred things however small. [30]

Meinong's first objection is not decisive. It is clear that when we claim that nobody can imagine something to be round and square, we mean to claim that even the most practiced imagination does not achieve this feat. But his second objection appears formidable on first sight. It comes down to the claim that the inability to imagine something cannot mean its impossibility, since there are things which we cannot imagine, but which are nevertheless not only possible but actual. But what this shows is, not that our explication is untenable, but merely that we have to formulate it more carefully. The fact that we cannot imagine a certain state of affairs does not automatically mean that this state of affairs does not obtain. We may not be able to imagine a thousand-sided figure, but this does not prove that there is no such thing. In this case we can easily produce such a figure. We can easily imagine how we would go about drawing such a figure. So-called *synthetic a priori* laws, then, are such that we can imagine neither an exception to them nor how to produce such an exception.

Meinong, we saw, insists that necessity is an irreducible feature of the world. He presents two arguments in defense of this thesis. One argument is directed against the Fregean reduction of necessity to lawfulness; the other, against the view that necessity depends on what we cannot imagine. In the *Hume Studies*, necessity appears in the form of evidence, that is, as a feature of mental acts. But later, after Meinong has embraced objectives as a category, necessity is also viewed as an objective feature of certain objectives.

5 *Causality*

The concept of causality, according to Meinong, consists of the two notions of necessity and of temporal contiguity. Necessity, he claims further, is a matter of compatibility and incompatibility, while temporal contiguity is a special case of inequality.[31] Meinong argues that necessity is an essential ingredient in causality. But I shall not discuss his argument. Instead, I shall turn to a problem which arises within Meinong's view.

Causation between *A* and *B*, according to Meinong, involves necessity. But he also agrees with Hume that we are never acquainted with such causal necessity. Meinong tries to reconcile these two assertions. His solution to the problem is, to say the least, farfetched. It consists, in essence, of the assertion that while equality and compatibility are ascribed to ideas, the causal relation is always predicated of real things, that is, of those unknown (partial) causes of our ideas which we can only infer. In the case of the former relations, we concentrate on our ideas and wonder only later whether the results of our investigation are applicable not only to our ideas but to the real things themselves. In the case of causality, there can be no question but that we must be talking about the real things. But even in this case, according to Meinong, the subject cannot transcend the mental realm which alone is given to him, so that the application of causality to real things must find some kind of mental expression. This mental expression consists in the fact that causal judgments are possible only in connection with ideas which are subjects of existential judgments. We make causal inferences from given impressions (*Empfindungen*) to the real things outside of us which cause them. The outside thing, Meinong says, 'has to be conceived of as something of which we cannot assert anything else but that it is a partial cause (a more precise determination of this point can be omitted here) for the production of a mental phenomenon.'[32]

These considerations show clearly that Meinong here thinks, along Kantian lines, of ideas as mental entities and of the real 'physical' world as being causally inferred from such ideas. Be that as it may, how does this conception of reality solve the problem of the unobserved causal necessity? Meinong comes to the conclusion that the foundations of causal relationships are never given to us. It is therefore not surprising, according to him, that the necessity which emanates from these foundations is not given to us either. Only if the foundations of a relation are given to us do we see that it obtains with necessity. The foundations necessitate the relation; and if the foundations are not given, the necessity is not given either. How does Meinong arrive at the conclusion that the foundations of causal relations are never given to us? His only argument amounts to claiming that we could never justify our attributing the relevant causal relation to ideas. He says:[33]

> The assumption that the complex $A B C \ldots N$ is the cause of x is not grounded in these ideas, but in experience which has always shown x attended by this complex, or in some auxiliary experiences; hence the assertion of causality cannot be aimed at the *ideas A B C ... N* and x, but at the *things*, which are represented by these ideas.

Meinong thus turns the table on us. He argues that since causality is a matter of necessity, and since this necessity is not grounded in the ideas themselves, the causal judgment cannot be about these ideas. It must be about the physical causes of these ideas, the real things. But our objection to this line of reasoning is obvious: If the foundations of causal relations are never given to us, how do we know that causality is a matter of necessity? We must re-evaluate Meinong's argument for the contention that necessity is a feature of causality in the light of his admission that we are never presented with the foundations of causal relations. Our objection, then, is this. If the foundations of causal relations are never given to us, and if necessity emanates from these foundations, how can we possibly know that causality involves necessity? We may perhaps guess that necessity is an ingredient of causality, but we cannot be sure about the matter. Indeed, Meinong will argue in later publications that there is such a thing as *evidence for surmise (Vermutungsevidenz)*, and that on the basis of experience we may arrive at this kind of evidence for the existence of a necessity which is not accessible to rational insight.[34] We may surmise, in other words, that necessity attaches to a certain relation, even though this necessity is not given to us.

6 *Identity*

Meinong has some grave reservations in regard to the identity relation.[35] He argues that the identity relation would have to be a relation with just one foundation and that such an entity would simply no longer be a relation.

But if the presumption is against the existence of a relation of identity, what are we saying when we assert identity? Meinong answers:

'I can find only one common feature in all these uses: identity is asserted of something insofar as it is related at once to several other things.'[36] And he concludes:[37]

> The expression 'identity' simply does not express anything else but that we are dealing with *one* thing and not two, a determination which is very important in case that two relations with one foundation each are given, since it concerns their second foundation, but which would be entirely useless as long as one deals with only *one* thing, since one knows anyway that *one* thing is not two things.

Meinong makes here three points altogether. First, there can be no relation of self-identity since it would have to have just one foundation. Second, assertions about identity would be trivial, useless, futile, etc., if they were meant to assert self-identity. Third, all informative identity statements assert that two relations, for each one of which we are merely given one foundation, have the other foundation in common.

In regard to the first point, Russell once expressed a similar concern: 'The question whether identity is or is not a relation, and even whether there is such a concept at all, is not easy to answer. For, it may be said, identity cannot be a relation, since, where it is truly asserted, we have only one term, whereas two terms are required for a relation.'[38] But Russell concluded later in the same work: 'Thus identity must be admitted, and the difficulty as to the two terms of a relation must be met by a sheer denial that two terms are necessary. There must always be a referent and a relatum, but these need not be distinct; and where identity is affirmed, they are not so.'[39] It seems to me that Russell's conclusion points the way to the proper reply to Meinong's objection. We must distinguish two very different notions from each other. Every relation has (at least) two *places*; it has a direction (sense) from one place to another. But these two places may be occupied, if I may put it so, by the very same entity. The common use of the expression 'term' tends to obscure this fact. Sometimes, 'term' is used in the same sense in which I just used the word 'place,' as when we speak of two-term relations. At other times, though, it is used for the entity that fills the place, as when we distinguish between the different terms of a relation. It does not matter, of course, how we express this distinction, so long as we make it. Let us say that every relation must have at least two *terms*, but that the *entities* which enter into the relation need not be two. In these words, Meinong is right when he asserts that the very notion of a relation involves that it has at least two terms. But he is wrong when he concludes from this that one and the same entity cannot occur as the first term as well as the second.[40]

Meinong's second point reminds us of Wittgenstein's remark: 'By the way, to say of *two* things that they are identical is nonsense, and to say of *one* that it is identical with itself is to say nothing.'[41] To assert that something is self-identical may indeed be useless, as Meinong claims, but it is certainly not to say nothing. The trivial, the obvious, the useless, is still something. It is even more obvious that to say of two things that they are identical is not to say something nonsensical. It is simply to say something false. Granted that we may be saying either something obvious or something false, it does by no means follow that there can be no relation of identity.

In my view, Meinong's two objections against the relation of identity can be met. But this does not detract from his third point. To the contrary, it really reinforces it; for it shows how the importance of the identity relation is to be explained. Meinong, in effect, describes a way out of the following dilemma posed by Frege.[42]

If identity is a relation, then it is either a relation between entities or between expressions. Take the first possibility first. If identity holds between entities rather than their expressions, then the sentence '$A=B$' must represent the very same state of affairs as the sentence '$A=A$' as long as A is the same as B. These two sentences say the same thing, namely, that something is identical with itself. But if this is so, then it could not possibly be the case that the first sentence is 'informative' while the second is not. It could not be the case that the first sentence enlarges our knowledge of the world while the second does not. But it is clear that some sentences of the form '$A=B$' are indeed informative, while no sentence of the form '$A=A$' ever is. For example, the knowledge that the morning star is identical with the evening star, as Frege points out, constitutes a remarkable astronomical discovery. We seem to be forced to conclude that identity cannot be a relation between entities.

Consider, then, the possibility that it is a relation between expressions. A sentence like '$A=B$,' according to this alternative, tells us that the expressions 'A' and 'B' are used for the same entity.[43] The sentence tells us something about a certain linguistic convention, but it says nothing about the non-linguistic world. But it is again clear that sentences of this kind sometimes convey non-linguistic information; witness the statement about the morning star and the evening star. Thus it seems to follow that identity cannot be a relation between expressions either.

In order to avoid this dilemma, one must distinguish between mere labels on the one hand and descriptions on the other. The dilemma does indeed arise because of a confusion between these two ways of representing entities. All examples of informative identity sentences, as it turns out, contain definite descriptions. To see clearly what is involved, let us first consider a 'language' without descriptions and with at most one label for an entity. All true identity statements of that language would be of the form '$A = A$,' and all false identity statements would be of the form '$A = B$.' None of these identity statements would be informative in the sense here discussed. Next, assume that there is added to this language, for purely capricious reasons, another label for the entity A, say, the label 'Z.' We now have two true identity statements, namely, '$A = A$' and '$A = Z$,' but the state of affairs represented by the second sentence is precisely the same as the state of affairs represented by the first. Hence, neither one is informative. Of course, it may be the case that someone does not know that 'Z' is in this language a label for A, so that he does not know what the second sentence says. But this fact has nothing to do with identity at all. The same person will also not know, for example, what the sentence 'Z is tall' says. The first horn of the dilemma does not appear, because a counter-example such as 'The morning star is identical with the evening star' is not of the form '$A = Z$,' since 'A' and 'Z' are mere labels.

If someone tells us that 'A' and 'Z' are used for the same entity, then we know that '$A = Z$' is true, and conversely. But from this we must not conclude, with Wittgenstein, that the identity statement says the same thing as the statement: ' "A" represents the same entity as "B".' The latter is really an identity statement, too, but one that involves descriptions: 'The entity represented by "A" (in our language) is identical with the entity represented by "Z".'

Finally, assume that we enlarge the language further by introducing two (true) descriptions of A, say, 'the entity which is F' and 'the entity which is G.' Compare now the two sentences (1) 'The entity which is F is identical with the entity which is F' and (2) 'The entity which is F is identical with the entity which is G.' The first sentence says that a certain entity is F and that it is self-identical. It differs from '$A = A$' and '$A = B$' in that it says that the entity under study has the property F. Thus we may say that it conveys some information about the world which is not conveyed by the two identity statements with labels. Sentence (2) says even more; it is even more informative. It says that a certain entity is F, that a certain entity is G, and that the former is identical with the latter. To put the matter differently, the state of affairs represented by (1) is clearly quite different from the state of affairs represented by either '$A = A$' or '$A = Z$'; and the state of affairs (2), in turn, is quite different from the state of affairs represented by (1). Thus, as soon as we turn to identity statements with descriptions, the first horn of the dilemma disappears, because it is plainly not the case that (1) and (2) represent the same state of affairs.

It may be objected that (1) and (2) must represent the same state of affairs, since (2) follows from (1) by the principle of substitution of identicals. But this would be a wrong application of the principle. (1) and (2), one must realize, do not represent states of affairs of the forms '*A=A*' and '*A=Z*,' respectively. Rather, they represent states of affairs of the following kinds: (3) *The entity which is F is identical with itself* and (4) *The entity which is F and the entity which is G are identical with each other*. The principle of substitutivity simply does not apply in these cases. [44]

We are, at last, in a position to describe Meinong's way out in contemporary terms. Meinong, in making his third point, says that all informative identity statements involve two relational descriptions. They are all of the same form as, say, the statement 'The son of John is identical with the brother of Mary.' Here we have an assertion to the effect that the second term of the relation of *being a son of* in regard to the first term, John, is the same entity as the second term of the relation *of being a brother of* in regard to the first term, Mary. In short, according to Meinong, informative identity statements are of the form: The entity which stands in the relation R to B is identical with the entity which stands in the relation S to C.

Meinong's characterization of informative identity statements seems to be too narrow if we take it literally. We must also include among informative identity statements those statements which contain descriptions in terms of properties rather than relations. Furthermore, identity statements with just one description (relational or non-relational) and one label must be counted as informative. However, if we conceive of the part-whole relation between a complex and a constituent property as one of the relations Meinong has in mind, then we can easily account in Meinong's terms for identity statements with descriptions involving properties. For example, sentence (2) then asserts that the entity which stands in the whole-part relation to F is the same entity as the entity which stands in the whole-part relation to G. If we interpret Meinong's view in this fashion, we see that he comes very close to a proper understanding of the informative nature of certain identity statements.

Meinong applies his view on informative identity statements to a particular case. He considers a situation where two people have the same idea, say, an idea of a golden mountain. He remarks, first, that in this case there exist two different ideas since there occur two mental acts of presentation. But these two ideas are equal. Since there occur two mental acts of presentation, each one has its own instance of the idea of a golden mountain. According to Meinong, when we say that two persons have the same idea, we can only mean that there occur two ideas *of the same entity*. Notice how the facts here assert themselves in spite of Meinong's general confusion between ideas and their intentions; in this context, he cannot but help make the correct distinction.

In the next step of his explication, though, Meinong gets bogged down, because of his insufficient grasp of what the intention of a general idea is. He argues as follows:[45]

> However, if two presentations through their contents [ideas] indicate such a common intention, then it is not sufficient that they be simply equal; for this equality means that whatever is adequate to the presentation P_1 must also be adequate to the presentation P_2, but not that an individual which corresponds to P_1 and an individual which corresponds to P_2 are the same individual. For, if P_1 and P_2 are general presentations, then they have with equal contents also identical extension, that is, the totality of the individuals subsumed under them must be the same. But since the general presentation as such is not as yet the presentation of a collective, since the abstractum *fish* thus does not represent several, even less all, fish, but only *one* fish, although without a determination of the individual features, therefore every *single* fish is indeed adequate to P_1 as well as P_2. But just because the trout corresponds to P_1, the carp to P_2, trout and carp are not identical. One can therefore speak of identity only if not more than *one* thing *can* correspond to the two contents; and this is the case only if the contents [ideas] are not only equal, but are also individually determined. The same can therefore only be presented through individual presentations with equal contents.

This passage shows very clearly a series of mistakes, mistakes which we already mentioned at the end of the last chapter. First, Meinong mistakenly believes that the intention of a general idea is not a property; the intention of the idea fish is not the property of being a fish. It is clear why he would make this mistake. At this point, he simply does not distinguish between the property on the one hand and the idea of the property on the other. Second, Meinong argues that the idea fish cannot intend the class of all fish, since it does not even intend *some fish*, not to speak of *all fish*. He thus identifies the class of all fish with the entity represented by the expression 'all fish.' This is his second mistake. Of course, to call this a mistake is not to deny that to the class there belong all those entities which are fish.[46] But, third, if the idea fish intends neither the property nor the class, what does it intend? Meinong claims that it intends *a fish* (any fish); it intends a single fish, but not any particular fish. His answer, I think, may be interpreted in terms of the traditional common name doctrine. According to that doctrine, the word 'fish' is a common name of all individual fish; it names neither the property *fish* nor the class of all fish. What does it mean to commonly name something? I have argued elsewhere that there is no sensible answer to this question.[47] The notion of a common

name is inherently confused. I, for one, cannot make sense of the
assertion that, say, 'fish' names every single fish, but does not name
either this or that particular fish, or the property of being a fish, or the
class of all fish.

Be that as it may, however, we can look at Meinong's view in terms
of this doctrine. The general idea fish, we may say, *intends commonly*
every single fish, just as the common name 'fish' is said to *name commonly*
every single fish. But now we can see, even in Meinong's context, that
something must be wrong with this notion of commonly intending.
Meinong, we recall, argues that the two equal ideas cannot have the
same intention; for one of these ideas may intend a trout, another a
carp, and a trout is not a carp. For this argument to work, we have to
assume that to have a general idea fish may mean to have a general
idea of a fish which is a carp or it may mean to have a general idea of
a fish which is a trout, and so on. But this is surely false; for the general
idea *fish* is surely not the same as the general idea *fish which is a trout*.
Perhaps, Meinong means to say that one idea would intend a certain
fish which happens to be a trout, while the other intends a certain fish
which happens to be a carp, and the two fish are not the same. But this
clashes with the notion of a common idea. A general idea – by definition, so to speak – can only commonly intend every single fish, it
cannot possibly intend just one fish. To say that it intends just one
fish, but an individually undetermined fish, we must remember, is, on
our explication, just another way of saying that it intends all individual
fish commonly. That is the sense we have tried to make of the otherwise unintelligible notion of a single, but individually undetermined
fish.

However, there is another interpretation of Meinong's view. Perhaps he means to say that what the general idea fish intends is whatever
the expression 'a fish' represents. If so, then his argument breaks down
again; for then it does not seem to be possible for the one idea to intend
a fish which is a trout and for the other idea to intend a fish which is a
carp. Both ideas would then have to intend whatever the expression
'a fish' represents. But let us not worry about the soundness of
Meinong's argument. Instead, let us ask what kind of an entity *a fish*
could possibly be within the framework of Meinong's ontology.
Meinong says that a fish is 'one fish, although without a determination
of the individual features.' I think that what he has in mind, though
not too clearly, is the following. Assume that something is a fish if and
only if it has the three properties F, G, and H. A particular fish (more
accurately: a 'slice' of a particular fish), according to Meinong's analysis,
is then a complex object, consisting of instances of F, G, and H,
together with a particular place and a particular moment. I shall
represent such a complex C_1 in this way: ' $<F_i, G_i, H_i, P_1, M_1>$.,

Another particular fish, C_2, would be represented by the expression: '$<F_j, G_j, H_j, P_2, M_2>$.' Thus while '$C_1$' and '$C_2$' are labels of these complexes, '$<F_i, G_i, H_i, P_1, M_1>$' and '$<F_j, G_j, H_j, P_2, M_2>$' are abbreviations of descriptions, namely, of the two descriptions 'the complex (object) consisting of F_i, G_i, H_i, P_1, M_1' and 'the complex (object) consisting of F_j, G_j, H_j, P_2, M_2,' respectively. Assume next that we wish to consider 'a fish, but without its individuating features.' We must then drop, first of all, the places and moments from these complex objects. But if we omit these individuating features, then the instances involved turn into properties. We must remember that properties, according to Meinong, are mysteriously turned into instances by being associated with individuating features, that is, with places and moments. Thus we arrive at the following complex object: $<F, G, H>$. This, then, is what Meinong thinks of as the referent of 'a fish.' I shall call such complex objects, which consist entirely of properties, 'natures.' Meinong, at this early stage in his philosophical development, does not explicitly acknowledge that these natures belong to his ontology. We shall see that natures, as time goes on, play a more and more important part in Meinong's thought until, at long last, they are discussed at great length under the heading of 'Incomplete Objects.' For the moment, we must keep in mind that Meinong's ontology contains, from the very beginning, these clandestine entities.

7   Some Real Relations

In the last main section of Meinong's work on relations, the horizon suddenly broadens. Meinong's study leaves the Humean framework. He suddenly realizes that there may be many more kinds of relations than he has so far discussed. More importantly, it suddenly occurs to him that there must be relations which are fundamentally different from the relations he has so far acknowledged. He sees that the view with which he started out is false. Not all relations, he argues now, are created by a mental activity. In addition to such *ideal* relations, he now maintains, there are also *real* relations.

He mentions three important examples of real relations. First, there is the relation between 'a presentation and the content toward which it is directed.'[48] This very description shows that Meinong here confuses two very different relations with each other, so that his subsequent discussion becomes ambiguous. We must distinguish between the intentional relation between an idea (content of a presentation) and what the idea is an idea of, on the one hand, and between the relation which holds between an idea and the act of presentation to which it belongs, on the other. The latter relation is presumably the same as the association relation that ties instances into a perceptual object. In the same fashion, certain mental entities are bound together to make up a certain mental experience, for example, a presentation, or a judgment, etc. Meinong confuses here the intentional relation with the association relation. The reason for the confusion, we may surmise, consists in in his fundamental confusion between the intention of an idea and the idea itself.

Keeping this ambiguity in Meinong's exposition in mind, we may continue. Meinong claims that this first example of a real relation differs from the earlier mentioned ideal relations in two respects. The real relation does not hold between two ideas but between an idea and a presentation. Furthermore, this relation is not the product of any mental activity; we are as passive in regard to this relation as we are in regard to the foundations of ideal relations.

The second real relation mentioned by Meinong holds between ideas when they form a complex idea. [49] Meinong argues that there must be a relation that individuates complex ideas. He reminds us that perceptual objects are individuated by places and moments, but that mental entities do not contain places, and that different ones can occur simultaneously. Since he cannot find any feature that does for mental complexes what places do for non-mental ones, he feels compelled to postulate a certain relation which somehow guarantees that simultaneous mental complexes can be distinguished from each other. This argument, too, is rather confused and confusing. If Meinong is really worried about the individuation of mental complexes, a relation like that of association alone will not do. On the other hand if he is really worried about how instances form complexes, then the fact that there are no places for mental complexes is irrelevant.

One could interpret what Meinong says about the first two real relations in the following way. He means to talk, first, about the intentional relation between an idea and its intention, and, second, about the association relation among ideas which form complexes. Accordingly, he is maintaining that the intentional relation and the association relation are both real rather than ideal relations. That this interpretation is not the only plausible one, however, is clear from what Meinong says about these two relations. But it also follows from the fact that Meinong later holds that, while the association relation is indeed a real relation, the intentional relation is quite obviously an ideal relation.

The third and last example of a real relation is the relation which, according to Meinong, must hold between the foundations of ideal relations, on the one hand, and these relations, on the other. Since the foundations are the *condition* for the occurrence of the corresponding idea of the relation, Meinong argues, this relation cannot simply be a causal relation. Here, too, we find a confusion. There is, on the one hand, the question of how the foundations of a relation are related to the relation. This, it appears, is what Meinong wants to talk about. On the other hand, there is the different question of how the idea of a relation is related to the ideas of its foundations. Meinong argues that the third example of a real relation cannot be the relation of causality by switching from the latter question to the former. What he says is, in effect, that the relation between an idea of a relation and the ideas of its foundations may be causal, but that the relation between an ideal relation and its foundations cannot be causal. It is clear that Meinong's contention that the foundations of a relation must be related to the relation invites an infinite regress. In the background lurks Bradley's argument against relations. We shall return to this topic in a later chapter.

Meinong thus claims that, in addition to the ideal relations discussed earlier, there are also quite different relations, namely, real relations. His next task is to distinguish between these two kinds of relations as precisely as possible.

At first, he tries to make this distinction in terms of the following criterion: while ideal relations are relations between presentations, real relations are relations between real things.[50] But this criterion contradicts his earlier claim that the ideal relation of causality is a relation between real things rather than presentations. In order to avoid the contradiction, Meinong repeats his earlier contention that the causal relation reduces to necessity and temporal contiguity, and, ultimately, to relations of compatibility and comparison. And these relations, he re-affirms, hold between presentations, not real things. But if this is true, then it is not clear at all how Meinong can continue to hold, as he does, that causality holds between real things. How are we to reconcile the two assertions (a) that causality reduces to comparison and compatibility between presentations and (b) that 'if someone wanted to assert causality between merely presented objects, this would be the same as if one wanted to tell a true story about a prince from a fairy tale'?[51]

His second criterion is in terms of mental activity: ideal relations are produced by mental activity, while real relations are passively given. Meinong proposes to speak of relations of spontaneity and relations of receptivity. This criterion explains the use of the terms 'ideal' and 'real.' If a relation is merely the product of a special mental activity, according to Meinong, then it does not belong to the foundations as such and without this activity. Such a relation is therefore *subjective* or *ideal*. On the other hand, if the person merely perceives the relation, then the relation must really hold between its terms.[52] Such a relation is therefore *objective* or *real*. At this point, Meinong identifies ideal relations with relations which are a product of the mind and real relations with relations which exist independently of any mental activity. Later on, Meinong will hold that all relations are objective, independent of mental activity. But he will retain the distinction between ideal and real relations.

As soon as Meinong realizes that he has now taken the fateful ontological step of admitting relations as non-mental entities, he has second thoughts about his original approach; for what else but ontological prejudice could have made him believe in the first place that such relations as equality, compatibility, etc., are mental rather than non-mental? Do we not believe that the relation of equality holds just as objectively and without any mental activity between two instances as any so-called real relation? What could be more 'objective' than the fact that two instances of the same pitch stand in the equality relation to each other? Moreover, do we not also believe that this relation holds between 'real entities' rather than our ideas of them? Meinong tries to save his position concerning the mental nature of ideal relations by two arguments. [53] These arguments are merely versions of the two arguments with which we started this chapter.

He argues, first, that the realistic position can at best only hold for equality but not for compatibility relations; for, of two incompatible mental phenomena, only one can exist. Meinong talks here about mental phenomena, but his argument can be generalized. The incompatibility relation cannot exist between real things, but only between ideas, because of two incompatible things, only one can exist. Meinong assumes that a relation must hold between two existents, and he concludes that, since of two incompatible things only one can exist, the incompatibility relation must really hold between the ideas of the incompatible things. By a similar argument one could try to prove that ideas have fishtails. Since there are no mermaids, one could argue, the property of having a fishtail which one usually predicates of mermaids cannot really belong to mermaids, but must belong instead to what does indeed exist when we think of mermaids, namely, our ideas of mermaids.

Meinong argues, second, that even equality and inequality must hold between ideas; for these are relations of comparison and one cannot compare what is not presented. Phenomena are comparable only in so far as they are presented to us, and to be presented is to be a presentation. The fallacy of this second argument is the typical idealistic fallacy: From the admitted fact that one cannot compare what one has no ideas of, one concludes that what one compares are one's ideas.

Meinong's third and last distinction between real and ideal relations is also the most important. Ideal relations are said to be known independently of experience; they are known *a priori* from mere presentations.[54] Real relations, on the other hand, are known only on the basis of empirical data. That a certain ideal relation holds between two entities follows from the very nature of the foundations of this relation. This is not the case for real relations. We may know all there is to know about the terms of a real relation and yet not know in what real relation they stand to each other. The paradigm case of an ideal relation – as far as its epistemological status is concerned – is the relation of inequality between two (instances of) colors. The paradigm of a real relation is the association relation between a color and a place. Why this particular color (instance) is at just this particular place cannot be answered by means of rational insight.

Meinong, as I said earlier, retains the distinction between real and ideal relations even after he has abandoned the notion that some relations are created by the mind. He gives up what I have here called the first criterion as soon as he distinguishes between an idea and its intention. The second criterion is retained, but in a different form. Ideal relations, Meinong will eventually hold, are not produced by an activity of the mind, but can be known only by such an activity. What requires the activity is, not the relation, but the idea of the relation. To have an idea of an ideal relation, according to this later view, requires a certain mental activity, while this activity is not necessary for the idea of a real relation. But the main distinction between real and ideal relations remains the third one. That an ideal relation holds, can be known *a priori*; that a real relation holds, can be known only *a posteriori*.

In the second *Hume Study*, Meinong's most significant achievement is his recognition of mind-independent relations. The greatest fault of this work consists in the pervasive confusion between ideas and their intentions. But this confusion does not last very long. Meinong, just like Husserl, comes to see that one must distinguish, not just between a mental act and its content, but between the act, the content (idea) of the act, and the intention (object) of the act. And just as it does for Husserl, this distinction opens up for Meinong a vast new field of philosophical inquiry. Husserl discovers phenomenology. Meinong, in the same vein, proclaims the discovery of a new philosophical discipline, the theory of entities. Such is the historical importance of the act-content-intention distinction to which we turn next.

III

Ideas and their Intentions

In 1894, there appeared a rather slim book by K. Twardowski, a student of Brentano's, which influenced the course of philosophy.[1] In this book, Twardowski argued that the intention of a mental act – its 'object' – is in no sense of the term 'immanent' to the act. He argued, in other words, that the intention of a mental act is never a part of that act. Twardowski, therefore, distinguished between the content of an act of presentation – what I shall sometimes call an 'idea' – and the object of this act. Without this distinction, I am convinced, there would be neither phenomenology nor a theory of entities. Meinong, as we shall see presently, adopts Twardowski's distinction. He even presents the same arguments for it as Twardowski. For this reason, we shall briefly turn to Twardowski's work in order to assess the soundness of one of Meinong's most basic and enduring views.

1   *Twardowski's Distinction*

Twardowski introduces a three-fold distinction for mental acts of presentation.[2] First, there is the act itself. Second, there is the content of this act; this content is a part of the act. Third, there is the intention (the object) of the act. This intention is, not a part of the act like the content, but stands to the act (to the content) in an indefinable relation, the so-called intentional relation. In more familiar terms, Twardowski distinguishes between the act of having an idea, the idea, and the entity of which the idea is an idea.

Twardowski then argues, in defense of his distinction, that the content and the object of a presentation could not possibly be the same.[3] To this end, he presents three arguments and considers, but rejects, a fourth.

The first argument is as follows. If one makes a true judgment which denies an object, then one must have a presentation (an idea) of the object which one judges and denies. But in order to deny something, one must have a presentation (an idea) of what one denies. Hence one has presentations (ideas) even of those things which do not exist. But this shows that the content of a presentation must be distinguished from its object; for the former exists in such cases, while the latter does not.

The full force of Twardowski's argument is somewhat obscured by his formulation of it in terms of Brentano's particular theory of judgment. In essence, Brentano's early theory of judgment holds that all judgments are affirmations or denials of individual things.[4] To see how this works in a particular case, consider the apparently predicative judgment: *This house is green*. Brentano's transformation of this judgment into its 'correct' form proceeds in two steps. First, he translates this judgment into an existential one: *This green house is (exists)*. Second, he eliminates existence in favor of acts of affirmation: *This green house is affirmed*. All that remains of the predicative state of affairs is an individual thing, the green house. The rest is mental attitude.

Twardowski also embraces another part of Brentano's philosophy of mind, namely, the notion that every mental act other than a presentation is based on a presentation.[5] Keeping Brentano's theory of judgment in mind, it is easy to see how this notion works in the case of judgment as well as other mental acts. Every judgment, we just saw, is either the affirmation or the denial of an individual thing. What happens is that the individual thing is brought before the mind by means of a presentation; then the additional act of affirming or of denying occurs. Similarly, in the case of loving. A presentation puts a thing before the mind, then the additional act of loving occurs.

Twardowski's first argument, as I said, is formulated in terms of Brentano's theory of judgment. But it could be reformulated as follows. When we judge, for example, that the winged horse Pegasus does not exist, there occurs the thought that the winged horse Pegasus does not exist. This thought exists. It consists of certain ideas, among them the idea of the winged horse Pegasus. This idea must exist, too. But, of course, there is no such thing as Pegasus. Thus while the idea of Pegasus exists, its object does not. Therefore, the idea cannot be identical with the object.

The second argument has three sides to it, as it were. Twardowski points out, first of all, that the objects of ideas have very different properties and stand in very different relations from their ideas, and conversely. For example, a mountain is a spatially extended thing, while an idea of this mountain is not spatially extended. Then Twardowski makes this same point once more in a more forceful way about a contradictory entity. This is the second side of his argument. Consider, for example, the round square. It is perfectly clear that it cannot possibly be the idea of the round square to which one attributes contradictory properties; for the idea exists, and it could not possibly exist, if it had these properties.

But when Twardowski compares the properties of ideas with the properties of their objects, he also claims that nonexistent objects have properties. For example, he claims that the golden mountain is golden – while its idea is not – and that the round square is round as well as square – while its idea is neither. This is the third side of Twardowski's argument. It is crucial for Meinong's later view, although it is unimportant for the argument under discussion. Without the assumption that even nonexistent entities have properties and stand in relations, it is safe to say, there could be no theory of entities – nor could there be, I might add, phenomenology. We shall discuss Meinong's defense of this assumption later.[6] But I might as well admit now that I think that it is false. The golden mountain, since there is no such thing, cannot be golden. Nor can the round square be either round or square. Nor, finally, is it true of Hamlet – as some contemporary philosophers are fond of holding – that he is indecisive. Rather, what is the case is that the golden mountain *is imagined* to be golden, the round square *is conceived of* as round and as square, and Hamlet *is judged to be* indecisive. But, of course, there is a world of difference between the two statements that the golden mountain is golden and that it is imagined to be golden.

Twardowski's third argument for a difference between content and object rests on the fact that there are different descriptions of the same entity:[7]

A further proof for the real, not merely logical, difference between the content and the object of a presentation follows from the existence of so-called equivalent presentations [*Wechselvorstellungen*]. According to the customary definition, such presentations have the same extension but different contents. An example of equivalent presentations is: *the city located at the site of the Roman Juvavum* and *the birthplace of Mozart*. These two names have a different meaning, but they both designate the same thing. Now, since the meaning of a name, as we saw, coincides with the content of the presentation designated by the name, and since what the name names is the object of the presentation, we can also define presentations as presentations *in* which a different content but *through* which the same object is presented. But the difference between content and object is thereby already given. For one conceives of something quite different when conceiving of the city which is located at the site of the Roman Juvavum from what one conceives of when conceiving of the birthplace of

Mozart. These two presentations consist of very different parts. The first contains as parts the presentations of Romans and of an antique city forming a fortified camp; the second presentation contains as parts the presentations of a composer and of the relation in which he stands to his native city, while the relation to an old settlement formerly occupying that site, which was presented by the first idea, is absent. In spite of these great differences between the parts of the contents, both contents intend one and the same object. The same properties which belong to Mozart's birthplace also belong to the city located at the former site of the Roman Juvavum; the latter is identical with Mozart's birthplace. The object of the presentation is the same; what distinguishes them are their different contents.

This third argument rests, in my opinion, on a fundamental mistake. In one sentence, the mistake consists in identifying the entity described by a definite description with the object intended by the idea which is expressed by the description. Twardowski claims in regard to the two descriptions: (1) 'the city located at the site of the Roman Juvavum' and (2) 'the birthplace of Mozart' that they have a different *meaning*, but designate the same *thing*.[8] Then he goes on to claim that the meaning of an expression is the content expressed by the expresssion, while the thing designated by the expression is the object intended by the content. From this conception it follows that the descriptions (1) and (2) express different contents, but designate the same object. It follows, in other words, that the two descriptions express different ideas, but designate the same intention. Now, if this is true, then it also follows that, in the case of so-called equivalent presentations, the contents of the presentations cannot be identical with their objects.

Twardowski is wrong when he assumes that the objects of the two presentations are the same. Yet he comes very close to seeing the true state of affairs. He says that one conceives of something quite different when one conceives of the city located at the site of the Roman Juvavum from what one conceives of when conceiving of the birthplace of Mozart. If what one conceives of is the object of one's presentation – as seems natural – then it follows immediately from this remark that the two presentations must have different objects rather than the same object. Not only are our ideas (contents) different in these two cases, but what is before our minds, the objects of our ideas, are different, too. This fact becomes even more obvious when we notice that Twardowski says that the first content contains as a part the idea (content) of Rome, while the second content contains as a part the idea (content) of a certain composer. How could the first content possibly contain the idea of Rome, without bringing Rome before the mind; and how could the second possibly contain the idea of Mozart, without bringing Mozart before the mind? But if the first content puts, among other things, Rome before the mind, while the second does not, and the second puts, among other things, Mozart before the mind, while the first does not, then what the two contents present to the mind cannot be the same. Hence their objects cannot be the same.

Twardowski does not draw this conclusion, even though it is implied in what he says. Instead, he convinces himself that the two contents must have the same object, by pointing out that the city located at the Roman site has all the properties of Mozart's birthplace. He appeals to Leibniz' principle. But from this indubitable fact follows merely that the two described things are the same, not that the intentions of the two ideas are the same. Only if one mistakenly identifies, as Twardowski does, the intention of the idea expressed by a description with the entity described by the description does his conclusion follow.

Since Twardowski is wrong in identifying the intention of an idea with the entity described, his third argument – unlike the first two – is not sound. The two descriptions do not only express different ideas, they also have different intentions. Nor could it be otherwise; for a difference in ideas always means a difference in intentions. What could have misled Twardowski is a certain ambiguity in the term 'object.' We may quite naturally say that two descriptions describe the same object or that one has different ideas of the same object. But then we must realize that this use must be distinguished from another in which 'object' means 'intentional object'. This is another good reason for our avoiding the term 'object' in this context and for speaking instead of the intention of an idea.

Twardowski briefly considers and then dismisses a fourth argument, an argument advanced by Kerry. According to Kerry, content and object cannot be identical in the case of general presentations; for a general presentation has only one content, but many objects. Its objects are all those entities which fall under the presentation. We are reminded of Meinong's view that a general presentation somehow intends all the entities which fall under the presentation, but without intending the class of these entities. Twardowski rejects Kerry's argument. In this regard, he is on the side of the angels. But his own positive view on general presentations and on universals is thoroughly confused and confusing.[9]

To sum up. Of the three arguments presented by Twardowski, the first two are sound. Ideas must be distinguished from their intentions, because we have ideas of entities which do not exist. In such cases, the idea exists, its intention does not. And ideas must also be distinguished from their intentions because they have different properties.

The intention of an idea may be round, heavy, and hard, while the idea is none of these. Twardowski's third argument, though, is not sound. It involves the mistaken identification of the entity described by a description with the intention of the idea expressed by this description.

2 Meinong's View

Meinong's paper 'Über Gegenstände höherer Ordnung und ihr Verhältnis zur inneren Wahrnehmung' marks two important advances in his philosophical development.[10] He adopts Twardowski's distinction between the content and the object of a presentation. And he also acknowledges explicitly that complexes and relations form two categories of his ontology. The paper has two parts which correspond to these two main topics. In an introduction, Meinong makes Twardowski's distinction. Then he turns to the proper subject of the paper, namely, objects of higher order. These two parts of the paper are relatively unconnected. In this section, we shall look at Meinong's version of Twardowski's distinction. In the next chapter, we shall discuss the ontological problem of objects of higher order.

Meinong, at the beginning of his discussion of presentations, has a footnote to Twardowski: 'Much that is suggestive and helpful about this can be found in the work by K. Twardowski, "Zur Lehre vom Inhalt und Gegenstand der Vorstellungen" (Wien, 1894), which is here merely mentioned, since a discussion of it in detail would lead us too far afield.'[11]

He then argues that content and object of a presentation differ. He lists Twardowski's first two arguments, namely, that objects may not exist, even though their contents exist, and that contents and objects have different properties. In connection with the first argument, Meinong criticizes Brentano's earlier notion of an immanent object. To say of the golden mountain that it exists in the imagination, according to Meinong, is not to say of it that it has some kind of existence. There exists in this case neither a transcendental object nor an immanent one. To express the matter without ambiguity and without inviting confusion, one should say that what exists is the imagining of a golden mountain, the conceiving of it. To say this is to imply that the act and its content exist. In brief, to speak of the imagined golden mountain is, not to speak of an immanent object, but to speak of the imagining of a golden mountain. Meinong notices almost immediately that this criticism invites the very question which the notion of an immanent object was supposed to answer: How can a presentation (or content) intend the golden mountain, when there is no such thing to be intended? But he brushes the problem aside:[12]

That it [the presentation] can 'have' an (immanent) object, even
though the latter does not exist, may well appear at first somewhat
strange; however, on closer inspection, one finds in this very fact
the nature of the concept of an object especially clearly expressed,
a more thorough discussion of which would lead us too far
afield.

Thus while Meinong insists on distinguishing between content and
object even for nonexisting objects, he does not as yet face up to the
problem of nonexisting objects.

In regard to Twardowski's second argument, Meinong mentions a
number of crucial properties which distinguish contents from objects.
First, Meinong claims that there are objects which are not real, while
all contents are real since they are parts of real mental experiences.
Second, Meinong points out, very astutely, that while all contents
exist simultaneously with their acts, the intentions of these acts may
have existed in the past or may exist in the future. Third, while some
objects of presentations are nonmental, all contents are mental entities.
Fourth and finally, there are such properties as blue, warm, and heavy
which some objects have, but which contents never have.

The other two arguments of Twardowski's are only mentioned in a
footnote.[13] He agrees with Twardowski that to the same object there
may correspond different contents. But he disagrees with Twardowski
– and sides with Kerry – in regard to the argument from general
presentations. Meinong thinks that a general presentation has a number
of objects.

Granted that the content of a presentation must be distinguished
from its object, can we characterize this content any further? Meinong
argues that all acts of presentation must have something in common,
namely, something by virtue of which they are all presentations.[14]
They must possess a common property which characterizes them as
presentations rather than, say, as judgments or desires. Of course, all
judgments must similarly have something in common that accounts
for their being judgments. But acts of presentation cannot be merely
characterized by this common property; for they are often presentations
of different objects. Presentations cannot be completely alike, if they
are presentations of different objects. However one may conceive of
the relationship between a presentation and its object, Meinong claims,
the difference between their having different objects must somehow
rest on a difference between the presentations themselves. And whatever it is that presentations of different objects differ in, it is this entity
which is called the content of the presentation. This content exists, it
is real, it is present, and it is mental, even if the object does not exist,
is not real, is not present, and is not mental.

Meinong tries here to give an argument, not for the difference between content and object, but for the existence of contents. There have been philosophers, otherwise sympathetic to an ontology of mental acts, who have denied the existence of contents. Moore is a case in point. He claims that 'it is impossible to verify by observation the existence of any internal qualitative difference between every pair of acts which have different objects.'[15] Moore simply denies that he is ever acquainted with such entities as contents. This denial, of course, does not mean much in our context; Meinong, Husserl, and many other philosophers insist equally stubbornly that they are acquainted with contents. As a matter of fact, the whole of traditional philosophy is in this matter on Meinong's side rather than on Moore's. This becomes obvious as soon as we realize that what Twardowski and Meinong call contents are the ideas and concepts of the tradition. What Moore claims, we must emphasize, is that he is not acquainted with any ideas or concepts. Moreover, extending his denial to 'propositional' mental acts, he is also saying that he is never acquainted with thoughts, or wishes, or hopes, but only with the thinking, the wishing, and the hoping. To deny the existence of contents, in short, is to deny the existence of ideas, concepts, notions, and the like on the one hand, and the existence of thoughts, wishes, hopes, and the like on the other.

Tradition aside, what are we to make of Meinong's argument for the existence of contents? How does Moore respond to it? Meinong claims, in effect, that there must be something in or about a presentation that distinguishes it from another presentation with a different object. Moore agrees with this, but he interprets it to mean something entirely different. According to him, two presentations with different objects are indeed distinguished from each other; they are distinguished by the fact that the first presentation intends a certain object, while the second intends a different object. They are distinguished from each other by the fact that they stand in the same intentional relation to two different objects.[16] Meinong, of course, has something else in mind when he insists that the two presentations must be distinguished in some way. Just as an act of presentation differs from a judgment in that the former has a certain *property* which the latter lacks, and conversely, so two presentations with different objects must differ in that the one has a certain (non-relational) *property* which the other lacks, and conversely. These properties are the contents. These properties are the ideas and concepts of the tradition.

There is a closing remark by Meinong about the 'transparency' of contents.[17] The content, he says, always remains in the background in favor of the object.[18] There are linguistic reasons for this; for what a speaker wants to talk *about* is not what his words *express*, but what they *mean.* And what words mean are not the contents, but the objects of presentations. There simply are no words for the contents as there are words for the objects, so that one has to talk about the contents indirectly, as it were, by talking about their objects. In this fashion, one speaks of a certain idea or concept as the idea *of a mermaid* or the concept *of blue.*

A mental act, according to Meinong, is a complex consisting of two instances. One instance determines which kind of act it is. For example, all presentations contain instances which are equal to each other, but to no other kind of act; all judgments contain instances which are equal to each other, but to no other kind of act; and so on. The second sort of instance determines the intention of the act; it gives the act the 'direction' toward its particular intention. This instance is the traditional idea or concept. Furthermore, every act has an intention. This intention is not a part of the mental act.[19] It stands in an entirely different relation to the act.

This ontological account raises at least four important problems. First, there is the problem of the nature of the intentional relation: What kind of relation is it? Meinong arrives later at a straightforward answer. The intentional relation is an ideal relation which holds with necessity between its terms. Second, there is the problem of nonexistent intentions: How can a relation connect with an entity that has no being? Meinong's answer to this question in his later writings is not altogether clear. He thinks that every intention has at least 'Aussersein,' but it is not entirely clear what this means. Third, there is the problem of how to distinguish between sensory and non-sensory presentations. Presentations, we recall, are usually divided into intuitions and concepts. The former are sensory in character; the latter, not. What is at stake is a distinction between sensing and conceiving. Meinong, as we shall see, has a very hard time solving this problem to his own satisfaction. But the most pervasive as well as most difficult problem for him is the fourth problem: how to analyze complex contents into their simple constituents; in particular, how to reduce the contents of judgments to the contents of presentations. One important question is: do thoughts consist entirely of ideas? I shall remind the reader from time to time that some of Meinong's arguments, even though they seem to have little to do with these four problems, really revolve around them.

IV

Objects of Higher Order

Meinong's early ontology, to the extent to which he would acknowledge it explicitly, is very lean indeed. It comprises just one main category, the category of instances. His implicit ontology, though, is much richer. There are, most importantly, complexes of instances as well as complexes of properties; for a complex of instances is not itself an instance and a complex of properties is not a complex property. They must, therefore, belong to a different category. There are, furthermore, properties and relations. Meinong, we saw, presupposes them in his theory of abstraction and for his notion of equality. Finally, his ontology contains places and moments, since these entities cannot plausibly be viewed as instances. Meinong, it is clear, can hardly be accused of having started out with a penchant for ontological excesses. It is to his credit that he soon realizes that his implicit ontology is not the same as his explicit ontology; and with this realization, he loses his blindness to his own and other philosopher's ontological commitments. From then on, Meinong's philosophical inquiries are primarily ontological inquiries.

This conversion to ontology can best be seen in connection with the important paper 'Über Gegenstände höherer Ordnung und ihr Verhältnis zur inneren Wahrnehmung,' which appeared in 1899.[1] In this paper, Meinong asserts that complexes and relations are objects of higher order. He arrives at the views that complexes and relations form two (additional) categories and that complexes as well as relations are objective entities rather than products of mental activity.

Meinong's first discussion of complexes and relations, though, occurs in a much earlier paper, a review of Ehrenfels' influential article 'Über Gestaltqualitäten.'[2] Ehrenfels, a student of Meinong's, inaugurated with this article what was to be known as Gestalt theory and Gestalt psychology. It is rather fascinating to observe how these theories of epistemology and the philosophy of science take their beginnings with one single but very profound ontological problem.

Before we turn to Meinong's review article, it will be necessary once again to introduce some terminological distinctions. Needless to say, behind these distinctions hide a number of ontological commitments.[3] All the entities there are can be divided into *simple* and *complex* entities. This distinction is so fundamental that it cannot be defined in any way. But one can and must, of course, give examples. A specific shade of blue, for example, is a simple property; a square, not further divided by any lines, is a simple individual thing. On the other hand, there are such spatially complex entities as chairs, tables, mountains, etc. These happen to be temporally complex as well, but there are also temporal entities which are not spatial. Furthermore, the class consisting of all the natural numbers is a complex entity. Complex entities divide into categories depending on the kinds of entities they contain, the kinds of relations that hold among their parts, and the kind of part-whole relation involved.

From this point of view, the most important division of complex entities is that into *classes, structures,* and *states of affairs.* The four legs and the top of the table before me form a class (of spatial things). They are *members* of this class, that is, they stand in a unique relation to the class, the relation of membership. The table, though, is not a class but a (spatial) structure. The legs are not members of it, but are (spatial) *parts* of it. A structure, in distinction to a class, consists of certain entities which *stand in certain characteristic relations to each other.* In this case, the relations happen to be spatial, but they need not be spatial. There are structures of very different kinds. For example, the series of natural numbers forms a structure; in this case, the characteristic relation is the successor relation. Mathematicians investigate 'abstract' structures when they deal with lattices, groups, rings, etc.[4] Finally, there is the fact or state of affairs that the table is in front of me. This fact is neither a class nor a structure; the table is neither a member of it nor a part of it. I shall say that it is a *constituent* of this fact.

Meinong's complexes, to employ our terminology, are structures. Their characteristic relation is that of association. The ontological problem which I mentioned in connection with the beginnings of Gestalt theory is this: Are there structures? As the early Gestalt theoreticians conceived of it, the problem took the form: How are structures distinguished from mere classes?

1 Gestalt Qualities

Meinong agrees with Ehrenfels that a 'Gestalt' is more than the sum of its parts. This result follows, according to him, from an argument presented by Ehrenfels and quoted, in part, by Meinong:[5]

But one can 'assert at once that different complexes of elements, if they are nothing else but the sum of these, must be the more similar the more similar their individual elements are to each other.' If similarity, even equality, obtains nevertheless in the cases mentioned above despite greater or lesser dissimilarity of the elements, then 'the similarity between spatial and tonal configurations (*Gestalten*) rests on something other than the similarity between the elements. . . . Hence those configurations must be something other than the sum of the elements.'

Meinong adds: 'that from things unequal or dissimilar something equal or similar could be the sum, such an assumption, in my opinion, involves no less an incompatibility than the assumption of a yellow blue or a round square.'[6]

To make sense of the argument, we must give a non-literal interpretation of the expression 'sum of elements.' What Ehrenfels, Meinong, and others had in mind when they spoke of a sum of elements seems to me quite clear, despite the unfortunate choice of the arithmetic term 'sum.' A sum of elements is simply a class. So understood, the argument can be reformulated as follows. The degree of similarity between two classes can only be a function of the degree of similarity between their respective members.[7] Thus, if we encounter two complex entities which are very similar to each other, even though their parts are not, then we must conclude that these entities cannot be classes. This argument seems to me to be perfectly sound. It amounts to a proof that certain complex entities cannot be classes. If a melody, for example, were merely a class of tones, then it could not possibly matter in what temporal order the tones occur. But, of course, it does matter. A melody is thus a structure, characterized, not only by its tones, but also by certain relations among the tones. To understand why Ehrenfels, Meinong, and others thought of figures (literally: *Gestalten*) as complex entities, we must recall that they thought of spatial figures as composed of places. But we can make their point by considering, say, a square whose diagonals have been drawn. This square consists of four triangles in certain spatial relations to each other, but it is not identical with the class of these four triangles.

Granted, then, that there are structures as distinguished from classes, how do the former differ from the latter? Our answer is obvious: a class consists only of its members, while among the parts of a structure there is always a certain characteristic relation or relations. To put it suggestively – though misleadingly – what is 'added' to the members of the class is a relation. Of course, a structure is formed by certain entities *in* that relation; it is not the same as the class consisting of the members *and* the relation. Meinong, surprisingly enough, does not accept our answer.[8] He presents two arguments for his rejection. The first argument rests on Meinong's view that the relations of equality and similarity are somehow produced by the mind through acts of comparison.[9] It follows from this view that, unless there occur such acts of comparison, there are no such relations. Meinong simply appeals to introspection and claims that we cannot discover a large number of acts of comparison when we hear, for example, a melody. But, of course, if one can be aware of relations without any activity of comparing, then Meinong's argument breaks down. And, indeed, we would claim that the hearing of a melody involves, not only the hearing of certain tones, but also the hearing of certain relations among the tones. The similarity between two melodies is not just a function of the similarity between their respective tones, but also a function of the similarity between their respective relations. The lower limit of this kind of similarity, if I may put it so, is a mere isomorphism between two structures.[10] In the case of an isomorphism, neither the parts nor the characteristic relations of the structures involved need be similar in the sense here used.

Meinong believes that our view is even more obviously untenable when we consider spatial configurations; for in these cases there are no discrete entities, comparable to the tones of a melody, which are given to us and among which we could recognize relations. One can distinguish, according to Meinong, between as many places as one wishes, but before these places are distinguished from each other, no presentation of a relation between places can occur. This objection assumes that a spatial figure consists somehow of places, that these are the non-relational parts of it. But since we have earlier rejected places as part of the furniture of the world, we must deny this essential premise of Meinong's argument. Consider, then, two simple, undivided, squares, *A* and *B*, of unequal size. In this case, we are not dealing with spatial structures at all. Rather, we have two *simple*, spatial individuals before us which do not have any spatial parts. Their similarity in regard to shape is explained in terms of a certain property which they share, namely, the property of being square. Next, consider two 'squares' formed by small triangles and small circles, respectively. Now we are dealing with two structures. One of these structures consists of triangles, the other of circles. But these triangles and circles are arranged in the same way; the relations among them are the same. The similarity between the two structures is, in part, a function of these spatial relations.

A side remark of Meinong's reveals, I think, a deeper reason for his rejection of our view.[11] As it turns out, we are really talking at cross purposes. Recall our original question: What distinguishes a class from a structure? Meinong asks, instead: In what does the experience of a structure consist, granted that it involves the experience of the structure's parts? When we point to relations as the distinguishing feature, he takes us to mean that the experience of a structure consists of (a) experiencing its (non-relational) parts and (b) experiencing a relation (or relations). But this is, of course, not what we have in mind. To experience a structure, in our view, is to experience certain parts (which are not themselves relations) *as standing in relation* to each other. But never mind this talk about what we experience, the point can also be made in purely ontological terms. We must distinguish between two quite different questions. First, there is the question what does a structure consist of, what are its parts (in the wider sense)? Second, there is the question of what there is altogether, when there is a structure. A structure consists of certain non-relational parts and certain characteristic relations; this distinguishes it from a class. But what there is, is not just the parts, relational and non-relational, but also the structure itself. Thus, in giving our earlier answer, we did not mean to deny – as Meinong might assume – that there are structures in addition to their parts, relational and non-relational.

In order to see how Meinong might be led to confuse the two questions, we must turn to the positive part of his view. Meinong objects to the term 'Gestaltqualitäten' and proposes to talk, instead, about *founded contents*. Recall that this review of Ehrenfels' article was written before Meinong had adopted Twardowski's distinction between content and object. The whole discussion, therefore, suffers from an idealistic bias. In what follows, let us overlook this feature and think of contents, not as mental entities, but as non-mental entities. A melody, then, is in Meinong's terms a founded content which is founded on its tones. The tones are called the founding contents.

But now Meinong notices suddenly that this is the very same analysis which he has given of relations. The ideal relation of equality between two instances, for example, is also said to be a founded content; and the two instances are the foundations or the founding contents of the relation. Since the two analyses agree completely, complexes and relations are in danger of collapsing into each other. And Meinong does indeed identify the two or, rather, he holds for a brief moment that they are two aspects of the same thing:[12]

Relations cannot obtain where there is something simple: hence, no relation without [some] complex. But also no complexes whose components do not stand to each other and to the complex as a whole in relation at least in so far as they are parts of the whole. It is, strictly speaking, the same objective state of affairs which presents itself as complex and as relation, depending on the point of view, as it were, from which it is seen: relation, in particular, is the complex considered from the point of view of one (or several) of the components.

In the very next sentence, though, Meinong maintains that the concepts of relation and of complex are irreducible to each other and are part of the basic, indefinable data.

Meinong's ontological inability to distinguish between complexes and relations has an epistemological side to it; it raises the question as to why the ideas of the foundations are sometimes followed by the idea of a complex, sometimes by the idea of a relation. Meinong's answer is rather vague. He talks about a fusing of the founded with the founding ideas. The general import of this view is that in certain cases the founded idea is so intimately fused with the founding ideas that it is almost impossible to separate them out. But such a separation is presumably required for the occurrence of the idea of a relation. According to Meinong, a complex is simply more intimately fused with its foundations than is a relation.

Meinong's ontological problem arises because two very different relationships are treated alike as that of foundation to founded entity. According to our distinctions, certain entities are *parts* of structures, but the relationship between a relation and its terms is not that of being a part of.[13] Thus while the two entities A and B may be a part of the structure S, they are not a part of the relation R in which they stand to each other. Meinong, on the other hand, assumes that the relationship between S on the one hand and A and B on the other is the same as that between R on the one hand and A and B on the other. He identifies these two relationships because he is not very clear about the nature of either one. And this is due, we may surmise, to his psychological approach to the whole matter. As he sees it, there occur certain ideas, the foundations, and then there occurs a certain further idea, the founded idea; and this process is the same for ideas of relations and ideas of complexes. The psychological approach, in turn, points to an ontological confusion. Let me explain.

Consider two instances, F_i and G_i, and the complex $<F_i, G_i>$. This complex, like any other complex, is characterized by the association relation and the part-whole relation. In forming the complex, F_i and G_i are associated with each other. F_i and G_i are parts of the complex. Meinong, as we have seen, does not pay sufficient attention to these two important relations. Instead, he stresses the fact that the complex $<F_i, G_i>$ is a third entity in addition to the two entities F_i and G_i, and he thinks of the relationship between the complex and its parts somewhat vaguely as that of 'founded' to 'founding' entities. When it comes to relations, nothing really changes in his assay of the situation.

A relation between F_i and G_i, for example, is thought of as a third entity in addition to F_i and G_i, which is, just as the complex, founded on these two instances. But, of course, this founding relation cannot really be the part-whole relation which characterizes complexes. Meinong, however, can easily be misled because he is thinking of instances of relations rather than of relations. While it makes no sense, for example, to think of the relation of being to the left of as *consisting* of two chairs which happen to be to the left of each other, the idea that an instance of this relation, namely, the instance associated with these two chairs, may consist of the two chairs has a smidgen of plausibility. So that we do not confuse complexes with relations, I shall from now on depict relation R_1 between two entities E_1 and E_2 by the expression '$[E_1, E_2]$.' The context will have to make clear whether we are talking about a relation or an instance of a relation, and also what particular relation we have in mind. Such are the ambiguities attached to Meinong's theory of relations.

Meinong, we saw, identifies so-called Gestalt qualities with founded contents. Something seems to be amiss; for the quality of a Gestalt should be a quality of a founded content, not the content itself. Meinong blurs the distinction between a thing and its properties. But this blur comes as no surprise. Removing the blur, we shall distinguish between a structure and its properties (and the relations in which it stands to other entities). A Gestalt is a structure; a Gestalt quality, a property of such a structure. The development of Gestalt theory after Ehrenfels revolves, not so much around the ontological problem of whether there is the category of structure, but around the question of whether the properties of structures can be *reduced* to properties of and relations among their parts. Of course, this question can only be answered intelligibly after a notion of reduction has been explicated. The most incisive discussions of Gestalt theory usually provide a number of possible explications.[14] Fortunately, we need not consider these various notions of reduction. From an ontological point of view the issue is clear: Can a structure have a property F, even though none of its parts has F? Or, as it is sometimes put: Are there emergent properties?

It seems quite obvious to me that there are such properties.[15] Consider a square A with its diagonals drawn. It consists of four triangles which stand in certain spatial relations to each other. Now, A has the property of being square, even though none of its spatial parts has this property. We cannot claim that the sentence 'A is square' is merely short for a sentence about the triangles and their arrangement; for there are obviously squares which do not consist of triangles at all. However, it is true, of course, that four triangles, arranged in such a fashion, will form a square. This truth, though, does not yield an ontological reduction of the shape of the square to the properties of and relations among its parts. Structures, I conclude, have emergent properties.

But I do not wish to claim that they have all the properties anyone has ever attributed to them. For example, I do not believe in such emergent properties as 'the will of the people' or 'the mood of the crowd.' Nor do I wish to maintain that the properties of a structure somehow determine the properties of its parts. What the properties of a given structure are, is not to be decided *a priori*. It is a factual matter. I insist here on only two ontological points, namely, that there are structures, and that they can have properties other than those which their parts have.

2 Two Kinds of Dependence

Meinong returns to the topic of complexes and relations eight years later in his paper on objects of higher order. His view has matured. Ideas are no longer confused with what they are ideas of. Nor is he now in danger of confusing complexes with the relations which they contain.

Meinong now gives a definition of objects of higher order in terms of a unique kind of dependence:[16]

> There are, as we know, objects which have by nature an inner dependence. I do not mean that dependence of occurrence by virtue of which, say, color cannot be conceived of without extension. This dependence, too, may be based on the nature of color and extension; but one can still call it external [*äusserlich*] compared with that [which] I am tempted to call unfinished [*Unfertigkeit*], which, for example, belongs to the object 'inequality,' when one tries to isolate it from what is unequal. I cannot think of inequality without reference to objects to which it is attached, as it were, while it at least makes sense to hold that a thought of blue or yellow contains nothing about space, even though it is impossible to think of color without thinking of extension as well.

We are thus invited to compare and contrast two kinds of dependence: the mutual dependence between color and extension, on the one hand, and the dependence of a relation on its terms, on the other. What Meinong seems to have in mind is that, while it is equally true that color cannot exist without extension and relations cannot exist without terms, the very notion of a relation involves that of terms, while the notion of color does not contain that of extension. Let us pretend that we can make sense of this distinction. It is at any rate clear that relations require terms, that is, that the category of relation consists of entities which have terms. But it is also clear that the same dependence attaches to properties as well as relations. A property is always a property of something, just as a relation is always a relation between entities. Meinong, however, thinks of properties as parts of complexes. This explains why he does not view properties as objects of higher order. We encounter here the basic asymmetry between properties, on the one hand, and relations, on the other, characteristic of all ontologies in which individual things are conceived of as complexes of properties. In such ontologies, properties are not exemplified by anything, they are merely associated with each other. Relations, however, not being parts of complexes, must stand in quite a different relationship to the properties or complexes of properties between which they hold.[17] Meinong's distinction between two kinds of dependence, we see, is a direct consequence of his ontology of complexes.

We can therefore explicate Meinong's view in the following way. Certain instances depend on each other in the sense that they are *necessarily associated* with each other. This is one kind of dependence. However, relations depend on their terms in a different way. It is necessary that there are terms which *exemplify* them. Perhaps, one could also put the distinction in this way: while it is not part of the notion of an instance that it be associated with something else, it is part of the notion of a relation that it be exemplified by something.

Be that as it may, Meinong claims that the kind of dependence which characterizes relations as objects of higher order also characterizes complexes. They, too, are said to depend on their parts in this indefinable way which we have tried to elucidate. It is this similarity between relations and complexes which makes the notion of an object of higher order significant. However, from our point of view, as we just stressed, there is no such similarity. A complex depends on its parts simply in that it *consists* of them; a relation, on the other hand, does not consist of its terms, but is *exemplified* by them. A relation depends on its terms simply in that it is exemplified by them; a complex is not exemplified by its parts nor by anything else.[18]

As examples of non-relational objects of higher order, Meinong mentions such complexes as a melody and a red square. The tones of the melody are the entities on which the melody is founded; in the case of the red square, a certain connection between color and shape establishes the complex. So far there is nothing new in his exposition. But Meinong also mentions examples which are neither melodies nor spatial configurations, namely, numbers.[19]

While Meinong does not tell us what kinds of entities numbers are, he does tell us that expressions like 'four nuts,' 'six people,' and 'nine planets' represent objects of higher order.[20] And he also distinguishes implicitly between three non-relational kinds of objects of higher order.

First, there are the 'numerical' objects of higher order just mentioned; then there are classes or, as he puts it, objective collections; finally, there are 'ordinary' complexes, that is, those objects of higher order which involve the association relation. His ontology is rapidly becoming more complex.

3 The Principle of Coincidence

In his review of Ehrenfels' paper, Meinong was not too clear about the relationship between relations and complexes. We saw that he came very close to identifying them. This confusion is now no longer present. A complex, he explains, is more than just a class of parts. In order for a and b to be parts of a complex, they must stand in some relation R to each other, that is, they are only parts of a complex because of the relation R in which they stand to each other. Furthermore, in order to conceive of a and b as parts of a complex, one must conceive of them as terms of a relation R. Conversely, if we assume that a and b stand in the relation R, then this cannot possibly mean that in addition to a and b there exists the relation R, which, together with a and b, forms a class. Rather, a and b must belong to a complex by virtue of the fact that they stand in the relation R to each other. Hence, if the relation obtains between a and b, then there exists, *ipso facto*, also a complex which has the terms of the relation as its parts. And if one conceives of a and b as standing in the relation R, one must conceive of them as parts of a complex. In this fashion, we arrive at the following principle: Wherever there is a complex, there is a relation, and conversely.

Meinong goes on to claim that this principle does not just assert a factual connection. A relation is a part of the complex; in addition to the relation, a complex contains as parts the terms of the relation, that is, just those entities on which the relation depends in the same manner as the complex. This relationship of partial identity – between the terms of the relation and the non-relational parts of the complex – and mutual dependence is called 'partial coincidence.'[21] Meinong adds, as a measure of his newly found realism, that this partial coincidence belongs to relations and complexes independently of their being conceived of.

The complex C is formed, according to this view, by a and b standing in the relation R. But this can only mean, according to Meinong, that a and b stand to R in the relations R' and R'', respectively, or, at least, that both stand to R in the relation R'.[22] Let us assume that the relation between a and R is the same as the relation between b and R, and let us call this relation R'. Now, if this relation is required, then another relation R'' is required to connect R' with, say, a. And so on. An infinite regress appears. However, Meinong does not think that this constitutes a serious difficulty. He compares it with the fact that the division of a line leads to an infinite series of ever smaller lines; and he points out that the relation R occupies a rather privileged position in the infinite hierarchy of relations, since all the other relations may be of the same kind. This latter assertion amounts to making a distinction between various relations R, S, T, etc. on the one hand, and an 'exemplification relation' on the other. The relations R', R'' and, similarly, the relations S', S'', etc., are then one and all the exemplification relation.

It is true that this infinite regress is not a vicious one. Meinong merely claims that any relational fact involves infinitely many further relational facts or, to be more precise, that if a relational fact exists, infinitely many further relational facts also exist. But, of course, this claim may be either true or false. I think that in this form it is almost certainly false. Nor is it very difficult to see which assumption leads Meinong to postulate an infinite series of relations. It is the assumption that a relation R can only hold between its terms a and b, if R is, in turn, somehow related to its terms. But this assumption is false. A relation relates its terms, but is not related to them. It is indeed hard to see how two non-relational entities like a and b could be in any way connected with each other, unless there existed a relation between them. But it would be a mistake to extend this idea to relational entities as well. If I may use an analogy, Meinong argues just like someone who concludes that there must be, in addition to ordinary glue, also super glue; for, since two wooden boards can only stick together when they are glued together, so glue can only stick to a board when it is glued to it by means of super glue. Just as the difference between wooden boards and glue is of importance if one wishes to avoid this silly conclusion, so the distinction between relational and non-relational entities is of importance if one wants to avoid the Bradleyan regress. What Bradley's argument shows is, in the last analysis, that relations behave quite differently from non-relational entities when it comes to being related to something. Bradley, needless to say, is comparable to someone who concludes from our glue and board example that there simply can be no glue at all.

In a footnote by Auguste Fischer to the reprint of Meinong's article in the *Gesammelte Abhandlungen*, another difficulty is noted.[23] In order to conceive of a relational fact, say, the fact that a and b stand in the relation R, one would have to conceive of an infinite number of further relational facts involving the relations R', R'', etc.; for one could not conceive of R as holding between a and b, unless one conceived of R as 'having something to do' with a, say, and this, in turn, would presuppose a further conception of the relation R' as being somehow involved in the case. And so on. But now it is quite obvious that the conception of some relational fact does not involve an infinity of further conceptions. Hence something must be wrong with Meinong's view. However, Meinong does not reach our conclusion outlined above. He claims in a later work that this problem merely shows that presentation (conception) alone cannot acquaint us with relations (and complexes). [24] Relations and complexes, according to this later view, are grasped by the mind by means of judgments and assumptions. Here we have one of the many unsolved problems which Meinong later attacks in terms of a newly discovered kind of mental act, namely, assumptions.

If we subscribe to the principle of coincidence, the question arises whether complexes with more than two parts involve relations with more than two terms. Assume, for example, that the complex C consists of the non-relational parts $a, b,$ and c. Meinong considers the possibility that in this case there are two two-term relations, R and R', such that R holds between a and b, and R' holds between b and c. The complex C would thus be formed by means of two two-term relations instead of one three-term relation. A complex could then contain more than just one relation. Now, if we want to preserve the principle of partial coincidence, Meinong remarks, then we must conceive of C as being composed of two complexes, namely, the complex formed by virtue of the relation between a and b, and the complex formed by virtue of the relation between b and c. A third relation would have to tie the two complexes together into the complex C. According to this view, a complex would either involve just one two-term relation or else it would be more complicated and consist of a number of complexes with two-term relations. Meinong rejects this view on the ground that it does not agree with most of our experience. [25] He directs our attention to a case where we conceive of six objects either as a definite or indefinite plurality, and he asks: Who could believe in this case that first only parts of objects are united into a complex, and then two of these pairs into another complex, and so on? He concludes, therefore, that it is mere prejudice to believe that no relation can have more than two terms.

With this conclusion, we can most certainly agree. What seems doubtful, though, is the implied position that every complex with more than two non-relational parts must contain a relation with more than two terms. Meinong seems to imply that the relation of a complex always has as many terms as the complex has non-relational parts. But it is hard to see why this should be the case. Take the series of natural numbers; it forms a complex. Is there any reason to assume that its characteristic relation is anything other than the two-term relation of being the next in the series, the so-called successor relation?

At any rate, two things are of historical interest. First, Meinong acknowledges now, not only that relations exist independently of human minds, but also that there are relations with more than two terms. Second, he argues that the principle of coincidence requires such relations.

4 Real and Ideal Objects

In the second *Hume Study*, Meinong distinguishes between ideal and real relations. Ideal relations are conceived of as mere mental entities, while real relations are thought of as given to rather than produced by the mind. Meinong changes this explication. He offers a new and less idealistic one. And he extends this new distinction between what is ideal and what is real to cover complexes as well, so that he can now speak of a dichotomy between real and ideal objects of higher order.

Objects, according to Meinong, are *real* if and only if they either exist or are such that, even though they do not exist, they could exist by their very nature. For example, a house, a chronograph, a book, but also color, tone, electricity, and the like are said to be real objects. Ideal objects, by contrast, are entities which cannot be said to exist, even though they must be affirmed in some sense. Absence, limit, the past, etc. are claimed to be the traditional examples of what is non-real and, hence, ideal. Meinong adds a number of new examples to this list. He says that the similarity between a copy and the original, though it does not exist, must be affirmed. [26]

He mentions, as another example of an ideal object, the number four. He claims that in the case of the earlier mentioned four nuts, the number four does not exist, in addition to the nuts, as a piece of reality. Rather, this number, like any other number, is an ideal complex. Thus there are ideal relations like the relation of similarity, and there are ideal complexes, for example, the number four. A color, that is, an instance of a color, which is located at a certain place forms, together with the place, a real complex. Meinong maintains that the principle of coincidence demands a real relation for a real complex. In this particular case the real relation which is characteristic of this real complex is the relation of association between instances.

Meinong's explication of the distinction between real and ideal objects rests on a distinction between two kinds of being. Certain entities are said to *exist*, while others are claimed to *obtain*. For purposes of translation, I shall from now on call the second mode of being, the being of ideal objects, *subsistence*. Real objects are said to exist, according to this convention, while ideal objects merely subsist. Notice that real and ideal objects are no longer characterized in terms of what is mental and what is not mental. Nevertheless, certain epistemological considerations lurk in the background. Meinong has a second criterion up his sleeve. Real objects, according to this criterion, are known *a posteriori*, while ideal objects are known *a priori*. What really convinces Meinong, for example, that the association relation is a real relation is the fact that he cannot possibly understand – in the sense of having a rational insight – why this particular color instance should be associated with this particular place. In contrast, that a certain color instance is similar to another color instance can presumably be known *a priori*.

Meinong alludes to this second criterion in the section of his article which is called 'Objects of experience and founded objects.' It is part of the nature of real objects that they are perceivable; ideal objects, on the other hand, are not in this sense perceivable. But if they are not perceivable, how do we know that there are such entities? Meinong faces here a very formidable problem. His solution of the problem is not too clear, but the gist of it is that the ideas on which perceptual judgments are based are passively given, while the ideas by means of which we are acquainted with ideal objects are produced by the mind and, hence, require a certain mental activity. [27]

Meinong considers, as an illustration, a comparison between two colors *a* and *b*. Such a comparison involves this: that the idea of *a* enters into a real relation with the idea of *b*, thus forming a complex idea. Meinong's next sentence reveals the crux of the matter: 'The operation which aims at the creation of this relation leads then, under sufficiently favorable circumstances, to the occurrence of a new idea, in this case, the idea of inequality.' [28] The new idea is, of course, not the idea of inequality in general, but the idea of inequality between *a* and *b*. This inequality, as a rule, is not just presented but also known by means of an evident judgment.

Meinong's analysis involves three important steps. First, he claims that the comparison between *a* and *b* consists in the idea of *a* and the idea of *b* entering into a real relation, and thus forming a real complex. Second, the occurrence of this complex idea is said to be followed, under favorable circumstances, by the occurrence of a further idea. This is the idea of the inequality between *a* and *b*. Third, and finally, there occurs usually also a judgment, based on this idea of the inequality between *a* and *b*, to the effect that *a* and *b* are unequal. This analysis raises a whole series of unanswered questions. For example, what is the intention of the complex idea formed from the ideas of *a* and of *b* by the real relation? Since this is an idea, although a complex one, it must have an intention. One might think for a moment that the relation of inequality between *a* and *b* is its intention, but this is denied by Meinong. Rather, there occurs presumably another idea in the wake of the complex idea under discussion, and this one is the idea of the relation. Again: what is the nature of this latter idea? Is it complex or simple? If it is complex, how does it differ from the complex idea consisting of *a* and *b* in the real relation? We shall see that these and similar questions haunt Meinong from now on. The ultimate problem is that of how complex intentions can be presented by complex ideas or, in one sense of this Kantian terminology, how the synthetic unity of apperception is to be understood.

The difference between this case and a case of perception consists presumably in the fact that in this case the idea of inequality between *a* and *b* is not given, like a sense-impression, but is acquired through an activity, an activity which somehow consists of two ideas' entering into a real relation. When we perceive a certain color at a certain place, this activity is presumably absent. What, precisely, happens in this case? Meinong does not tell us. But we must infer that he would hold that no activity of comparison is necessary in order for there to appear the idea of the relation of association between the color and the place. In short, ideas of ideal relations require a comparison, while ideas of real relations do not. But is this really true? Do we have to compare, say, green and red in order to know that they are different? I am inclined to believe that we do not. The following view seems to me to be very plausible. What we compare, in truth, are always entities in regard to one or more of their properties, not two properties by themselves. For example, we may compare two chairs in regard to their colors, or we may compare two colors in regard to their saturation, but we cannot really compare two colors as such or two chairs as such. When we compare, say, the two chairs in regard to color, we *pay attention* to their colors – rather than other properties and relations – and *notice* whether they have the same color or not, or whether they have similar colors, etc. Of course, it is part and parcel of this view that, say, the relation of inequality between the colors of the two chairs is just as much 'passively' given to us as the colors themselves. The only 'activity' which occurs consists in one's paying attention to certain properties rather than others.

The judgment that *a* and *b* are unequal is said to be evident. *a* and *b are* not just unequal, they *must* be unequal. According to Meinong, the 'must' here expresses that kind of logical necessity which is based on the natures of *a* and *b* on the one hand and of the relation of inequality on the other. If a color and a place are associated with each other, then this relation of association is somehow built upon its terms, too, but its terms could also have entered into a different relation: one can imagine this color at a very different place, and one can imagine this place to be differently colored. In order to mark this difference, Meinong proposes to say from now on that only ideal relations have *foundations*; the terms of an ideal relation are called its foundations. And he hints that there exists a special relation which connects the terms of an ideal relation with the relation.

As it turns out, real and ideal objects of higher order differ from each other in three connected respects. First, real objects exist, while ideal objects merely subsist. Second, real objects can be known *a posteriori*, while ideal objects are known *a priori*. Third, real objects are perceived, while ideal objects are given to us by means of 'idea production.'

5 *Spatial Complexes*

Meinong also discusses, among other things, two rather difficult problems, namely, the problem of how places combine into spatial figures and the problem of how entities which exist at different times can form an object of higher order. We shall take up these two discussions in the present section and the next one.

Consider a square A which is uniformly colored blue. This square has no spatial parts. Of course, one can imagine it to be divided into two rectangles or four triangles, but imagined parts are not real parts. Nor can we say that the square consists of four straight lines. These lines are not *parts* of the square, in the sense here intended, but constitute its *boundaries*. But if A has no spatial parts, then it cannot be an object of higher order. This, in essence, is our objection to Meinong's claim that all spatial figures are objects of higher order. [29] The square A does not even have spatial parts; how could it then consist of places, as Meinong claims?

Meinong's attempt to answer this objection is of truly heroic proportions. Nothing less than the existence of places is at stake and, hence, what is ultimately in question is his ontology of complexes of properties. Meinong first points out that the fact that A is a unity (*Einheit*) does not speak against its being an object of higher order; for every complex is such a unity. We may easily concede this point to Meinong. It does not touch upon our objection.

Next, Meinong admits that the square A has no parts in the sense that it is not further divided into smaller squares, or triangles, etc. But since we could draw certain lines and thus divide A into certain parts, Meinong raises the question of whether or not something has parts even if it is not divided but is merely divisible; and he answers this question in the following way: [30]

> However, what is divisible cannot possibly be simple; and what is not simple, but rather complex, seems to have to have [i.e., seems to be such that it must have] parts. But the difficulty is first of all of a terminological nature. What is divisible must contain the stuff for distinction. However, the differences which it contains do not have to separate out into natural unities; in reality,

when the latter is the case, then there is no longer mere
divisibility, but division.

Meinong then proposes to distinguish between determinate and
indeterminate parts. Indeterminate parts are those differences which,
according to him, are contained in undivided entities which are
divisible. And he tries to answer our objection in terms of this distinction between two kinds of parts.

It may fairly be objected to Meinong's solution that it is nothing
short of a merely verbal maneuver. To say of an entity that it contains
differences or that it has indeterminate parts, is to say nothing more
than that it is divisible. The notion of an indeterminate part, when
taken any other way, is simply an absurdity, comparable to Locke's
indeterminate triangle. What is divisible is indeed different from what
is not divisible; for it can be divided. But that something *can* be divided
into (determinate) parts does not mean that it *is* already divided into
a different sort of part. In short, a possible part is not a kind of actual
part. Meinong himself notices a peculiarity in this notion of an indeterminate part; for, as he remarks, indeterminate constituents can
only be made out after they have first been stripped of their indeterminacy, that is, after they are no longer indeterminate parts but genuine
parts.[31]

Meinong, returning to our main objection after a number of further
considerations, claims now that this objection only holds, if the parts
of objects of higher order cannot be indeterminate parts. What our
objection really shows, he thinks, is that the apparently simple square
A is an object of higher order, but an object of higher order which is
built, not upon determinate parts, but on indeterminate parts. In
general, the lesson we are supposed to draw is that complexes and
relations may be based on indeterminate parts just as well as on
determinate parts. But Meinong seems to be somewhat unhappy with
this way out, as well he should be; for he returns to the topic again in
a later article, and he also remarks, in the article now under consideration, that there is possibly still another answer to our objection.[32] He
maintains, first, that in regard to space and time, a point can be nothing
but a limit, while this is not equally certainly the case in regard to
color or tone continua. Second, he claims that if these latter continua
consist of punctiform elements, then our objection would not apply
to them, since they are not really continuous after all, but have parts
instead.[33] These remarks are rather brief and not altogether clear.
Even if what he says about colors and tones is true, there remains the
objection in regard to the square *A*, since Meinong himself admits
that *A* does not consist of spatial points. Furthermore, these remarks
call our attention to another problem: if there are no spatial points,

OBJECTS OF HIGHER ORDER

then what are the places Meinong talks about? Are they mere 'limits'? For that matter, what is a limit? Meinong, it is clear, is here grappling with the deepest issues of the ontology of space (and time).

6 *Temporal Complexes*

Consider a melody whose tones, naturally, occur successively at different moments. Meinong's problem arises from the following argument. If this melody consists of its tones such that one cannot possibly be aware of the melody without being aware of every one of its tones, then one cannot hear the melody *before* all of its tones have been presented; one cannot be aware of the melody before the last tone has occurred. However, since the melody consists not just of the last tone, but of all its tones, it seems that when one is aware of the melody, one must be aware of all its tones, not just of its last tone. It therefore seems to be the case that one can only be aware of a melody if all its tones are *simultaneously* presented. But plain experience seems to show that the tones are not simultaneously presented. Hence it seems to follow that we cannot really be aware of a melody at all. Surely, something must be wrong with this argument.

Meinong calls our attention to his newly adopted distinction between an idea and what the idea is of and declares that we must distinguish between the act-time and the intention-time.[34] The occurrence of an idea is temporally determined by the act-time; in other words, an idea is said to occur when the act of having it occurs. Meinong makes now two crucial assertions. First, act-time and intention-time do not have to coincide, as shown by the fact that one can now remember things that happened in the past. Second, intentions with durations can be presented in durationless mental acts. I think that both of these assertions are true. An individual thing which is before my mind need not exist simultaneously with my thinking of it.[35] Furthermore, when I am aware that, say, tone T is followed by tone T', I am aware of a temporal relation between these two tones, but my awareness itself has no duration.

How, then, do we hear a melody? There exists presumably a series of successive tones, T, T', and so on, and these tones are presented in a series of successive ideas, T, T', etc. It is clear that the melody M is not presented through the idea T, nor is it presented through T', and so on: none of these ideas presents M. Hence, since we are aware of the melody, there must occur another idea, O, by means of which we are presented with the melody M. But this idea, like all ideas, is, of course, a momentary entity without a duration.

Meinong now considers three alternatives to his conclusion that there must occur the new idea O of the melody M.

First. Someone may object that our awareness of M simply consists in the occurrence of the successive ideas T, T', etc. To be aware of a melody, according to this view, is to be aware in successive mental acts of successive tones. Nothing more is involved. Meinong replies that this account may be appropriate for our awareness of classes, but not for the presentation of a temporal complex.[36] He thinks that it makes sense to say that we have heard a class of tones, if we have heard each tone, one after the other. But a melody, he reminds us, is not a class of tones.

Meinong, I believe, is correct when he rejects this analysis of what it means to hear a melody. But he concedes too much when he grants that this analysis applies to our awareness of classes. In the sense in which we always talk here about awareness, presentation, etc., it is obvious that a series of awarenesses of entities is not the same as an awareness of a series of entities. Meinong's mistake, as well as his opponent's, is elementary: he confuses a class of ideas with the idea of a class. At any rate, Meinong is correct in his rejection of the first alternative.

Second. According to the second alternative, the various ideas T, T', etc., enter into some kind of (real) relation with each other, forming a complex idea C; and this complex idea C is the idea of the melody M. Thus we do not really have a mere succession of ideas, but a complex idea – spread out over some time – which consists of those successive ideas. Meinong rejects this second possibility for reasons which are not entirely clear to me.[37] If I understand Meinong correctly, he is arguing that the mere fact that certain ideas stand in certain relations to each other does not as yet suffice to bring before the mind anything other than what the ideas present to it singly. He implies here a fundamental principle which he will later articulate and embrace explicitly. Consider two ideas, I and I', which are ideas of the entities E and E', respectively. According to the principle, no matter what real relation may obtain between I and I', I will never intend anything else but E, and I' will never intend anything else but E'. Hence, the complex idea consisting of I, I' and the real relation cannot present any new entity. We shall return to this view and discuss it in greater detail in one of the next chapters.

Third. It may be said that the awareness of the melody consists in the successive hearing of the single tones plus the presentation of something else; something, however, that does not consist of the tones and, hence, is not to be identified with the melody. Meinong objects to this alternative that it is impossible to have an idea of a complex without having ideas of all its parts.[38] What this objection comes down to, I take it, is that the added idea cannot be an idea of the melody, since, by assumption, it is not an idea of the tones as well.

Put positively, Meinong asserts that an idea of the melody must be, in some sense, an idea of its tones. It is impossible to have an idea of a complex, he seems to be saying, which is not also an idea of its parts. We can easily see now that Meinong has backed himself into a corner. He holds, on the one hand, that the idea of a complex must also be an idea of its parts. The only sense which this requirement seems to make is that the idea of a complex must be a complex idea, consisting of the ideas of its parts. But then he also holds, on the other hand, that the parts of a complex idea can never present anything other than their usual intentions, so that the complex idea as a whole cannot present anything other than what the constituent ideas present singly. In brief, Meinong holds that a simple idea cannot present a complex, and he also holds that a complex idea cannot present a complex. Assumptions, as we shall see, are later used to solve this puzzle: presentations, Meinong will hold, do simply not suffice to acquaint us with objects of higher order; somehow, assumptions enter into the picture.

If we do not share Meinong's confidence in the power of assumptions, how can we avoid the unpalatable conclusion that complex objects cannot be presented to the mind by ideas? Obviously, we must reject one or the other of the two basic assumptions mentioned a moment ago. Let me indicate what tentative line I shall take in the following chapters. I shall agree with Meinong that a complex idea cannot present anything other than what its constituent ideas present singly. Hence complexes cannot be presented by complex ideas. This leaves only the alternative that they are presented by simple ideas. What was Meinong's argument against this possibility? He argued, as you will remember, that the idea of a complex must also be an idea of its parts; and he takes this to mean that the idea of a complex must consist of ideas which are ideas of the parts of the complex. It is at this spot, I submit, that Meinong's line of reasoning is faulty. Though it may be true, properly understood, that the idea of a complex is an idea of the parts of the complex as well, it simply does not follow that the idea of the complex must therefore be a complex idea. If we see the problem in this light, we realize that what is at stake is the dogma that a complex object can only be presented by a complex idea. Meinong accepts this dogma, while we do not.

Meinong concludes, after having discussed these three alternatives, that the presentation of a melody involves, aside from the ideas of the successive tones, a new idea which cannot occur earlier than the last idea of the last tone.[39] This new idea is the idea of the melody. It is, in distinction to the third alternative discussed above, an idea of all the tones of the melody. However, Meinong does not tell us whether the additional idea of the melody is simple or complex. He does not realize that his objection to the second alternative implies that this idea cannot be complex, while his objection to the third alternative seems to imply that it cannot be simple either. The problem of how complex entities are presented to the mind remains, therefore, unresolved in Meinong's article on objects of higher order.

Let us summarize Meinong's new ontology. At this point, Meinong's *explicit* ontology comprises two kinds of *objects*, 'ordinary' objects and objects of higher order. All ordinary objects are *instances*. Objects of higher order divide into (instances of) *relations* and *complexes* (of instances). They can also be divided into *real* and *ideal* objects of higher order. The latter distinction has two sides to it. It is derived from an ontological distinction between two modes of being, existence and subsistence. It is also based on an epistemological distinction between *a posteriori* and *a priori* knowledge. With the explicit recognition of the category of objects of higher order, an important epistemological question appears on the scene: How are we acquainted with objects of higher order? Meinong's arguments, we have seen, imply that neither simple nor complex ideas can acquaint us with objects of higher order.

V

Assumptions and Objectives

Meinong's most famous book is called *On Assumptions*.[1] The topic indicated by its title hardly warrants its fame. From an ontological point of view, the discovery of one more kind of mental act is not very exciting. But the title is somewhat misleading. What Meinong discovers is not just another kind of mental act, but another ontological category, the category of states of affairs. He calls these new entities *'objectives.'* From now on, Meinong's ontology distinguishes between the two basic categories of objects and objectives.

Yet, the title of Meinong's book is not wholly inappropriate. In the first edition, the edition here under discussion, he talks mainly about assumptions; objectives occur for the first time in the seventh chapter.[2] They are added, one is tempted to say, as an afterthought. Meinong discovers objectives because he has to solve the problem of what the intentions of assumptions are. Now, here is a most intriguing question: Since Meinong, just like Brentano, always acknowledged the existence of judgments, why do the newly discovered assumptions rather than the familiar judgments lead him to objectives? In other words, what is there in or about assumptions, but not in or about judgments, that opened his eyes to the existence of objectives?

According to the tradition – Cartesian as well as Kantian – there are two kinds of fundamental *intellectual* mental acts, namely, presentations and judgments. Both Brentano and Meinong accepted this view. Presentations were thought of as intending things – objects, in Meinong's terminology. What judgments intend, on the other hand, was never quite clear. According to Kant's *Logic*, for example, a judgment is really a kind of presentation. If so, then its intention would have to be a kind of object, perhaps a complex object. Thus what is required for the discovery of states of affairs – starting from the inside out, so to speak – is a realization of the uniqueness of judgments.

Brentano fully realized that judgments are not a sort of presentation. He insisted on the irreducibility of judgments. Yet, he never acknowledged the existence of anything but individual things. The reason for this blind spot lies in his particular theory of judgment. Brentano held, as I said, that judgments are irreducible to presentations.[3] But judgments, like all other mental acts, are said to be based on presentations. A presentation brings an object before the mind, as it were; when a judgment is added, a new and peculiar way of being conscious of this object is added: the object of the presentation is either affirmed or denied in the mental act of judgment. The situation is similar in the case of love or desire. In order to love an object, the object must be brought before the mind. This is the function of a presentation. But something else must be added, namely, the act of loving. Once an object is present to the mind, different attitudes can be adopted toward it: it may be affirmed or denied, loved or hated, desired or abhorred, etc. Brentano sees the uniqueness of judgment, not in its having a special kind of intention, but in the two attitudes of affirmation and denial.

1 *Assumptions and Negation*

Meinong begins his main argument for the existence of assumptions by a brief review of his earlier view on judgments. This earlier view, as I said, is essentially Brentano's. The two features of affirmation and denial are thought to be essential to all judgments. Meinong now argues that there are really two quite different aspects to every judgment.[4] There is, first of all, the fact that, if someone makes a judgment, then he believes something, he is convinced of something. Second, every judgment is either positive or negative; it has a position, as Meinong puts it, in regard to yes and no. For example, if you judge that A exists, you are convinced of something, namely, of A's existence; and your judgment is positive. If you judge that A does not exist, then you are also convinced of something, but this time your judgment is negative. Similarly, if you judge that A is F, you are convinced that A has the property F, and your judgment is positive. If you judge that A is not F, you are also convinced of something, but your judgment is negative. Now, once it is seen that every judgment involves a conviction and that it is also either positive or negative, then it may be realized that one can find the polarity of positive and negative without any conviction. Assumptions, like judgments, are either positive or negative but they lack the conviction of judgments. For example, if I assume that A is F, my assumption is positive, but it lacks conviction; I am not at all convinced that A is F. If I assume that A is not F, the assumption is negative. According to Meinong, assumptions occupy a position halfway between presentations and judgments. They are more than mere presentations, because they are either positive or negative. But they are not as yet judgments because they lack the feature of conviction.

By splitting up affirmation and negation into conviction on the one hand and a position in regard to yes and no on the other, Meinong overlooks an essential ingredient of the original theory of judgment.[5] Judgments themselves, according to this theory, can be either affirmative or negative. To see what this claim comes down to, let us change terms and speak of belief and disbelief instead of affirmative and negative judgments. A belief or disbelief, in distinction to an assumption, carries with it a conviction. Furthermore, a belief may be either a belief in a positive state of affairs or a belief in a negative state of affairs; and the same holds for a disbelief. From a phenomenological point of view, it is quite obvious that a belief in a positive state of affairs is not the same as a disbelief in its negation. Nor is a disbelief in a state of affairs the same as a belief in its negation. Thus it is clear that we must distinguish, not only between positive and negative judgments and assumptions in Meinong's sense, but also between positive and negative judgments in Brentano's sense.

Meinong is surely right in holding that there are mental acts of assuming, that these acts are not to be confused either with presentations or judgments, and that judgments involve what he calls a conviction, while assumptions do not. As to the positive and negative features, they are usually attributed to the intentions of judgments and assumptions rather than to the acts themselves. What is positive or negative, roughly speaking, is the state of affairs which is either judged to hold or assumed to hold. This distinction rests ultimately on the assumption that we are able to distinguish between positive and negative states of affairs or, better, that the distinction between these two kinds of states of affairs is ontological rather than epistemological in nature. Very roughly, a negative (simple, non-quantified) state of affairs is one that contains negation; a positive state of affairs is one that does not contain negation. At any rate, it is clear that Meinong's primary opponent – the orthodox Brentano student, so to speak – will hold that what Meinong calls assumptions are nothing but presentations of a certain kind. To assume that A is F, for example, will be said to consist in presenting to oneself an AF.

Meinong tries to discredit this alternative. He claims that negation can never be a matter of mere presentation. If this is true, then it follows that the assumption that A is not F cannot possibly consist in a presentation of an A which is not F. As Meinong sees the dialectics of the situation, what he has to show in order to make his point is that there are no negative objects; for example, that there is no such object as a not-red house. Recall in this connection how Brentano's theory of judgments depends on the existence of such objects. Meinong presents an intricate and ingenious argument to this effect.[6] The argument has three main steps.

First. Meinong asserts that if one thinks of, say, not-red, one must think of red. In other words one cannot think of a negative object without thinking of the corresponding positive object. Hence, if there are negative objects, then they must be built upon positive objects; and this means that they must be objects of higher order.

Second. All objects of higher order, as we have seen earlier, are either perceptual objects or are objects whose ideas have to be produced by a mental activity. Meinong next asserts that negative objects, if there were such things, could not be perceptual objects. They must be what Meinong sometimes calls 'founded objects.'

Third. But all founded objects are connected with their foundations with necessity. For example, red and green are not just unequal, they *must* be unequal; they are necessarily unequal. But while there may be negations which hold with necessity, there are also negations which do not; there are also negations which are merely contingent, as we might say. For example, that there is a non-red house is a contingent fact. Thus if there were negative objects, some of them would not be necessary objects. Hence these objects could not be founded objects. But since they are not perceptual objects either, they could not be objects at all.

Assuming that Meinong's argument is sound, we must conclude that negation is not a matter of objects. Meinong will hold later that it is a matter of objectives instead.

Meinong's argument is really an argument to the effect that there must be a category of entities other than objects. He argues that a negative object, if there were such a thing, could not be a simple object. If it cannot be simple, then it must be complex, that is, it must be an object of higher order. Then he tries to show that it cannot be an object of higher order either, for it can be neither a perceptual object of higher order nor a founded object. Thus it can be neither a simple object nor a complex object and, hence, not an object at all. Or, rather, there can be no such object. But since negation does occur, there must be entities other than objects to which it 'attaches.'

There are two important issues here. First, are there or are there not entities other than objects? Second, what is the ontological nature of negation? Among those who concede ontological status to negation, there are three main answers to the latter question. Some philosophers hold that negation attaches, if I may so put it, to states of affairs. This is, for example, Frege's view.[7] I am inclined to accept it. Other philosophers think of negation as attached to properties and relations. This is the view which Brentano would hold, if he conceded ontological status to negation at all. It is the view directly attacked by Meinong in the argument outlined above. Finally, some philosophers hold that negation attaches to the copula, so that we may speak of positive and negative exemplification. According to the first view, there are only positive and negative states of affairs; all properties are positive, and there is only one relation of exemplification. According to the second view, there are positive and negative properties and relations; states of affairs are positive or negative by virtue of containing positive or negative properties or relations, and there is again only one relation of exemplification.

Meinong's argument is an argument both against the second as well as the third view, assuming his understanding of complex properties and of relations. It is therefore of interest even to those philosophers who hold these two views but do not deny the existence of states of affairs. Let us look at the three main steps of the argument. The first step comes down to the assertion that negative properties or negative exemplification must be objects of higher order or, roughly speaking, complex entities. While this may be conceded for negative properties, it appears doubtful for negative exemplification. Those who hold that there are these two modes of copulation usually hold that both relations are simple, unanalyzable, or primitive. Meinong, of course, thinks of all relations as objects of higher order; and this is the reason why his argument applies to this view, if we accept his analysis of relations.

In step two, Meinong assumes that a negative property, if there were such a thing, could not be perceived. Many contemporary philosophers would find this assumption unexceptionable, although I think that it is plainly false. If there were such a property as, say, not-green, then, in my view, one would see this property quite literally with one's very eyes when one sees, say, that a certain billiard ball is not green.[8] At any rate, the most dubious assertion occurs in step three of Meinong's argument. He assumes here that all ideal objects of higher order are connected with their foundations by necessity. This means for negative objects of the type here envisaged that, say, the object *non-red house* would necessarily have to exist. But why should this be the case? Meinong could have argued instead, it seems to me, that all the examples of ideal objects of higher order previously considered are different from the negative objects now under scrutiny in just this respect, namely, that while complexes and relations of the former kind are indeed necessarily founded on their foundations, the same does not hold for negative objects. In short, he could have turned his whole argument around, so that its conclusion would have been instead that there are non-perceptual objects of higher order which are not by necessity connected with their foundations.

2 *Assumptions and Sentences*

Meinong's second argument for the existence of assumptions concerns the meaning of sentences. His goal is clear: he wants to establish the fact that sentences do not always express judgments, but may express assumptions.

He repeats a few remarks from his paper on objects of higher order about the meaning of words which, in turn, echo similar remarks by Twardowski.[9] Both philosophers make a distinction between what a word expresses and what it represents. What a word expresses is always a presentation; what it represents, if it is not a syncategorematic word, is an object.[10] Meinong's view can be summed up as follows. The word 'sun' represents the sun. It expresses the idea of the sun. When someone utters this word, his utterance is a sign that he has the idea. Thus there are really three things involved: the intention of the idea is the referent of the word, the idea is what is expressed by the word, and the utterance of the word is a sign (indication) that someone has the idea.

So much for the meaning of words. What about the meaning of sentences? As Meinong sees it, the question is: is the characteristic which distinguishes between words and sentences to be found on the side of what sentences represent or on the side of what they express? And he argues that this characteristic difference must lie on the side of what sentences express. Nothing could substantiate better my contention that, at the beginning of his book, Meinong has not yet discovered objectives. Here is his argument:[11]

> Whenever we are dealing with a sentence, a referent is indeed not lacking: the latter is constituted by the referents of the words which are combined in the sentence into a complex and by the objects of higher order which are built upon the *inferiora* consisting of these latter referents. In the present context, we do not have to determine the number of such *superiora*. But to the unlimited multiplicity of such referents, there corresponds nothing which is common to sentences. Rather, it seems always possible to retain what is in the restricted, real, sense the object expressed by a sentence, even if we discard the sentential form. I do not mean at all that one can, as Brentano does, reproduce the whole sense or even the real sense of the sentence 'The man is sick' by the sentence 'The sick man exists.' But it seems to me to be indisputable that in the words 'the sick man,' which do not at all constitute a sentence, the whole object-material, in the more restricted sense, is retained which the sentence 'The man is sick' contains.

Meinong has a footnote to this passage in which he calls attention to the fact that he is talking here only about the object of a sentence in a restricted sense and that another sense will be discussed in chapter 7. This is, of course, the chapter in which he introduces objectives. This footnote seems to have been added later in order to mitigate a clear inconsistency in Meinong's view. The argument just cited does not merely have to be slightly modified; if there are objectives, it would have to be dropped entirely.

Meinong concludes from his argument that the characteristic of sentences, as compared to words, must be sought on the side of what they express rather than what they represent. Sentences, he points out, express judgments; words, by themselves, never do. What he wants to show is that sentences do not always express judgments, but sometimes express assumptions. He mentions three considerations to this effect.[12]

First, Meinong points out that there are independent sentences which do not express judgments; for example, questions, imperatives, etc. In asking a question, one obviously does not express a judgment; for a judgment is what one is after, but does not as yet have. What one expresses, according to Meinong, is a desire; a special kind of desire, so to speak, namely a desire for knowledge. But, more importantly, one makes an assumption. For example, if I ask 'Is this chair taken?', I express a desire to know something and I make the assumption that this chair is taken. Now, this analysis sounds odd for at least two reasons. Firstly, it comes as a surprise that Meinong says that questions express desires; for what he seemed to be after is a case of a sentence which expresses an assumption. Secondly, even if we forget the point of the discussion for a moment. it may still appear strange to us that a question is said to express a desire. We are not denying that someone who asks a question may have a desire to know the answer; what we are doubting is that the question itself expresses this desire. What we have stumbled upon is a general flaw in the act-philosophies of Brentano's students. There is a tendency among these philosophers to reduce the great variety of different kinds of mental act to just a few kinds. In this particular case, a mental act of questioning is somehow identified – at least in part – with an act of desiring. I see no reason for denying that the mental acts expressed in a question or a command are neither judgments, nor assumptions, nor desires, nor anything other than what they seem to be, namely, acts of questioning and acts of commanding.

What the existence of questions shows, from this point of view is, not at all that there are assumptions, but rather that there are states of affairs or objectives. What is in question, properly speaking, is never an object, but always an objective. But this is not what Meinong has in mind at the moment.

Meinong points out, second, that certain dependent sentences (clauses) do not express judgments. Consider the two sentences: 'I am convinced that it will rain today' and 'I doubt that it will rain today.' If we assume that the clause 'it will rain today' is the expression of a judgment in the first sentence, then we must assume that it also expresses a judgment in the second sentence. But is it clear that it cannot express a judgment in the second sentence; for the speaker does not judge (affirm) that it will rain today, but doubts that it will rain today. But if that clause does not express a judgment in the second sentence, then it does not express one in the first sentence either. Or consider the sentence 'My friend believes that it is going to rain today.' Surely, the speaker who utters this sentence does not express the judgment that it will rain today. He may very well believe that it will not rain today. We can agree with Meinong's conclusion that the dependent clauses in these cases do not express judgments. But, again, we do not have to follow him when he makes the additional assertion that they express assumptions.

Third, Meinong calls our attention to certain compound sentences and claims that their constituent sentences cannot express judgments. For example, a hypothetical judgment of the form *If P, then Q* does not express a judgment that *P* and a judgment that *Q*. Someone may believe that the hypothetical judgment is true, even though he also believes that the antecedent as well as the consequent are both false. Similarly for disjunctions: the speaker may not wish to assert both disjuncts. In general, as Meinong says, all deductions are of this kind: one may affirm a certain deduction without affirming either its premises or its conclusion.

3 *Assumptions and Intentions*

Meinong attempts to show also that assumptions play a role in intentionality. It is *the* fundamental fact of epistemology, according to him, that if one correctly judges that one feels a pain or that one has a certain wish, then it is true that the feeling or the wish exist. This fundamental characteristic of all justified existential affirmations is called *the transcending of these judgments toward a reality*. Reality, of course, comprises both existents and subsistents. Meinong claims that it is obvious from the fundamental fact of epistemology what the intention – he says 'object' – of knowledge is: It is that object which is justifiedly affirmed.[13]

But if the notion of intention is thus clear in the case of an evident affirmative judgment, the same does not at all hold for either false affirmative judgments or true negative judgments. Meinong attempts to clarify the notions of intentionality and of an intention for judgments of this sort, and he thinks – as we might expect – that this can only be done if we avail ourselves of assumptions. Meinong, to put it succinctly, is up against the problem of nonexistent intentions.

Consider, then, a true judgment of the form: *A does not exist.* Meinong's first point is that the intentionality of a judgment cannot depend on whether the judgment is correct or not, or on whether it is positive or negative. He concludes that it is the underlying presentation – which no judgment lacks – that deserves to be called intentional in the primary sense. What makes a judgment intentional, what gives it an 'object,' is always the presentation on which it is built. But this conclusion leaves us with the crucial question: 'Even if it is the presentations which in the first instance have the objects, what kind of a having is it, if what the respective presentation has may very well not exist?'[14]

Meinong's answer is neither illuminating nor tenable.[15] He talks about a disposition of certain presentations to yield, under favorable circumstances, justified true judgments, and he identifies this disposition with the intentionality of presentations without intentions. For example, the presentation on which a false affirmative judgment is built *intends the object A* only in the sense that it *could*, under certain circumstances, intend the object *A*, namely, if it were the basis for a justified true affirmative judgment. Meinong raises immediately an objection against his own answer. Dispositions, he maintains, cannot be perceived. Thus if certain presentations do not intend objects, but merely have the ability to do so under certain circumstances, then this ability cannot be perceived. But we can perceive that all ideas without exception intend something and what these intentions are. Hence it cannot be the case that the intentionality of certain ideas consists in nothing but their having a certain disposition. Meinong tries to answer this objection in terms of a further distinction between actual and merely potential intentionality, but it is clear that his first attempt to solve the problem of nonexistent intentions has failed. Thus he tries a new line of reasoning; in the process, he takes back some of the things which he has just asserted.

He starts again with the true affirmative judgment.[16] Here we have the paradigm of what intentionality is; nor is the intention itself lacking. Next, Meinong claims that false affirmative judgments do not pose a problem either. Of course, we should protest that in the latter case there is no object; hence the problem appears already in full strength. But let us keep quiet for the moment. According to Meinong, the problem arises, when we turn to mere presentations. On the one hand, a mere presentation does not seem to be intentional; for it acquires its intentionality only through becoming the basis for an affirmative judgment. On the other hand, inner awareness leaves no doubt that even such mere presentations are already intentional. Meinong now cuts the Gordian knot by asserting that what we are dealing with in such cases are not really mere presentations, but are already presentations connected with affirmative assumptions.

Consider, for example, the idea of a round square. We cannot hold that this idea has an intention in the sense that it can serve as the basis for a true (justified) existential judgment; for there is no such entity as a round square. On the other hand, we cannot deny that this idea is intentional; for inner awareness clearly shows that it is. But if we now hold that the condition of intentionality for ideas does not depend on there being certain true affirmative judgments, but on the existence of certain affirmative assumptions, then the difficulty disappears. Even though there can be no justified affirmative judgment concerning a round square, there can be an affirmative assumption; one can assume that a round square exists. Meinong concludes:[17]

> For this reason it is advantageous to base the concept of intentionality upon the assumption instead of the judgment. This can be done in regard to intentionality in the sense of mere potentiality as well as in regard to the actual 'directedness' toward an object. Accordingly, intentionality is to be defined as the ability of a presentation to be the basis for an affirmative assumption: A presentation is thus said to be directed toward an object if its content is turned into the content of an affirmative assumption.

Recall Meinong's original reason for denying actual intentionality to ideas in general: there are ideas whose objects do not exist. But the same holds for certain affirmative assumptions. If I assume that a round square exists, I have an assumption whose object does not exist. By parity of reason we should therefore have to say that this assumption is not actually intentional: it is only potentially intentional in the same sense in which the idea of a round square is only potentially intentional, namely, in the sense that harks back to the actual intentionality of true affirmative judgments. And does not the same argument apply to false affirmative judgments as well? In other words, if we admit, as Meinong seems to concede in regard to false affirmative judgments and affirmative assumptions, that mental acts can be intentional, even though their objects do not exist, what reason does then remain for denying the intentionality of ideas?

In the second edition of *Über Annahmen*, Meinong admits that the view we have just discussed comes down to the admission that certain ideas simply have no intentions, and that this admission clashes with all our experience. As Meinong now sees his earlier analysis, he starts out with the idea that an idea is intentional if and only if its object exists. Then he proceeds to call an idea intentional if its object could exist. And, finally, he even calls ideas like that of the round square intentional, even though the object could not possibly exist. What occurs here, he now sees, is more than a mere weakening of the notion of intentionality; intentionality disappears altogether.[18]

It remains to show the importance of assumptions for negative judgments. Meinong maintains that every negative judgment refers back to some kind of affirmation: 'In order to negate of A that it is, say, C, for this there seems to be occasion and opportunity only if it has occurred to the judging subject to affirm the C of A.'[19]

If this is true, then the negative judgment that the round square does not exist must have been preceded by some kind of affirmation. But it is obvious that this affirmation cannot consist in the corresponding affirmative judgment. In order to judge that the round square does not exist, one does not have to judge first that it does exist. Rather, the affirmative act is in such cases an assumption. Every negative judgment, Meinong concludes, presupposes an affirmative assumption.

This conclusion also explains how a negative judgment can be intentional. Intentionality, we have been told, is primarily a matter of assumptions. A negative judgment, Meinong merely adds, derives its intentionality from the presupposed affirmative assumption. What about negative assumptions – where do they get their intentionality? Meinong's answer is short and to the point: they, too, presuppose affirmative assumptions (or affirmative judgments) and get their intentionality from these affirmative assumptions (or judgments).

4   Assumptions and Objects of Higher Order

Meinong, as we saw, has a difficult time explaining how objects of higher order are apprehended. He now suggests that assumptions are essentially involved in their apprehension. He approaches this main topic by two kinds of presentations, intuitions (*anschauliche Vorstellungen*) on the one hand and conceptions (*unanschauliche Vorstellungen*) on the other. How does the 'sensory impression,' the intuition, of a red cross differ from the mere non-sensory conception of a red cross? Meinong had tried to answer this question in an earlier article, but he has been rather dissatisfied with the answer and tries to find a better one.[20]

The difference between intuition and conception cannot lie on the side of the object, since one and the same object – for example, the red cross just mentioned – can be either intuited or conceived of. Meinong concludes tentatively that it must somehow involve the contents of the respective acts of presentation. He takes for granted that there are no simple conceptions; simple objects, in other words, can only be intuited, but cannot be conceived of. Thus the problem of distinguishing between intuitions and conceptions arises only in regard to complexes. But complex objects are apprehended by presentations with complex contents. The question now becomes whether there is a difference between the complex contents of certain intuitions and the complex contents of certain conceptions. Meinong asserts that these complex contents are formed by means of two different real relations. Thus the complex content of an intuition contains one real relation; the complex content of a conception, another.[21]

Just as there are no simple conceptions, on Meinong's view, so there are no negative intuitions. All negative presentations are conceptions. While one can, for example, form a conception of a cross which is not red, one cannot have an intuition of it. Of course, one could have an intuition of, say, a blue cross, and it would then be true of this blue cross that it is not red, but this is not the same thing as to have an intuition of a cross which is not red. If negation can thus only occur in connection with conception, then it follows, according to Meinong's earlier considerations, that mere presentation cannot be all there is to conception. Whenever a negative conception occurs, an assumption must be involved. Moreover, even positive conceptions must really involve assumptions. For, the conception of a cross which is not red does not consist of a presentation of a red cross plus some kind of negative assumption about this cross; rather, it involves the assumption that a cross is not red. Hence, it stands to reason that a positive conception involves an affirmative assumption as well.[22] We arrive therefore at the conclusion that all conceptions involve assumptions. And this means, of course, that conception cannot after all really be a kind of presentation, if we mean by presentation, as always, an irreducible kind of mental act.

Meinong draws a further conclusion from these deliberations:[23]

> But this yields without further ado the important result that the 'combination' [of contents] by itself is, so to speak, logically indifferent. The combination of the presentations 'cross' and 'red' (of course together with a proper relation) does not as yet decide whether the cross is presented as red or not red, [whether] the red is presented as shaped like a cross or not shaped like a cross.
>
> This means that the combination by itself does not as yet suffice to connect the objects of the partial presentations into a complex object. Rather, this is achieved by an added assumption which, by virtue of its positive or negative quality, gives to the complex which it completes its positive or negative character, which conceptions always have.

Meinong is in a bind. He wants to hold that several ideas which stand in a certain real relation to each other form a complex idea. He also argues that this complex idea does not as yet determine an intention, that is, a particular complex object; an act of assumption must be added, before this complex object is put before the mind. But how can there occur a complex idea which does not have an intention? And what is it in or about the assumption that 'completes' the complex idea so as to make it an idea of an object? What remains mysterious in Meinong's account is the relationship between the complex content of the conception as such and the content of the assumption. If the assumption intends something other than what the mere conception intends, as Meinong implies, then the content of the assumption must be different from the content of the conception. But in what this difference consists Meinong does not tell us. He seems to assume that the two contents are the same.

If conceptions really involve assumptions, perhaps even intuitions – at least intuitions of complex objects – involve assumptions. Of course, intuitions cannot be negative, but it may be the case that the intuition of a complex object involves an affirmative assumption. If so, then we arrive at a view that can be summarized as follows.[24] (1) The only simple presentations are intuitions. (2) All complex objects are either intuited or conceived of; in either case, an assumption is involved. This assumption has a complex content. (3) What distinguishes the content of an intuition from that of a positive conception is a difference in real relation. Meinong, at this point, neither accepts nor rejects this view. Instead, he turns to the more general topic of how complex objects are given to the mind.

He immediately faces what appears to be an insurmountable difficulty. How can one apprehend two objects, A and B, in the relation R? It certainly will not do to have the three ideas of A, of B, and of R simultaneously. Nor will it do to think in addition of some other relation R', a relation which supposedly connects A and B with R. The most obvious answer to our question, an answer which Meinong has taken for granted all along, is that the three ideas must form a complex idea C. In order to form this idea, they must stand in some real relation E with each other. Meinong introduces a thought which casts doubt on this obvious answer.[25] First, he raises the question of whether the intentional relation between an idea and its intention – more generally, between a content and its intention – is a real or an ideal relation. He rejects the view that intentionality is a kind of similarity. It is, on his view, a unique, indefinable relation. But one thing seems to be absolutely certain in regard to this relation:[26]

I mean the classification of this relation as belonging to one of the two main classes of ideal and real relations which exhaust the total field of relations. Very simple considerations throw light on this matter. If what I apprehend [*erkenne*] is itself real, hence a piece of reality, then it will most certainly not be touched in any way by my apprehension – as we may here say for the moment with not very great but sufficient precision. What is apprehended, moreover, does not have to be something real: the insight into an equality, or a possibility, for example, has something ideal as an object. The act of apprehension and the content on which it is based, of course, is always real: however, something real can never stand to something ideal in a real relation, but only in an ideal relation. But if the relationship between the apprehension and the apprehended is independent of the real or ideal nature of the latter, then it follows for a real object of apprehension that the apprehension can only stand in an ideal relation to it.

Meinong thus holds that the intentional relation is an ideal relation. He asserts next that, since the intentional relation is an ideal relation, an idea cannot change its intention, no matter what happens to it, that is, no matter with what other ideas it enters into real relations. For, as Meinong explains it, since ideal relations belong to terms once and for all with necessity, they cannot be affected by the external fate of these terms.[27] Thus if there exists a complex idea which consists of the idea of A, the idea of B, and the idea of R, then these three ideas must have the same objects which they had before they entered into the complex idea. But this means that the complex idea C cannot intend anything other than what its three constituent ideas intend separately. In particular, it cannot possibly intend the intention: A *and* B *in relation to* R. In general, complex ideas cannot intend complex intentions. How, then, are complex objects presented to the mind?

The problem arises because Meinong embraces the following two views: (1) that the intentional relation is an ideal relation, and (2) that ideal relations are not affected by real relations into which their terms enter.

Meinong draws the conclusion that no content of a presentation, be it either a simple or a complex content, can intend an object of higher order. And he goes on to argue that, where presentations fail, assumptions jump into the breach. These further arguments are not very clear. Nor can they possibly be convincing; for it is obvious that the only solution of the problem of how complexes are apprehended is to maintain that they are presented to the mind by simple contents; and this Meinong cannot bring himself to admit.

Are there any other solutions? Meinong, as I said, could hold that the complex consisting of A, B, and R is presented by a simple idea; an idea, of course, which is not identical with either the idea of A, or the idea of B, or, finally, the idea of R.[28] Or he could hold that this complex is brought before the mind, not by means of a presentation at all, but by means of an assumption, where the assumption – and this is crucial – has a *simple* content. According to this second possibility, there occurs a certain presentation with a certain complex content, and there also occurs – in connection with this presentation – an assumption. But this assumption does not have the same content as the presentation. It is this additional content of the assumption which intends the complex object.

Meinong introduces a distinction between primary and secondary intentions.[29] For example, if we judge that A and B stand in the relation R, then the relation R is the primary object of this judgment, while A and B are its secondary objects. Next, he asserts that while every judgment and every presentation has a primary intention, only certain presentations have secondary intentions, namely, all presentations of objects of higher order. The object of higher order is the primary intention of such a presentation; the entities on which this object is built are its secondary intentions. Now, in order for a presentation to intend an object of higher order, it suffices that, in addition to the presentation, there occurs an affirmative judgment or assumption. But this is not sufficient for the presentation to have its specific secondary objects; for, as Meinong puts it, there remains a certain indeterminacy in regard to the secondary objects of the presentation. The judgment or assumption affirms the relation R, not the instance of R which holds only between A and B. Meinong, therefore, concludes that this indeterminacy is removed by means of presentations whose primary intentions are the secondary intentions of the earlier mentioned presentations.[30] According to this conception, the presentation of A and B in relation to R is different from the presentation of C and D in the same relation in that in the first case there occur presentations with A and B as their primary objects, while in the second case there occur presentations with C and D as their primary objects. In the first case, there also occurs an assumption, say, which has as its secondary objects the two entities A and B, while in the second case the secondary objects of the corresponding assumption are C and D.

Last but not least, Meinong claims that the foregoing analysis solves the problem of how objects of higher order can be given to the mind. He says that in order to have a presentation of A and B in the relation R, an assumption is required which has R as its primary, A and B as its secondary objects; and that this is achieved when the content of R enters into an appropriate real relation to the contents of A and B. He claims that one can therefore not present to oneself the relation as existing between A and B, but merely assume it. What one usually thinks of as the presentation of A and B in relation R is in reality always an assumption.[31]

Meinong, I think, is mistaken. He has merely substituted an enigma for a mystery. The only contents involved are the three ideas of R, of A, and of B. These enter into a real relation and form the complex idea C. If Meinong's earlier argument is sound, as he still assumes, then C cannot intend an object of higher order. Now we add to this complex idea an assumption. This assumption is said to have R as its primary object, A and B as its secondary objects. But never mind this complication; it does not change the situation in the least. What is important is the fact that this act of assuming *does not have a new content*. But if it does not have a content other than C, how can it bring before the mind anything new? How, in particular, can it bring before the mind the object of higher order? Meinong assumes that the activity of assuming somehow achieves what no complex idea can achieve, namely, the mind's acquaintance with complex entities. How the act of assuming achieves this feat, however, is the enigma. At times, Meinong seems to think that this act somehow creates the complex idea C; at other times, he thinks of C as already finished and at the disposal of the act of assuming. But even if we assume that the assumption creates the complex idea C, since this idea does not suffice for the apprehension of a complex object, nothing is gained for our understanding of the apprehension of complex objects.

We see that Meinong does not accept either one of the possible solutions mentioned earlier. He does not accept either one of these two ways out, we may surmise, because he cannot accept the notion that a *simple* content – either a content of a presentation or a content of an assumption – can intend a complex entity. Instead, he claims that judgments and assumptions somehow establish a connection between, say, A, B, and R, so that the mind is presented with a complex entity.

Before we close, a very common objection to Meinong's basic assumptions about complex ideas must be mentioned.[32] Meinong maintains, we recall, that the complex idea C^*, consisting of the three ideas A^*, B^*, and R^* in a certain real relation R', cannot intend the object of higher order O (A and B in the relation R). It may be objected that Meinong is mistaken: while it is true that A^*, B^*, and R^* do not present O while they are unconnected, this no longer holds as soon as they enter into the relation R' with each other. R' makes the difference, so to speak. But Meinong could retort, legitimately in my opinion, that the occurrence of R' can make no difference in what is brought before the mind since R' is not an idea (content). By definition, as one says, contents and contents alone are responsible for the intentions of the mind. If there is a difference in intentions, then there must be a difference in contents. But a real relation between contents is not itself a content. Hence it can make no difference to what is before a mind whether A^*, B^* and R^* enter into the real relation R' or some other real relation R''. Hence it follows, as Meinong has claimed all along, that the ideas A^*, B^*, and R^* can never intend the complex object O, no matter how they are connected by means of real relations. As I see it, there is only one way of avoiding Meinong's conclusion. One must hold that relations between ideas can themselves be ideas. For example, in our case, one could hold that the object O is presented by a complex idea consisting of A^* and B^* in the relation S, where S is an idea of the relation R. S then fulfills two functions: it connects A^* with B^*, and it also intends R. I cannot accept this way out because I do not think that an idea of a relation can be a relation. [33]

5   Objectives

More than once, in the course of the first one hundred and fifty pages of his book, Meinong is on the threshold of discovering states of affairs. This is particularly true of paragraph 34 – a few pages away from the chapter on objectives – which is called 'The thetic and synthetic functions of judging and assuming.' He starts the discussion with a brief criticism of Brentano's view on judgments. [34] He remarks that Brentano's view would have to be extended so as to take into account subsistence as well as existence; some judgments would be of the form *A subsists*. More importantly, Meinong does not think that categorical judgments of the form *A is B* can be reduced to existential ones in Brentano's fashion. He considers an analysis of them according to which they are judgments about the subsistence of an instance of a relation. The judgment that *A is B* thus becomes a judgment to the effect that a certain instance of the relation R subsists. [35] The intention of the judgment is therefore an object of higher order, and all the difficulties of the last section reappear now in connection with what I shall call *predicative judgments*.

Meinong claims that there is an additional difficulty: (an instance of) the relation R, although it is supposed to be the main object of the predicative judgment, cannot be found. [36] There seems to be no presentation of it. It does not seem to be the case that (an instance of) the relation R is somehow before the mind when predicative judgments are made. Meinong concludes from this alleged fact that predicative judgments must really be quite different from judgments of being of the type *A exists* or *A subsists*: the subsistence of (an instance of) the relation R cannot really be the subject matter of a predicative judgment. Consequently, he now distinguishes between the thetic and the synthetic functions of judgments. Judgments of being have a thetic function, while predicative judgments have a synthetic function. He says that the predicative judgment 'approaches *two* contents of presentations, puts itself, in a manner of speaking, *between* the objects of the two presentations and thus connects them in a certain sense with each other.'[37]

Turning back to thetic judgments about objects of higher order, Meinong notices that, according to his earlier account, even thetic judgments have a synthetic function. They, too, establish a connection, namely, a connection between the primary object of the judgment, the complex O or the relation R, and the secondary objects, the parts of O or the terms of R. But this case differs from the predicative case in that a presentation of the relation occurs in the former but not in the latter case. In either case, though, judgment (or assumption) is said to create a relation, to establish it, or however one may want to put it. We recognize here the idealistic gambit of ascribing to the mind the power to produce relations. Although Meinong has by now acknowledged the mind-independent subsistence of relations, in these particular cases he resorts to his old move. But only for a moment. In the very next paragraph, he takes it all back. The judgment can at best connect contents with each other, he now claims, but not connect the objects of these contents. It can only establish a relation between the contents A^* and B^*, not between A and B themselves. Meinong finally throws up his hands in despair: 'The problem of how it is possible to apprehend a complex without an idea of the respective relation must, indeed, remain without an attempted solution within the context of this chapter.'[38]

At this very late point in the book, Meinong conceives of the intention of a predicative judgment as (an instance of) a certain relation R. Its intention is thus an object of higher order. The only thing that makes him doubtful about this conception is the alleged fact that (an instance of) the relation R does not seem to be before the mind when a predicative judgment is made. He is perfectly happy with an analysis according to which objects are the intentions of judgments. In the next chapter, though, he suddenly discovers objectives. But even then he does not realize that he has discovered a new category of entities. Instead, he thinks that these objectives are just another kind of object of higher order. That there is a fundamental difference between objects on the one hand and objectives on the other dawns on him only very slowly.

After having given one analysis of existential and predicative judgments, Meinong suddenly gives an entirely different one.[39] He claims that what one knows when one knows that an election took place without incidents is not the object *incident*, but something that cannot be represented by a single word, but only by a sentence beginning with 'that.' In our case, what one knows is *that the election took place without incidents*. What one knows in this case has a positive character, even though the judgment itself is negative.

Now, that the election took place without incidents is not a piece of reality, but it is nevertheless something factual, as Meinong puts it. This entity can itself become the object of an affirmative judgment; for we can say such things as: 'that the election took place without incidents is a fact', or 'that the election took place without incidents, that is (exists).' And this means, according to Meinong, that the entity under study must be an object. But, of course, it is not identical with the object of the judgment that the election took place without incidents. The object of this judgment, as the term 'object' has been used throughout, is an incident or the like. Thus we need a new term for this new kind of object. Meinong proposes to use the word 'object-ive.' Thus the judgment that the election took place without incidents has an object and an objective. The object is the election – Meinong, for reasons which I do not understand, says it is 'an incident which took place'; the objective is that the election took place without an incident. To take a more obvious example, if one judges that John is tall, the object of the judgment is John; its objective, that John is tall. Notice that the objective of one judgment can be the object of another, according to this distinction. [40] This shows, of course, that objects and objectives do not form mutually exclusive categories. We are therefore working with three different notions of object. 'Object' means, first, the intention of an idea. Second, it signifies an ontological category. In this sense of the term, objects are contrasted with objectives. An object is an entity which is not a state of affairs. Third, the object of a judgment is the entity which the judgment is about.

So far, Meinong has only considered true judgments. But false judgments have their objectives, too. Every judgment, be it true or false, has therefore an objective, just as every judgment has an object. But it does not follow from the fact that a certain judgment has an objective that this objective has being (exists or subsists). [41] In the case of false judgments, the objective is merely an immanent one, just as the object of a false existential judgment is merely an immanent object.

Now follows an argument for the subsistence of objectives. [42] If we judge that *it is the case that* the case has not been closed, for example, we must ask what it is that is said to be the case. According to Meinong, it is not the judgment which is said to be the case; nor is it the object of the judgment. This leads us to the objective as the entity which is the case. Similarly, if we judge incorrectly that A does not exist, then we can also judge that *it is not* that A does not exist. It is clear that what is not in this case can be neither the judgment, since it does exist, nor the object A, since it exists, too. In short, since there are judgments of the form *It is (the case) that* P whose object is neither the judgment itself nor the object of the corresponding judgment that P, we are led to conclude that there must be something else which is the object of the judgment that it is (the case) that *P*. This something else is the objective.

This conception of objectives raises the following problem. Let us distinguish between judgments of different levels: the judgment *that P is* is of first level, the judgment *that P is* (subsists) is of second level, and so on. Now, the judgment of first level rests on a certain presentation; the content of this presentation somehow provides the 'material' for the judgment. If we now turn to the second level judgment, this judgment, too, must be built on some kind of apprehension of its object. Meinong is puzzled. He thinks that one will have to admit that a judgment can have as its object an objective which is apprehended by means of another judgment, without an intermediary by means of presentation. But this means that it is possible to think of something of which one has no presentation. [43]

In his characteristic fashion, Meinong follows up a number of possible ways of avoiding this consequence of his view. First, he falls back on the old standby: mental activity. Judgments may perhaps produce ideas in the following fashion. If an object *A* becomes the object of an affirmative or negative judgment, a new idea is produced, and this idea is the idea of the objective *that A is* or *that A is not*. This would mean that the objectives are founded on the object *A*; and Meinong objects to this possibility that two different objectives, the affirmative and the negative one, would have the very same foundation, namely, the object *A*. He is not very clear at this point. He seems to adopt a tentative view to the effect that judgments and assumptions may put entities before the mind so that this is no longer viewed as an exclusive function of presentations. What presents the judgment of second level with its object, according to this view, is the judgment of first level. Meinong's discussion at this point may be obscure, but the source of his trouble is not.

Meinong holds two opposing views. On the one hand, he still clings to the notion that all the intentions of the mind are placed before the mind by presentations. On the other hand, he also believes that there are objectives in addition to 'ordinary' objects. It is part and parcel of the notion of a presentation within the Brentano tradition that a presentation cannot place before the mind anything but an 'ordinary' object. So, if there are objectives, then they must be placed before the mind by a mental act other than a presentation. Yet presentations are the only acts, in Meinong's view, that present us with entities.

Now, Meinong has just claimed that judgments and assumptions can present us with objectives, but this claim cannot be made to agree with the rest of his view. It is not enough just to say that judgments present us with objectives, he must also explain how this takes place.

In particular, he must explain how a judgment can present us with anything other than an 'ordinary' object, when it does not have any other content than the one supplied to it by its underlying presentation. This is the crux of the matter: do judgments and assumptions have their own contents or do they get their contents from their presentations? Meinong, we saw, holds that it is the content of a presentation that puts an entity before the mind. He has also been holding that the content of a judgment or assumption is simply the content of the underlying presentation. And from these assertions it follows that judgments and assumptions cannot put before the mind anything else but what their presentations present to the mind. Hence there arises the problem of how we can be presented with objectives.

The obvious solution of the problem consists in the acknowledgment of contents other than ideas. Earlier, I said that I shall call propositional contents 'thoughts.' A judgment, we could hold, has a content just like a presentation. But while the content of a presentation is an idea, the content of a judgment is a thought. Thus there are two kinds of contents, ideas and thoughts, and the contents of judgments and assumptions are not the same as the contents of presentations. In particular, the content of a judgment is not the same as the content of the presentation on which it is based. As a matter of fact, we might have to give up this very notion that *one* presentation supplies the material for a judgment. Several ideas, it stands to reason, are involved in a thought. Thus the content of a judgment may consist of the contents of several presentations. It is easy to see how this whole line of reasoning clashes with the essentials of Brentano's theory of judgment. Hence it clashes with much of what Meinong still takes for granted at this point of philosophical development.

At any rate, I claim that Meinong does not realize at first that objectives form their own category. Additional confirmation of this claim comes from another consideration.[44] Meinong had maintained earlier that the judgment that A is B can apprehend a complex entity consisting of A and B without there being any idea of the relation R between A and B. He did not explain how this feat is achieved, but merely asserted that predicative judgments can in fact achieve it. Meinong now claims this miracle for other cases. He claims that in many cases where a complex is apprehended, the essential relations, required by the principle of coincidence, are not presented at all. Or, rather, he claims that, even though they do not seem to be presented, they really are. When one judges that A is B, for example, there exists presumably a presentation of A and a presentation of B; furthermore there exists also the objective *that A is B* and this objective is the intention of the judgment. The objective is thus put before the mind by the judgment itself, not by any presentation. Meinong now claims that the missing relation is simply the objective. Thus the relation is given after all, but it is given, not by a presentation, but by the judgment. One cannot find this relation, Meinong adds, as long as one looks for an entity that is given in an act of presentation. If one realizes that some entities are given by means of acts other than presentations, then one can also see that the relation is actually presented to the mind. In sum, 'the judgment apprehends objects in relation with each other in grasping the objective which connects them.'[45]

Relations are here identified with objectives. Hence these objectives are simply objects of higher order. This is the confirmation I promised in the last paragraph. Of course, nothing could be further from the truth than that relations are objectives or, in general, that objectives are merely objects of higher order. If we wish to retain a distinction between simple and complex entities of whatever kind, we may wish to say that objectives are *entities* of higher order. Entities of higher order would then divide into objects and objectives. In our terminology, structures as well as states of affairs are in some sense complex entities and may therefore be brought under one heading, say, as complexes. But, of course, there is a fundamental ontological difference between structures on the one hand and states of affairs on the other, and they form mutually exclusive categories.

Aside from this mistaken identification of a relation with an objective, there is a new and partially correct idea involved in Meinong's attempted solution of the problem of how relations are presented to us. He says that a judgment apprehends objects in relation by apprehending the objective *which connects them*. What he should have said is that a judgment apprehends objects in relation in apprehending the objective *in which* they are connected. It is true, indeed, that the judgment does not just reduce to a presentation of the relation R; it is the judgment itself which somehow presents us with the relation. This is the sound part of Meinong's idea. But, of course, the same holds not only for the relation R, but also for A and B: they, too, are given to us in the judgment. The judgment thus does not only present us with the relation – mistakenly identified with the objective – but also with its terms, and it presents us with all three entities *because it presents us with an objective of which these entities are constituents*. Meinong could not possibly agree with this last conclusion. Our view, as he sees it, implies that one can judge something without having an idea of what one judges. But this objection rests on an ambiguity in the notion of having an idea of something. We merely deny that, in order to judge that A is B, there have to occur certain *separate acts* of presentation before the act of judgment can occur. We do not deny that one has an idea of, say, A in this case, in the sense that the thought that A is B is, among other things, a thought about A. We claim that one is *eo ipso* acquainted with the constituents of an objective, if one is presented with the objective. One is acquainted with these constituents by means of the thought which intends the objective. Meinong, on the other hand, believes that one can only be acquainted with the constituents of the objective by means of separate acts of presentation.

So far, we have noticed in the chapter on objectives a tendency to think of objectives as just another kind of objects of higher order. But at the end of the chapter, the opposite tendency suddenly becomes visible. Meinong here pursues a line of reasoning which leads him to the inevitable conclusion that almost everything is an objective, that there really are very few, if any, objects. The main premise of this line of reasoning is that whatever cannot be apprehended by a mere presentation must be an objective. We noted earlier Meinong's inclination to assign greater and greater responsibility for the apprehension of entities to judgments and, especially, assumptions. For example, objects of higher order, that is, relations and complexes are said to be apprehended by means of judgments and assumptions. Add to this assertion the premise just mentioned and what follows is the peculiar view that complexes and relations are really objectives. But let us look at the twists and turns of Meinong's actual line of reasoning.

He starts with the assertion that, instead of saying 'I assert that A exists,' one can say 'I assert the existence of A.'[46] Similarly, instead of saying (a) 'I do not deny that the blackboard is black' or (b) 'I do not deny that green is different from yellow,' we can say (A) 'I do not deny the blackness of the blackboard' and (B) 'I do not deny the difference between green and yellow.' But if this is true, then the difference between objective and object seems to vanish; for how, say, does *difference* differ from *being different, blackness* from *being black*? And are not difference and blackness objects – the former a founded object; the latter, an object of experience? But if they are not objects, must we then not also conclude that all relations, even all attributes as they are represented by grammatical *abstracta*, are really not objects but objectives?

Consider the case of difference or, in general, the case of a relation R between A and B. Meinong argues as follows.[47] The relation R as holding between A and B cannot be the intention of a presentation, as earlier arguments have shown, but must be the intention of a judgment or assumption. It follows that R *as holding between A and B* must be an objective. Now, if R *between A and B*, as can hardly be doubted, is the same as R *as holding between A and B*, then it is clear that R *between A and B* must be an objective rather than an object. One may be misled into thinking that it is an object because one fails to make a sharp distinction between the mere relation R on the one hand and the relation R *between A and B* – an *instance* of R – on the other.

Meinong seems here to acknowledge the mere relation R in addition to its instances. And this raises the problem of what kind of entity R is; for, while it may be plausible to assume that the instance is an object of higher order based on A and B, this no longer makes any sense for the pure relation R, divorced from all specific terms. This problem aside, though, there are several mistakes involved in Meinong's argument. We must distinguish between the following three expressions: (1) '(the relation) R', (2) 'The R between A and B', (3) 'that R holds between A and B.' According to our view, (1) represents a certain relation, (2) *describes* that same relation, while (3) represents a state of affairs. [48] Using Meinong's terminology, we would say that (1) and (2) represent the same object, while (3) represents an objective. Meinong thinks that (2) represents an entity other than what (1) represents: the latter represents a pure relation; the former, an instance. This is his first mistake. Second, and more importantly for what we are about, he thinks of the instance, not as some kind of unanalyzable, simple entity, but as being in some nebulous way a complex involving the entities A and B, namely, the object $[A, B]$. This conception leads him, third, to hold that the instance cannot be the intention of a presentation, but can only be intended by judgments and assumptions. What is really given to the mind, accordingly, is R's holding between A and B. Fourth, he identifies this latter objective with the instance of R. Now, I do not think that there are instances, but if there were any, then Meinong, I think, would be wrong in conceiving of them as being complex. An instance of R, for example, would be a simple, indefinable relation. But be that as it may, even if the instance of R is complex, Meinong's argument to the effect that it can therefore not be presented by a presentation is not sound. We saw how this argument evolves from his inability to explain how complex objects are intended by complex ideas. Meinong, in short, identifies the instance $[A, B]$ with the objective *that R holds between A and B*; his doctrine about the apprehension of objects of higher order by means of judgments and assumptions serves as a verbal bridge that facilitates this identification.

Just as Meinong identifies the relation R between A and B, that is, $[A, B]$, with the fact of R's holding between A and B, so he also identifies the referent of the abstractum 'blackness' with the objective (*something's*) *being black*. [49] What the relation R in isolation is to the instance $[A, B]$, the property black is to blackness: blackness is the being black in regard to a specific thing. Since it does involve this kind of relationship to a specific thing, it cannot be apprehended by means of a presentation alone, as can the pure property black. Hence it cannot really be an object, but must be an objective.

By arguments of this sort, Meinong arrives at the surprising conclusion that almost all entities which were previously thought to be objects are really objectives. All complexes and relations, for example, are now recognized to be objectives. Even attributes like *blackness* are now identified, as we just saw, as objectives. Are there any objects left? Meinong gives a guarded answer: 'If we do not count the few cases where we deal with something really simple, then mere presentation will only suffice in cases of pure intuition, and even this, strictly speaking, only with a certain ambiguity.'[50]

If we remove the ambiguity, then it turns out that only the objects of simple intuitions can be objects. What are these objects? Up to now, we have worked with the silent understanding that they are instances of properties and relations; for example, a certain instance of black as contained in a certain complex or a certain instance of similarity as shown by a certain couple of instances of colors are our paradigms of objects of intuition. But these instances are now identified with objectives. Suddenly, we seem to be faced with the possibility that all objects have vanished from the world. We are confronted with the possibility that the world consists solely of objectives.

Assume that Meinong is correct in holding that almost everything is apprehended by means of propositional mental acts rather than isolated presentations. Assume further that what such propositional mental acts intend are objectives. Does it follow that what appeared to be objects must really be objectives? Does it follow, for example, that the instance [A, B] must be an objective? Meinong seems to overlook another alternative. One could hold, and I think that this is indeed the correct view, that while certain entities or, perhaps, all entities can only be apprehended by means of propositional mental acts, this merely means that they are apprehended *within the context of an objective*; it does not mean that *they are* objectives themselves. For example, the instance of R just mentioned would be apprehended, say, in a judgment to the effect that this relation holds between A and B, but it would not be the intention of this judgment. What this proposal comes down to is the view that all mental acts are propositional; that there are no presentations – properly speaking – at all. In a sense, then, the intentions of all mental acts are objectives. But objectives have constituents; in particular, they have objects as their constituents. And all objects are presented to the mind as constituents of objectives. It is obvious that Meinong would have resisted any effort of ours to persuade him of this view; for it involves a complete reversal of the alleged function of presentations. Presentations, far from being the necessary foundations of all mental acts, turn out to be dispensable. Yet, such is the power of the view we have just sketched that Meinong, as we shall see, comes closer and closer to embracing it in his consequent investigations.

At the very end of this section on objectives, Meinong remarks that sentences do not only express but also represent something. What they represent are objectives. A sentence, therefore, expresses a judgment or an assumption and it represents an objective.

6 *Some Characteristics of Objectives*

Meinong, as I have repeatedly emphasized, does not at first grasp the true nature of objectives. He thinks of them as objects of higher order.[51] He even divides them into complexes and relations. But he is quite clear on several other features of objectives from the very beginning. For example, objectives, he insists, can at best subsist; they are never existents. Being, we have seen earlier, divides, according to Meinong, into existence and subsistence. We also saw that real complexes and real relations exist, while ideal complexes and ideal relations merely subsist. Meinong now adds that objectives, if they have being at all, subsist. A false judgment, in his view, intends an objective which does not have any being; it does not even subsist. This claim that objectives at best subsist clashes with an earlier view. Subsistence, Meinong had maintained, is the mark of necessity. But if every true objective has subsistence, even such a contingent objective as that the sun is shining on a certain day in Graz, then it can no longer be held that subsistence is the mark of necessity. Meinong, therefore, corrects his earlier view. If objectives have being, then they subsist. But among subsisting objectives, only certain objectives are necessary.

Subsistent entities, according to Meinong, are distinguished from existents by their special relationship to time. Subsistents are timeless. What holds for subsistents in general, holds for objectives in particular: objectives are not in time. Meinong's desk, he says, exists at a certain time. But that the desk now exists, this objective subsists now as well as in the future and in the past, even though it was not accessible to knowledge in the past and will be lost to knowledge in the future. This objective is no less timeless than the fact that a right angle is greater than an acute angle.

In the second edition of *Über Annahmen*, Meinong briefly defends this view of the timelessness of objectives against two objections by Marty.[52] He first deals with an obvious counter-example. Assuming that his watch works on Sunday but stops on Monday, the objective *My watch works today* would presumably subsist on Sunday, but would not subsist on Monday. Thus it would not be timeless in the sense intended by Meinong. But Meinong points out that the expression 'today' does not represent the same thing when it is uttered on Sunday and when it is uttered on Monday. We are really dealing in this case with two different objectives which happen to be represented by the same words. The objective *My watch works on Sunday* does subsist even on Monday, and the objective *My watch works on Monday* does not subsist even on Sunday.

Meinong then considers a second objection. From the point of view of one and the same *now*, the existence of the desk *obtains* as something present, it *obtained* a hundred years ago as something in the future, and it is *going to obtain* in a hundred years as something past. In other words, it was true that the desk will exist, it is true that it now exists, and it will be true that it has now existed. According to this conception of objectives, the objective concerning the existence of the desk obtains, but it obtains as something past, present, and future, just like the table itself. Meinong answers this objection by claiming that we must not put the desk and the existence of the desk in the same boat! If we say of the desk at a certain time that it exists as something future, we express ourselves rather badly: it would be more appropriate to say that the desk does not exist at that time at all. But the same does not hold true for the corresponding objective that the desk exists at a certain time: this objective subsists even at a time when the desk does not exist; the existence which, say, subsisted one hundred years ago was not *a future existence*, but merely the existence of something future. In brief, Meinong asserts that, while there are objects which exist in the future or have existed in the past, there are no objectives which subsist in the future or have subsisted in the past. Temporal characteristics belong to objects, not to objectives. One could, he points out, argue with equal force from a grammatical point of view, that objectives must have spatial locations; for we can say such a thing as: 'It happened in England that parliamentarism had its first political successes.'

But even if we agree that what subsists is, say, the timeless existence of a future object rather than the future existence of that object, we have to face up to the fact that we can talk about what subsists, what subsisted, and what will subsist. Now, when Meinong dealt with existence, he claimed that the temporal indication belongs to the object, not to the verb 'exists.' But in this case we do not have a corresponding object; what subsists (obtains) is the existence of some object. Thus we may ask where the temporal characteristic of the verb 'subsists' belongs, since it does not belong either to the subsistence of the objective or the existence of the object. Meinong admits this difficulty. He remarks, firstly, that the difficulty is partially a linguistic one, since language does not have *verba finita* without a *tempus*. And he also points out that objectives can be given a temporal characteristic, in spite of their timelessness, because they are apprehended in time by mental acts.

An objective which subsists, Meinong continues in his characterization of objectives, may perhaps also be called a *fact*.[53] But he has some doubts about this matter. He thinks, first, that necessary objectives can hardly be called facts; for example, the objective that 2 is smaller than 3, since it is not empirical in nature, is presumably not commonly called a fact. Meinong believes, second, that certain objects are often called facts; for example, it is customary to say that a muscle contraction is a physical fact.

Meinong claims next that all objectives can be divided into three groups. First, we get a division into objectives of being and predicative objectives. Objectives of being are of the form *A is*; predicative objectives are of the form *A is F*. Since being divides into existence and subsistence, objectives of being can be further divided into objectives of existence and objectives of subsistence.

Objectives have *modal properties*.[54] Under what conditions is an objective necessary? When is it impossible? Meinong answers that an objective O is necessary if and only if the judgment *that O is a priori* evident. An objective is impossible if and only if its subsistence is negated with *a priori* evidence. There exists thus a certain asymmetry: impossibility occurs only on the second level of judgment, so to speak; we must turn to a judgment about the being of O.

Objectives also enter into *relations* with each other. Above all, there are the familiar relations of compatibility and incompatibility. Then there are the relations of 'connection': the *if-then* and the *because* relations. Meinong thinks that, even though causal relations may be extended to objects, they really belong to objectives. Suddenly, Meinong realizes that objectives are everywhere; their characteristics, important for everything. Epistemology as well as logic, he now announces, is a matter of objectives. Once this is clearly seen, psychologism can be overcome. Epistemology, for example, is neither a science among sciences, nor is it the psychology of the knowledge process. Rather, it deals with the area where truth, necessity, compatibility, etc., are at home, and this is the realm of objectives.

VI

Being and *Aussersein*

In one of his major works, 'Über Gegenstandstheorie,' Meinong proclaims the existence of a hitherto neglected philosophical discipline, the so-called theory of entities.[1] In describing this new and vast field of inquiry, he is faced with a particular philosophical problem. Having held for some time that there are two modes of being, namely, existence and subsistence, he has to consider the possibility that a third mode of being may have to be added in order to account for the ontological status of such entities as the golden mountain and the round square. Meinong, as almost everyone knows, introduces at this point the concept of *Aussersein*. This chapter is about his doctrine of the *Aussersein* of the pure object.

The problem of a third mode of being, I said, arises in connection with the theory of entities. We shall discuss this theory in detail in chapter 8. But we shall now make a few preparatory remarks about it in order to show how it leads to what I have called the problem of a third mode of being.

Historically as well as structurally, Meinong's discovery of the theory of entities and Husserl's invention of phenomenology have the same source. Nor is there any significant difference between the two disciplines; Meinong's theory of entities is nothing but Husserl's phenomenology by another name. Meinong, not unlike Husserl, engages in long and tedious discourses on how his new discipline differs from traditional metaphysics, from logic, from mathematics, etc. Unlike Husserl, though, he never claims that the new discipline is characterized by a special method. The theory of entities differs from other 'sciences' primarily in its subject matter, not in its method. Today, most of us do not take the claims seriously that the theory of entities will yield a wealth of philosophical truths or that in phenomenology we have, at long last, discovered a 'scientific philosophy.' We view the claims made on behalf of these new ways of doing philosophy against the proper historical background, a philosophical climate in which the very possibility of metaphysics was in doubt. From this point of view, Meinong and Husserl were trying to show how philosophy as a respectable rational enterprise is possible. Those of us who have never doubted the respectability of philosophy look upon Meinong's and Husserl's achievements, not as consisting in the discovery of the one true philosophical method, but as consisting in the enlightening discussion of certain very fundamental philosophical problems.

When we approach Meinong's theory of entities or Husserl's phenomenology with this prejudice, then it appears that there are two assertions which form the very core of both of these theories. The first assertion is that every mental act whatsoever has an intention; the second, that intentions have characteristics quite independently of their ontological status. The theory of entities is merely the theory of intentions, irrespective of their modes of being. Such a theory is, of course, only possible if the second assertion is true; for only if intentions have properties and stand in relations to other entities irrespective of whether or not they have being, can there be any significant true statements about them and, hence, a theory about them that deserves the name. Both of these assertions were defended by Twardowski; and both are tacitly accepted by Meinong. I believe that the first one is true, while the second is false. Since my discussion of Meinong's view on being rests entirely on this belief, I shall have to devote a few remarks to Twardowski's argument that there are presentations without objects.

Since Twardowski accepts Brentano's view on judgments, the division into act, content, and object is, as we have seen, only applicable to presentations. The object and content of any act other than a presentation is simply the object and content of the presentation on which this act is built. The question now is: Are there presentations which do not have objects? Twardowski mentions that a number of philosophers have held that there are such presentations. For example, Bolzano gives as examples of presentations without objects such presentations as that of a round square, that of a green virtue, and that of a golden mountain. [2] Kerry, in a similar vein, claims that a presentation with incompatible parts has no object; and he mentions, as an example, the presentation of a number greater than zero which, when added to itself, equals itself. [3] Twardowski, though, thinks that these philosophers are mistaken. Every presentation has an object. Consider, for example, the presentation of an oblique square. Twardowski argues as follows: [4]

However, a more thorough examination of the situation shows that those who claim that under such a presentation there falls no

object are guilty of a confusion. This confusion is easily exposed
if one considers the three functions of names; for, here, too, we
find all three of the functions mentioned earlier, namely, to make
known, to express, and to represent. If someone uses the
expression 'oblique square,' he makes known that there occurs in
him an act of presentation. The content which belongs to this act
constitutes the meaning of this name. But this name does not only
mean something, it also represents something, namely, something
which combines in itself contradictory properties and whose
existence one denies as soon as one feels inclined to make a judgment about it. Something is undoubtedly represented by the name,
even though it does not exist. And what is so represented is
different from the content of the presentation; for, firstly, the
latter exists, while the former does not, and, secondly, we ascribe
properties which are indeed contradictory to what is represented,
but these properties certainly do not belong to the content of the
presentation. If the content had these contradictory properties,
then it would not exist; but it does exist. We do not attribute
obliqueness and squareness to the content of the presentation,
but, rather, whatever is represented by the name 'oblique square' –
and what, though it does not exist, is nevertheless presented – is
the bearer of these properties.

Twardowski then concludes: [5]

The confusion of the proponents of presentations without objects
consists in that they mistook the nonexistence of an object for its
not being presented. But every presentation presents an object,
whether it exists or not, just as every name represents an object,
regardless of whether the latter exists or not. Thus, even though
it was correct to assert that the objects of certain presentations do
not exist, one says too much if one asserts that no object falls
under such presentations, that such presentations have no objects,
that they are objectless.

Twardowski thus uses what I called the second assertion, namely, that
nonexistent objects have properties just as much as existent objects,
in order to substantiate the first assertion, namely, that every presentation has an object. Since the oblique square is really oblique and square,
it cannot possibly be identical with the corresponding content; for the
latter is neither oblique nor square. And he insists that one must keep
apart two entirely different questions, namely, whether or not a certain
presentation has an object, on the one hand, and whether or not the
object of this presentation exists, on the other. Put differently,
Twardowski claims that we must distinguish between the fact that the
intentional relation holds between a presentation (more precisely, the

content of presentation) and an object and the fact that the object of the presentation exists. Put still differently, he claims that the intentional relation holds between a presentation and an object, even if the object does not exist. Thus he implies that there is at least one relation, the intentional relation between presentation and object, which can hold even if one of its terms is not an existent. This view agrees very nicely with the previously mentioned assumption that nonexistent entities have properties just like existent objects; we merely have to add that they can also stand in a certain relation (or, perhaps, relations) to other entities. Twardowski's view that every presentation has an object and that nonexistent entities have properties and stand in relations is thus of one cloth.

I think that Twardowski is correct when he claims that every presentation has an object or, as I would have to say, that every mental act has an intention.[6] On the other hand, I do not agree with him that, say, the round square is really round and square. We shall return to this latter contention in a later chapter. As to the former, I shall venture to defend it against a most common objection. The claim is that the intentional relation can hold between a mental act and an entity which neither exists nor subsists, which, in short, has no kind or mode of being. Now, it is admitted by both sides that there are relations – for example, spatial and temporal relations – which hold only between entities which have being. The question is whether or not all relations are of this sort. While Twardowski maintains that there is at least one relation which is not of this kind, our opponent holds that there are no exceptions.[7] To prove our point, we call his attention to the intentional relation. Now, it would of course not be fair to reply to us that the intentional relation cannot really be a relation of the kind we have in mind, because all relations hold between entities which have being; for whether or not this last assertion is true is just the question. But our opponent may argue that the intentional relation cannot be of the kind we claim it to be, since this would mean that it is a relation with just one term, and the notion of a one-term relation is simply absurd. Something that has just one term – in the sense here contemplated – would simply no longer be a relation; it could at best be a property. In brief, our opponent argues that our notion of the intentional relation implies that this relation has just one term, and that such a notion makes no sense. This, I may add, is the only argument I have ever found against Twardowski's and our conception of the nature of the intentional relation.

But the argument rests on an equivocation in the notion of a term of a relation. The idea of a relation with just one term is indeed absurd. Relations have at least two terms. There simply is no such thing as a relation with only one term. But when we assert that the intentional relation can hold between an existing presentation and a nonexisting object, we do not imply that it is a one-term relation. The intentional relation is a two-term relation; it has two terms. But, and this is the crux of the matter, the two entities which are related by the relation need not both exist. The notion of a term of a relation is not the same as that of an entity which stands in the relation. How many terms a relation has is one matter; whether or not all entities exist among which the relation holds is quite another matter. We encountered this very distinction between term and entity earlier in connection with the relation of identity. Identity is a two-term relation; it is not, say, a three-term or four-term relation. Yet it never holds between two entities; it is a relation which entities have only to themselves. Just as we must not conclude from the fact that identity never holds between two entities that it is therefore a one-term relation and, hence, an absurdity, so we must not conclude from the fact that intentionality can hold between a mental act and a nonexistent entity that it is therefore a one-term relation and, hence, no relation at all.

Let us return to Twardowski's position. Every presentation has an object. Objects can have properties and stand in relations even if they do not exist. These are the two cornerstones of his view on nonexistent objects. Meinong accepts both of these assertions. They are also the cornerstones of his theory of entities.

1 The Beginnings of the Theory of Entities

Every presentation has an object. Is there a science that deals with objects as such? There are, of course, sciences which deal with certain kinds of objects; for example, psychology deals with mental acts, feelings, and other mental phenomena; botany deals with plants, flowers, etc. Metaphysics, too, deals with objects. But, according to Meinong, it does not deal with any particular group of existents, like the individual sciences, but concerns itself with the totality of existents.[8] Thus we find that the sciences as well as metaphysics deal with existent objects and only with existent objects. However, this restriction to existents – and here we are still following Meinong's train of thought – is nothing but a prejudice. That there can be knowledge of objects other than existents is shown by the fact that we can have knowledge of *ideal* entities. Such objects do not exist; they subsist. Hence there is also knowledge of subsistents. Meinong mentions three examples of ideal entities: the relations of equality and inequality, numbers and objectives. Notice that objectives are here called ideal *objects*. This raises a terminological problem. If we keep in mind that Meinong will eventually divide all entities (other than so-called dignitatives and desideratives) into objects on the one hand and objectives on the other, we cannot speak of a theory of *objects* as the all-embracing enterprise, but must speak – as I have done and shall continue to do – of a theory of *entities*. The notion of an entity is then co-extensive with that of an intention. The theory of entities, so understood, is the theory of intentions; we leave open whether or not all intentions must be objects, and we are prepared to admit objectives as intentions.

Notice also that numbers are said to be subsistents. Meinong explains that the whole of mathematics, since it deals with subsistents, is a part of the general theory of entities. Small wonder, therefore, that the traditional division of all sciences into the natural and mental sciences (*Natur- und Geisteswissenschaften*) cannot assign a fitting place to mathematics. This dichotomy merely applies to all those sciences which deal with existents, but it does not concern any inquiries into subsistents.

Granted that subsistents as well as existents can be objects of knowledge, is the theory of entities then to be identified with the theory of all subsistents and existents? Meinong thinks that this characterization would still be too narrow. It would leave out entities which neither exist nor subsist. It would leave out such entities as the golden mountain and the round square. Such entities must not be ignored; for they are presented to the mind. They are, in our terminology, intentions of mental acts. The theory of entities must deal with impossible entities as well as existents and subsistents.

Can we then define the theory of entities as the theory which deals 'with the given irrespective of its being, in that it aims only at knowledge of its characteristics (so-being)'?[9] Meinong believes that this definition is too general. A theory, he argues, consists of true sentences. Thus the theory of entities cannot really be interested in objectives irrespective of whether they subsist or not. Only subsisting objectives are of interest. Could we not then say that the theory of entities deals with *objects* irrespective of their ontological status, but it seeks to discover *objectives* about these objects which subsist? Meinong does not even accept this definition. He wants to bring into the picture another philosophical theme in order to characterize the theory of entities. To this effect, he reminds us of the traditional distinction between empirical and *a priori* knowledge or, as I shall also say, of the distinction between *rational* and *empirical* knowledge. Empirical knowledge, of course, is *a posteriori* knowledge. The theory of entities, he claims, is constituted by rational knowledge. 'What can be known about an entity from the nature of the entity, hence *a priori*, that belongs to the theory of entities.'[10]

2   *A Third Mode of Being*

The theory of entities, we saw, deals, not only with existents and subsistents, but also with entities which have no being at all; it deals even with 'absurd' entities like the round square. Meinong holds that knowledge about such contradictory entities is possible because of what he calls the principle of the independence of so-being from being: What an entity is, what properties it has, is not dependent on whether it has being.[11] Thus, not only is the golden mountain golden, as Meinong emphasizes, but the round square is both round as well as square. Meinong's principle simply coincides with what I called the second assertion at the beginning of this chapter, namely, Twardowski's claim that nonexistent entities have properties (and stand in relations).

That there can be knowledge about entities without being is even more clearly shown, Meinong maintains, when we consider only objectives of being, that is, objectives about the ontological status of entities; for we obviously know that the round square neither exists nor subsists. One could say, paradoxically, that there are entities for which it holds that there are no such entities. Properly understood, though, there is no paradox. The expression 'there are' does not mean the same in its two occurrences: it refers to existence and subsistence in its second occurrence; in its first occurrence, to something else. But what is this something else? Is it a third mode of being on a par with existence and subsistence? Meinong is now fully aware of the fact that these questions must be dealt with in a straightforward fashion; his earlier evasive discussion of the problem in the first edition of *Über Annahmen* simply will not do. He tries to describe the situation in a new way: It is as if the blue must have being in the first place, in order, that one can raise the question of its being or non-being. But in order not to fall into new paradoxes or actual absurdities, perhaps the following way of putting it may be allowed: Blue, and also every other entity, is in a certain way given prior to our decision about its being or so-being, in a way which is also not prejudiced against non-being. From a psychological point of view, one could also describe the situation in this way: if I am able to judge in regard to an entity that it is not, then it appears that I must first of all have grasped the entity, as it were, in order to assert of it non-being or, more precisely, in order to affirm or to deny non-being of it.[12]

Twardowski, quite obviously, could perfectly well agree with this description. But Meinong does not believe, like Twardowski, that the principle of the independence of so-being from being – conceived of as including relations – solves the problem of how entities without being can be given to the mind. Instead, he contemplates a third mode of being – a mode of being which would belong to every entity that neither exists nor subsists – because of the following argument.[13] Assume that the entity A neither exists nor subsists, that is, that it has no being. It is then true, according to Meinong's view, that the objective A *has no being* subsists. This objective has therefore being.

Now, an objective is a kind of whole which consists of certain parts. For example, the objective that A has no being contains as a part the entity A. But it stands to reason that a whole can only have being if all of its parts have being; for, otherwise, something could come from nothing. And this means, in our example, that the entity A must have some kind of being, since the objective A *has no being* has being. This kind of being can be neither existence nor subsistence. Thus the only possibility left is that A has a kind of being different both from existence and subsistence.

We have here an argument of an ontological rather than epistemological kind. This is all to the good. But a closer look at the argument shows that it does not really point in the direction of a third mode of being. First of all, if it is a mystery how a subsisting objective can consist of parts which neither exist nor even subsist, then it is no less of a mystery, one may claim, how a subsisting objective can consist of parts which, though they have some kind of being, do not themselves subsist. How can parts which do not subsist somehow 'add up' to something that subsists? How can something come, though not quite from nothing, from something much less? But let us assume that we do not raise this objection. What else can we do to avoid the conclusion that there is a third mode of being? Well, we could, second, deny the claim that objectives are wholes. But I do not think that this objection is sound. Objectives, as I said in an earlier chapter, are indeed complex entities. To my mind, there can be no doubt about this point; for we can clearly and easily distinguish among the constituents of different objectives. As a matter of fact, there is only one way of classifying objectives, and this is by means of their constituents. Of this kind, for example, is the division of objectives into objectives of being and objectives of so-being. Of this sort, I would add, is also the distinction between quantified objectives and non-quantified objectives, between conjunctions and disjunctions, and so on. If we, then, accept the premise that objectives are complex, the only other way of avoiding Meinong's conclusion is by rejecting the assumption that all wholes which have being must consist of parts which have some sort of being. Thus we are forced, third, to deny that a subsisting objective must have parts which have some sort of being. And this, I think, is ultimately the correct response to Meinong's argument. States of affairs, unlike other complex entities – for example, spatial and temporal structures – can contain entities which have no being. And this means, as one immediately sees, that the specific whole-part relation characteristic of objectives and their constituents has something in common with the intentional relation: Even though it is a two-term relation, it can relate entities which do not have any being. Assuming that there is only one kind of being, existence, we can put the matter this way: the relation between a state of affairs and its constituents is similar to the intentional relation between a content and its intention in that both relations can hold between non-existents.

It may be objected to this diagnosis of Meinong's argument, somewhat impatiently, that there is another, quite obvious, way out, namely, Russell's analysis in terms of the theory of descriptions. What Russell claims, in response to Meinong's arguments is that objects without being never enter into objectives.[14] The golden mountain, for example, is not a constituent of any state of affairs. Only entities with being can be parts of objectives. Whenever we talk about entities without being, the corresponding states of affairs contain, not these entities, but only whatever it is that certain definite descriptions represent. For example, since it is true that the golden mountain does not exist, the golden mountain is not a constituent of the state of affairs that the golden mountain does not exist. To see this clearly we must realize, according to Russell, that the definite description 'the golden mountain' is actually a complex expression of a certain kind, and that none of its constituent expressions represents the golden mountain.[15] What enter into the state of affairs are the referents of these constituent expressions; for example, the property of being golden.

Russell's analysis raises a very important problem: What precisely are the entities that a definite description contributes to a state of affairs? It is clear that Russell always has the relevant properties in mind, but this does not seem to be enough.[16] Consider the description 'the individual thing which is golden and which is a mountain.' Does the word 'individual' here represent an entity which is part of the appropriate states of affairs? Does the word 'the' – in analogy to such quantifier expressions as 'all' and 'some' – contribute to the constituents of the respective states of affairs? Russell, of course, defines definite descriptions, as one says, contextually. But this does not solve the problem, it merely pushes it one step back: we can now ask whether the word 'some' or the expression 'if and only if' as they occur in Russell's paraphrase represent entities and, hence, contribute constituents to certain propositions. What is at stake, in short, is the division of words into categorematic and syncategorematic expressions as applied to descriptions.

But let us assume that we have solved this problem. Let us assume, for the sake of the argument, that what a description contributes is the property mentioned in the description and this property only. Let us assume, furthermore, that unexemplified properties dissolve into exemplified simple properties. Does Russell's analysis avoid the conclusion of Meinong's argument? In the general form in which Meinong poses the argument, the answer, I think, is affirmative. Russell's theory of descriptions explains how there can be propositions about non-

existent entities since these entities do not literally enter into the propositions. But we can construct a version of Meinong's argument
which is not affected by the theory of descriptions. Even if we accept
Russell's theory, we still have to contend with false propositions,
nonexistent states of affairs, or whatever you want to call the entities
represented by false sentences. If we assume that there are complex
states of affairs – thus rejecting one kind of logical atomism – we
can ask how a complex state of affairs could possibly subsist, if
one or more of its constituent states of affairs has no being at all. For
example, consider the disjunction *P or Q* and assume that while *P*
subsists, *Q* does not. How can the whole *P or Q* have a part without
any mode of being? Russell's theory of descriptions does not answer
this question. [17]

My earlier contention that states of affairs may exist (or, as Meinong
would say, that they may subsist), even if one or more of their constituents do not exist, is to be understood in the light of what was
just said in the last paragraph. If we accept Russell's theory, Meinong's
problem is solved for all entities other than states of affairs. But since
I believe that there are such entities as *and*, *or*, and so on, I also believe
that there are complex states of affairs. And if there are such complex
states of affairs, I see no way of avoiding the conclusion that complex
states of affairs can exist, even if some of their constituent states of
affairs do not exist. Hence we must reject the principle that a complex
entity can exist only if all of its parts exist. More generally, we must
reject the principle that a complex entity can have being only if all of
its parts have being.

Meinong, at any rate, would not even agree with our claim that
Russell's theory of descriptions solves his problem for entities other
than objectives, that is, for the golden mountain and the round square.
Consider the true judgment *Ghosts do not exist*. According to Russell's
theory, the state of affairs judged in this case is more perspicuously
represented by the sentence: 'It is not the case that there are individual
things which are ghosts.' Now, it is important that the individual
things here mentioned are existents. [18] Thus what the sentence says
can also be expressed by the shorter expression: 'No existing individual
thing is a ghost.' A similar analysis, relying on the notion of existing
individuals, is forthcoming for a statement like 'The golden mountain
does not exist.' Meinong objects to this Russellian type of analysis:
'if on one occasion someone thinks about ghosts and denies their
existence, and on another occasion thinks about something actual
whether this be vaguely or precisely determined, and recognizes that
such an object is not a ghost, he is in each case thinking two totally
different thoughts.' [19]

Meinong's argument reduces to the claim that the sentence 'No existing individual is a ghost' expresses a thought to the effect that some actual thing or things is not a ghost rather than the thought that ghosts do not exist. Of course, it is hard to decide this issue between Meinong and Russell; for we have to rely in this matter solely on our intuitions about what certain sentences say. But I shall take Russell's side. Meinong's mistake, I submit, consists in confusing the thought that no existing individual is a ghost with another thought, a thought 'about something actual' for which one recognizes that it is not a ghost. What makes the difference between these two thoughts is that we have no particular thing or things in mind when we think that no existing thing is a ghost. It is true that the thought that the people in this room are not ghosts is not the thought that there are no ghosts. But it does not follow from this example and similar ones that the thought that there are no ghosts is not the same as the thought that no existing thing is a ghost. Meinong may have been misled by the slippery phrase 'something actual whether this be *vaguely or precisely determined.*' He seems to equate thinking that *no existing thing* is a ghost with thinking of *something actual* which is *vaguely determined*. But this identification must be rejected. When I think that all men are mortal, I simply do not think of a particular man or several particular men in a vague way.[20] Rather, I think of all men in a precise way. Thus our defense of Russell's position rests on two assertions. First, we insist that the thought expressed by 'Ghosts do not exist' is more perspicuously expressed by the sentence 'No existing thing is a ghost.' Second, we hold that to think of something actual (or some actual things) and to judge of it that it is not a ghost is not the same as to judge that no existing things are ghosts.[21]

3 *The Nature of* Aussersein

Meinong argues, as we saw, that a certain principle about the being of wholes and their parts speaks for there being a third kind of being in addition to existence and subsistence. The golden mountain, for example, would have this kind of being, since it occurs as a part of the subsisting objective that the golden mountain does not exist. But Meinong also casts doubt on the notion of a third mode of being. If there were such a mode of being, he points out, every entity whatsoever would have it. But this means that the usual dichotomy between being and non-being, which exists for other modes of being, disappears. Thus, in holding that there is this third mode of being, we are asserting that there is a kind of being to which there corresponds no non-being. Meinong does not think that this is a viable position. He asks, rhetorically we may assume: 'A being which is in principle unopposed by non-being, can one still call this at all a being?'[22] And he concludes that it would be better if one could avoid the assumption that there is a third mode of being.

We are back at the starting point: how are we to reconcile the earlier principle about the being of wholes and their parts with the fact that objects without being can be parts of subsisting objectives? Meinong now prefers to conclude that all these considerations show that the principle about wholes and their parts does not apply to objectives. We have here an exception to a general principle.[23] In the end, Meinong thus comes to the same conclusion as we did earlier.

But one can sense that he is not happy with his position. He tries to make it more palatable by embarking on a new train of thought. It is at this point that he introduces the important notion of *Aussersein*. Meinong acts as if what now follows substantiates his conclusion that objectives are a special kind of whole, but in reality it is an entirely new line of thought:[24]

> This is a position which speaks also for itself: if the whole contrast between being and non-being is only a matter of the objective and not of the object, then it goes without saying, after all, that neither being nor non-being can be essentially contained in the object by itself. Of course, this does not mean that an object could ever neither be nor not be. Nor is it to assert that it is purely accidental in regard to the nature of every object whether it is or is not: An absurd object like the round square carries in itself the guarantee of its non-being in every sense, an ideal object like inequality carries in itself the guarantee of its non-existence. But one could, if one likes to evoke models which have become famous, formulate what has transpired above by saying that the object as such – irrespective of occasional peculiarities or of the objective-clause which is always given – (one could perhaps say: the pure object) stands 'beyond being and non-being.' This may also be expressed in the following less engaging or also less assuming way, which, in my view, however, is more appropriate: The object is by nature beyond being (*ausserseiend*), although one of its two objectives of being, its being or non-being, subsists in any case.

The problem with *Aussersein* is that it is not at all clear what we are to understand by the *pure object* which allegedly has it. Being, according to Meinong, is a matter of the objective, not of the object. But this does not mean, he also assures us, that an object neither has being nor does not have being. What are we to make of these and similar assertions? Having pondered a number of possible interpretations of Meinong's remarks, I have settled on the following view as the one that seems to be least implausible.

Being, I take Meinong to say, is not an object of any kind.[25] Nor is it ever a constituent of an object. In these respects, it differs radically from the ordinary characteristics of objects. What there is, in the way of being, is, rather, certain objectives. Assuming that the object A has being, for example, there is then the 'pure' object A and a certain objective, A^*, which is the being of A. But this objective, and this is most important, does not consist somehow of A and being; it is, as I just said, A's being. A^* does indeed contain A, but it does not contain something in addition to A. In short, if A has being, then there are two entities, the 'pure' object A and A's being. The former is an object; the latter, an objective.

What happens when A does not have being? In this case, there is the objective of A's non-being, say, $-A^*$. But in this case, too, there is no such object as being. In order to find out whether A has being or not, it is no use to contemplate A by itself. What we must do, is to turn to the realm of objectives instead. If we find there the objective A^*, then we know that A has being; if we find there the objective $-A^*$, then we know that A has no being. The pure object A, as distinguished from the objectives A^* and $-A^*$, has therefore nothing to do with being. Neither existence nor subsistence ever occur in a complex $<\ldots>$ or a relation $[\ldots]$. This is the gist of our explication of what Meinong means by saying that the pure object stands beyond being and non-being, that the pure object has *Aussersein*.

This explication seems to agree fairly well with all the things Meinong says about *Aussersein*. (1) He claims that the contrast between being and non-being is a matter of the objective, not of the object. This means, if we are right, that the contrast occurs only when we consider objectives, and then in the distinction between A^* and $-A^*$. (2) Meinong also asserts that every object, nevertheless, either has being or does not have being. In our words, for every object A, there is either the objective A^* or the objective $-A^*$. (3) He says that it sometimes follows from the nature of an object that it does or does not have being. This means that the properties which go to make up an object (a nature) sometimes determine whether A^* or whether $-A^*$ has being. (4) The being or non-being of an object is said to be external to the object. Being or non-being are not parts, are not constituents, of the object. (Nor are they, we must add, constituents of the corresponding objectives). (5) The so-being of an object, by contrast, is internal to the object. This means that the characteristics of an object are constituents of the object. (6) Last but not least, there is the formula which Meinong attributes to Ameseder, a student of his, and which runs as follows: the object contrasts with the objective in that the former may, under favorable circumstances, *have* being, while the latter *is* itself being.[26] We can make some sense of this rather obscure slogan if we translate it into the following assertion: if the pure object A *has* being, the objective A^* *is* its being.

Ontologically speaking, Meinong's view on *Aussersein* comes to this. There are no such entities as existence or subsistence. And since there are no such entities, they cannot be parts of objects in the way in which properties (and relations) or instances of properties (and relations) are parts of objects. For example, neither the golden mountain, that is, the nature < Golden, Mountain >, nor the brown table before me, that is, the object < Brown$_i$, Table$_i$, Place$_i$, Moment$_i$ >, contain being or non-being as a part. But there are entities which, if I may put it so, do the duty of modes of being. These are objectives of being, that is, objectives of existence and objectives of subsistence. To say that A exists, for example, is not to say that an object called 'existence' is part of A; rather, it is to say that a certain entity, the objective A *exists*, subsists. This objective, however, does not contain, in addition to A, a constituent called existence.

Objectives, unlike other kinds of wholes, can contain entities which have no being, even when they themselves have being. Meinong, as we have seen, accepts this insight, albeit somewhat reluctantly. By introducing the doctrine of the *Aussersein* of the pure object, he adds a new twist to the earlier insight. We must no longer think of the object A, assuming that it has no being, as somehow containing its non-being within itself, so that what enters into the objective A *has no being* is an A which contains its non-being, which brings this non-being with it, so to speak. Rather, what enters into the objective of non-being is the pure object.

In conclusion, three remarks. First, it is clear that Meinong, like the early Russell, was at times tempted to think of *Aussersein* as a third mode of being, a mode of being in which every entity whatsoever, including the round square, participates. [27] Assuming that there is such a third mode of being, one could hold that every object contains or participates in at least one of the three modes. A table, for example, would contain existence; the inequality relation between green and blue would contain subsistence; and the round square would contain *Aussersein*. The objective that the round square does not have being would then contain an entity, the round square, which has some sort of being, though a rather inferior kind. Thus we would not have to hold that a subsisting objective can contain an entity which has no being whatsoever. We would merely have to accept the somewhat smaller mystery that a subsisting objective could consist, in part, of an entity with the lowly mode of *Aussersein*.

Second, our discussion has so far exclusively centered around the being of objects. But it is obvious that the theory of *Aussersein* raises a number of questions about the being of objectives. For example, if A

has being, then the objective $A*$ is said to subsist. Does this mean that there is another objective to the effect that $A*$ subsists, $A**$, and so on? Does this second objective, $A**$, contain subsistence as an entity or is it 'simple' like $A*$? Moreover, how are we to account for false beliefs or judgments? Assume that the objective O is not factual, that it does not subsist. Assume also that someone mistakenly believes O. What, then, is there before the person's mind when he believes O? Since O has no being whatsoever in this case, there seems to be nothing the person believes. But this is surely wrong. We know what it is that the person believes; and we can distinguish what he believes from what some other person believes, even if this second person believes an objective P which is as unfactual as O. It is clear that we can raise the same sort of questions about objectives which, when raised about objects, lead to the theory of *Aussersein*. What is the ontological structure of a situation where someone correctly believes that the objective O does not subsist? In order to grasp that O does not subsist, must not O be somehow given to the mind first? Shall we then have to speak of the 'pure' objective O? But how can objectives be pure in this sense, if they do not just have being but are being? Furthermore, the objective that O does not subsist seems to contain an entity, O, which has no being; and how can an objective which subsists consist, in part, of an entity without being? This, we recall, is the question that started it all.

Third, Meinong's theory of the *Aussersein* of the pure object does not really advance the dialectic of the problem of nonexistent intentions. Rather, it presupposes Twardowski's basic assumption that the intentional nexus can connect with an entity which has no being. Whether or not objects contain their being as constituents is really irrelevant: It is a fact, at any rate, that some objects have being while others do not, and that the mind can be related intentionally to those which have no being just as much as to those which have being.

VII

Empirical Knowledge: Perception and Introspection

In the last chapter, we saw that Meinong defines the theory of entities in terms of the traditional dichotomy between *a priori* and *a posteriori* knowledge. What can be known *a priori*, merely from the nature of the entities involved, that belongs to the theory of entities. Everything else is a matter of empirical knowledge. This characterization of the theory of entities demands a sharp distinction between *a priori* and *a posteriori* knowledge, between rational and empirical knowledge. Meinong attempts to clarify the notion of empirical knowledge in his work *Über die Erfahrungsgrundlagen unseres Wissens*.[1]

There exists another reason for Meinong's epistemological treatise. Meinong started out with a rather Kantian view about our knowledge of the external world. He thought that we infer the existence of external objects as the external causes of our mental acts: 'Accordingly, the outside thing has to be conceived of as something of which we cannot assert anything else but that it is a partial cause for the production of a mental phenomenon.'[2] However, since the time of the *Hume Studies*, Meinong's philosophy has changed in many important ways. He now distinguishes between the act, the content, and the intention of a mental phenomenon. He now believes that there are objectives. And he thinks of intentionality as an ideal relation. In other words, Meinong has acquired the tools for a more sophisticated theory of knowledge than the one outlined in the *Hume Studies*. In the book we are about to discuss, he wields these tools in a masterly fashion. Yet, in the end, he will again meet defeat. All that we can know about the outside world, he will come to conclude, is that some kind or another of object exists. Such is the fatal influence of the traditional arguments against the independent existence of sense qualities.

1 *Perceptual Judgments*

Meinong characterizes rational knowledge in the following way. He compares the *a priori* judgment that red is different from green with the *a posteriori* judgment that a stone which is dropped falls. His first point is that we must distinguish between empirical presentations (ideas) and empirical judgments.[3] A judgment which is not empirical may nevertheless involve empirical ideas. An *a priori* judgment can therefore not be defined as a judgment that does not rest on empirical presentations. The distinction between the *a priori* and the *a posteriori* between the rational and the empirical, concerns judgments, not presentations. More precisely, it is a distinction between justifications for making judgments.

An empirical judgment is justified in terms of past experience. A rational judgment, on the other hand, is not in this manner based on experience. One knows that red is different from green, according to Meinong, because of the very natures of the entities involved. Under favorable circumstances, Meinong continues, such a rational judgment is both evident and certain. This is the second feature of rational knowledge. Third, a judgment of this kind is also necessary. The difference between red and green, for example, is necessary. Fourth and finally, since only the natures of the respective entities matter for rational knowledge, only their so-being is of importance. Whether the entities judged exist or not, is therefore unimportant. Rational knowledge, in summary, (1) concerns the natures of the entities involved, (2) is under favourable circumstances evident and certain, (3) holds with necessity, and (4) is unaffected by the existence or non-existence of the entities involved.

A comparison with the judgment about the falling stone shows that this judgment has none of these four features. It does not follow from the nature of a stone that it will fall when dropped. Furthermore, no amount of experience, Meinong tells us, can ever yield the evidence required for full certainty. Thus we can never have this kind of evidence, evidence for certainty, for the judgment about the stone. Nor does this judgment ever hold with necessity. Finally, experience becomes silent as soon as we leave the realm of what exists. The judgment about the stone is about an existing stone and would have no meaning if there were no stones.

After this preliminary and rather brief characterization of rational knowledge, let us turn to the main topic, empirical knowledge and, especially, perception.

Meinong distinguishes between immediate and mediate experience, and restricts his inquiries to immediate experience. His first main thesis is that all empirical knowledge reduces to perception.[4] Immediate experience is thus identified with perception; and in order to find out what immediate experience is, we must inquire into the nature of perception.

Every perception, according to Meinong, is a judgment. Thus he rejects the notion that perception consists entirely in the having of a certain kind of presentation. To perceive is, not to have a special kind of presentation of an object, but to make a judgment. This does not mean that there are no perceptual presentations. It merely means that these presentations are not all there is to perception. A perception is thus analyzed into two mental acts: there occurs a certain kind of presentation, a perceptual presentation, and there occurs also an *existential* judgment. Does every perceptual presentation lead to the corresponding existential judgment? Meinong, in a very interesting aside, maintains that perceptual presentations can occur without the corresponding judgments.[5] According to him, ordinary hallucination does not differ, on the mental side, from veridical perception.[6] In hallucination, just as in veridical perception, there may occur an existential judgment in connection with a perceptual presentation. But, as he points out, there are also cases of hallucination where the person is not fooled, where the person knows that his experiences are hallucinatory. In these cases, there occur certain perceptual presentations. But since it is impossible to make a judgment if one knows that it is false, it follows that no corresponding judgments can occur. In these, admittedly abnormal, cases, we have no perception in the true sense. Meinong's analysis implies that perception takes place only when the person believes in the existence of the perceived entity.

Since every perception involves an existential judgment, it intends, at least in part, an existential objective. To perceive the tree is to have a certain presentation and to judge that the tree exists. Granted that we can, in this sense, perceive the existence of things, can we not also perceive that they have certain properties (and stand in certain relations)? In other words, are there also perceptions which intend objectives of so-being? Do some perceptions involve predicative judgments rather than existential ones? Meinong wants to hold that perception is restricted to existential judgments, that no perception involves a predicative judgment. But do we not say such things as that we see that the grass is green, that the sky is blue, and that this tree is to the left of that tree? It seems to be nothing but plain common sense that we do not only perceive that certain things exist, but also that these things have certain properties. Meinong himself notes that one may well come to the opposite conclusion from the one he draws, namely, to the conclusion that all perceptions involve predicative judgments. Yet, he is determined to defend the view that perception involves only existential judgments:[7]

Assume someone is looking out through a window for the first
time at a landscape unknown to him. It may then happen that he
says: 'The meadow before me is green,' and, perhaps, also: 'I see
that the meadow is green.' But can the being green of the meadow
really be the first thing he perceives? Can one recognize that the
meadow is green before one even knows that there is a meadow?
Obviously not; thus the judgment that there is a meadow must
be contained in what is experienced when one looks out through
the window.

This argument seems to derive its plausibility from an ambiguity
in Meinong's rhetorical question: 'Can one recognize that the meadow
is green before one even knows that there is a meadow?' If this question asks whether one can see that the meadow is green without having
first judged that it exists, then the answer, I think, is affirmative.
Meinong is simply wrong when he believes otherwise. When we con-
sult plain experience, we do not find these existential judgments pre-
ceding all our perceptions. However, it is quite true that one cannot
see that the meadow is green without seeing the meadow. Thus if
Meinong's question aims at asking whether or not one can see that
the meadow is green before one has seen the meadow, then the answer
is negative. To see that the meadow is green is, *eo ipso*, to see the
meadow. Does this mean that there occurs a perception of the meadow
prior to the seeing that it is green? If so, then we seem to be embracing
Meinong's analysis after all; for it is this perception of the meadow
that is analyzed into an existential judgment founded on a perceptual
presentation. However, when we admitted that one must perceive the
meadow in order to perceive that it is green, we did not wish to imply
that there must occur any particular act whatsoever prior to the perception that the meadow is green. There need occur neither an existential judgment of the type envisaged by Meinong, nor any other
particular kind of mental act. Granting for the sake of the argument
that there occurs a perceptual presentation, 'the very next perceptual
act' is the seeing that the meadow is green; and this seeing is also a
seeing of the meadow. In short, when one sees that the meadow is
green, one sees the meadow (and also the color green); for to see the
meadow is to see something 'about it'; it is to see some (predicative)
state of affairs in which it occurs.

But let us grant, to go on with the argument, that every perception
involves an existential judgment. Meinong wants to claim more,
namely, that predicative judgments are not a matter of perception at
all. To this effect he asserts that an existential judgment about the
meadow is a judgment about the meadow including its color, since no
act of abstraction has as yet taken place. Meinong implies that the com-

plex object which is the meadow can only be given to the mind independently of some of the properties of which it consists if a mental act of abstraction has taken place. Before such an act of abstraction occurs, the complex object is perceived as consisting of certain properties. If this is true, what becomes of the predicative judgment: this meadow is green? Meinong says that there are only two possible analyses of this judgment.[8]

The complex object which is the meadow may be analyzed into its parts while special attention is paid to the color which it contains. This does not mean, Meinong insists, that the predicative judgment is really of what he calls the *tautologous* form: (1) 'The complex containing green, property F, property G, etc., contains green.' Rather, the subject of the judgment, the complex, has not as yet been analyzed, so that the judgment is of the form: (2) 'This meadow is green.' It is clear that this claim clashes with the earlier assertion by Meinong that to perceive the meadow is to perceive it as consisting of its color. But let us neglect this obvious tension in Meinong's exposition. Assuming that the judgment is of form (2), how does it now follow that it cannot be a perceptual judgment?

Meinong argues that judgments of the form (2), though they are not tautologies, are nevertheless necessary and known *a priori*:[9]

> But this does not change the fact that here, too, one contrasts a whole, from which one has picked out a part, with this part and assigns it to the whole. The right to do this derives then from the nature of the whole on the one hand, of the part on the other, in the same way in which we noted above that the difference between red and green is justified by the nature of the judged objects. In one word, it is an *a priori* judgment.

According to the first possible interpretation of the judgment in question, then, it cannot be a perceptual judgment, since it is an *a priori* judgment; and it is an *a priori* judgment, on Meinong's view, because it asserts that a certain whole has a certain part, an assertion which is presumably true by virtue of the nature of the whole on the one hand and the nature of the part on the other. We can generalize: all judgments about the so-being of complexes, all ordinary predicative judgments, are known *a priori*. They are necessary, though not tautologous.

It is a rather popular view that a judgment of the form: (3) 'Complex C contains part P' is necessary.[10] But I see no reason for accepting it. If Meinong had claimed that the judgment in question is tautologous, then one could at least understand the rest of his argument. But we saw that he clearly distinguishes, as he should, between assertions of the form (1) and assertions of the form (2).

If so, then we may justifiedly ask for some kind of argument for the assertion that (2) is a necessary judgment, a piece of *a priori* knowledge. Meinong's interpretation of this judgment in terms of whole and part does not by itself constitute such an argument. We must raise the question: What is there in or about C that makes it necessary that P is one of its parts? And a similar question arises in regard to P: What is there in or about P that makes it necessary that P is a part of C? However, since P is really an instance, not a property, such that P 'by its very nature' is a part of this whole rather than any other, one may convince oneself that this second question at least can be answered. From our point of view, however, this merely shows that the notion of an instance is inherently confused.

Meinong's first interpretation of judgments of so-being makes all of them necessary. Only existential judgments are not necessary; only existential judgments are pieces of *a posteriori* knowledge. However, there seems to be an exception. Recall that Meinong had claimed earlier that the relation of association between, say, a color and a place is a real relation. If this is so, then it follows that the fact that this particular color is associated with this particular place cannot be known *a priori*. Thus there is at least one judgment which is not an existential judgment and which is *a posteriori*. This exception merely serves to reinforce our doubts about Meinong's view that objectives of so-being of the sort A *is* F, where A is a complex and F is a property, are necessary and known *a priori*. Consider the complex C, formed from a certain color F (instance), a certain place P, and a certain moment M. If the fact that F is associated with P and M is not necessary and is not known *a priori*, why should the fact that C contains F be necessary and known *a priori*? Is it not just as 'accidental' and beyond rational insight that this color F belongs to C as it is that F is associated with P and M? We cannot claim that the first case is different from the second because C is simply the complex object consisting of F, P, and M; for, then, we are really no longer talking about the judgment that C contains F, but rather about the quite different assertion that a complex which contains F, P, and M contains F; and we saw that Meinong insists that the judgment under consideration is of the former rather than the latter kind.

According to Meinong's second interpretation of the judgment under consideration, it concerns the word 'green.' What the perceiver judges in this case is that the property which is seen is the same entity as the property commonly called 'green.' 'Our judgment asserts or implies then an identity (*Übereinstimmung*). Now, whether two things are identical or not, this is decided again only from the natures of these things, [there is] again no difference from the above case of inequality.'[11] According to this second interpretation as well, the judgment under discussion turns out to be necessary. Since it is necessary and *a priori* it follows again that it cannot be a judgment of perception. The proof that all perceptual judgments must be existential is thus complete. A predicative judgment is either a judgment about a part-whole relationship or a judgment about a certain identity. In either case it is *a priori*; its objective is necessary.

If perception involves only existential judgments, how could we possibly express such a judgment in words? For example, granted that the judgment *This meadow is green* is already a matter of rational insight, what does the corresponding existential judgment look like? It is clear that the judgment *This meadow exists* will not do; for it involves a predicative judgment to the effect that the perceived object is a meadow. The proper expression of a perceptual judgment seems to reduce to a mere 'This exists.' Anything else, according to Meinong's theory, is no longer a matter of perception, but belongs to rational knowledge. If there ever was a philosophical position that flies in the face of common sense, this is surely it. There can be no doubt whatsoever that we see that there are green trees, that we hear the first tones of a symphony, and that we smell the aroma of a steak.

Meinong realizes that his view clashes with common sense, and he tries desperately to soften the clash.[12] He claims, firstly, that we so often express our perceptions in predicative judgments because we wish to convey the new and important parts of our experiences, and these are not the existential judgments, but the *a priori* predicative judgments which follow in their wake. We do not usually express our bare perceptions in words, because they are uninteresting, since they are obvious. This attempted explanation of why we all believe that we can perceive, not only that things exist, but also what properties they have, makes sense only if we have already accepted Meinong's view. Secondly, and more importantly, Meinong also maintains that the pure perception is always inexpressible. The complex of instances which is perceived cannot really be communicated. This is the reason why the sentences by means of which we do communicate about our perceptions are not really expressions of perceptual judgments. The most nearly adequate expression for such a judgment, as we just saw, is the sentence 'This exists.' And it is quite clear that this sentence by itself is not a good vehicle of communication.

This second claim, as well, presupposes Meinong's analysis of perception. But it also involves a very important epistemological point. How do we usually communicate about individual things? Language puts at our disposal two means of talking about individuals, namely, labels and descriptions. It is clear that one cannot communicate by means of a label unless the listener knows what it is a label of. For example, if I say '*A* is green,' the listener may not know which one of several things before us I have called 'A.' Hence he will not know what I am saying or, more precisely, he will not know of which one of several things before us I am asserting that it is green. On the other hand, a definite description may help to fix for him the object which I have in mind. If I say, for example, 'The book on my desk is green,' the listener will know what thing I am talking about. In this case, though, the description itself involves a predication. Descriptions, it is clear, often have to jump into the breach when we fail to communicate by means of pure labels.[13]

But before we jump to the conclusion that labels are worthless for purposes of communication, two further points must be stressed. First, the contrast between labels and descriptions is not restricted to expressions for individual things. Any entity whatsoever can be labeled as well as described. Second, and more importantly, communication must ultimately rest on labels and labels alone. One can only describe an entity by means of a property which it has (or a relation in which it stands to something else). One must, therefore, use a predicate (or a relation term) in the description. Now, either this predicate is already a label, or it, in turn, is a description of a property. If the latter is the case, then this property must be described in terms of a second property and we can repeat our alternatives. Since this process cannot go on indefinitely, it follows that all communications must begin with and rest on labels; descriptions, one might say, are only possible if there are labels. Ultimately, then, we all learn our first language by guessing at the beginning what certain labels mean. Such is the frail nature of language acquisition.

Granted that definite descriptions greatly facilitate communication about individual things (as well as other kinds of entities), it is an entirely different matter whether or not we can perceive those predicative states of affairs which are involved in descriptions. Meinong, as we saw, denies that we can perceive any predicative states of affairs.

Meinong raises two important questions.[14] Can nonexistence be recognized just as immediately as existence? If so, is a judgment to the effect that something does not exist a perceptual judgment? Meinong answers the first question in the affirmative. The non-existence of a certain table in a room, for example, is recognized just as immediately as its existence in another room. The answer to the second question is, according to Meinong, more difficult. But in the end, Meinong adopts the view that all perceptual judgments have a positive objective. Meinong says that it is obvious that one cannot perceive something which is not there. But it is not equally obvious that one cannot perceive the non-existence of something. I take him to mean by this last assertion that it is not obvious that a perceptual judgment cannot have an objective of non-existence. But such a judgment of non-existence, Meinong now argues, differs from a perceptual judgment in that the object of a judgment of non-existence can never be given to the perceiver by means of a perceptual presentation. Since perception – by definition, so to speak – involves perceptual presentations, Meinong excludes judgments of non-existence from perceptual judgments.

Meinong's general view, in spite of its sophistication in spots, is clearly a variant of the classical dogma that perception consists of sensation plus judgment. The senses are represented by so-called perceptual presentations. Judgment is added in the form of existential judgment. There can hardly be any doubt that perception does indeed involve the senses or, as I shall say, that it involves sense-impressions. But the classical view, and Meinong's as well, goes wrong when it adds judgments to these sense-impressions as the second essential ingredient of perception. Rather, what is added are certain irreducible mental acts of perception, namely, acts of seeing, acts of hearing, acts of smelling, etc. According to this alternative to the tradition, perception consists of two things: the having of sense-impressions and the occurrence of a mental act of perception.[15] A mental act of seeing, for example, is *sui generis*; it is not a judgment in any ordinary sense. The difference between seeing that there is a book on the desk and merely judging that it is on the desk does not consist solely in the fact that certain sense-impressions are present in the first case and absent in the second. The mental acts that occur in these two cases are themselves as different from each other as, say, a wishing is from a remembering. Why does Meinong – and his fellow students of Brentano – overlook the obvious phenomenological difference between, say, seeing and judging? Perhaps, they were under the spell of the traditional – if you wish, Cartesian – division of mental acts into presentations and judgments. I think that the following theme may have influenced their thinking on this point. Assuming that perception is somehow 'propositional,' that is, that it involves states of affairs, the only kind of mental act traditionally available for the role of intending states of affairs was judgment. Assuming, for example, that seeing is a matter of seeing *that* something is so-and-so, and given that the only kind of act which intends propositions, states of affairs, etc., is judgment, one simply jumped to the conclusion that seeing that something is so-and-so is identical with or, at least, involves judging that something is so-and-so. What one did not realize, to put it succinctly, is that there are propositional mental acts other than judgments. There are, in my view, such propositional acts as acts of seeing, acts of hearing, etc.[16]

All perceptual judgments intend existential objectives. Hence it follows from Meinong's view that ideal entities cannot be perceived; for ideal entities do not exist, they subsist. But if ideal entities cannot be perceived, how are we acquainted with them? It is clear that Meinong's ontology will eventually force him to acknowledge the existence of a special kind of mental act, a special capacity of the mind, by means of which we are in contact with the realm of ideal entities.

At any rate, Meinong's claim that we cannot perceive ideal objects points out a flaw in his division of complexes into real and ideal complexes. A chair, for example, is said to be a real complex; its essential parts are a color and a place. But a melody, according to Meinong, is an ideal complex. It follows that we cannot perceive a melody. But this goes against the grain; for we are all convinced that we do hear melodies. Meinong does not flinch, though. He merely remarks: 'One simply asserts that one hears a melody when one, in reality, hears the tones on which the melody is based.'[17]

Meinong devotes more attention to another consequence of his theory of perception. According to this theory, we can perceive only existents. Existents, for Meinong, are always individual; they are localized in space and/or time. Hence it follows that we cannot perceive anything which is not so localized. If follows, in particular, that we cannot perceive properties, as ordinarily understood; for properties, in this sense, are not localized in space and/or time. But this, too, goes against the grain. We seem to believe that one can perceive the blueness of the sky, the color of the meadow, and so on.

Meinong must therefore explain how we come to believe these things, when, in reality, properties are not perceivable. His explanation harbors no surprise. He merely asserts that we must distinguish between properties on the one hand and instances of properties on the the other. We must distinguish between, say, the color green and the green of this particular leaf. Now, while it is true that the color green, the property, is not localized and, hence, does not exist, the same is not true of the instance. This instance is an individual – in the appropriate sense – and thus localized in space and time. It does, therefore, exist. When we believe that we can perceive, not only individual things, but also properties, we are partially correct. What we can perceive are instances of properties, not the properties themselves. It is true, therefore, that we can perceive, not only complexes which constitute ordinary perceptual objects, but also instances of properties. But we are mistaken when we confuse these instances with the properties themselves. The property green, in distinction to all of its instances, can never be perceived. We get acquainted with it through a process of abstraction.

These remarks are interesting because they show that Meinong has changed his mind about the nature of instances and of properties. He used to hold that, say, the color part of the leaf acquires its particularity by being associated with a place (and a moment). By itself, this part was said to be universal. We were supposed to get acquainted with the property green by means of abstraction, and abstraction simply consisted in disregarding the associated place (and moment). Meinong sees now that this view is untenable. He realizes that color instances must be particular by themselves, that it makes no sense to claim that they 'become particular by being associated with a certain place.' He also realizes that if the particular instance is a part of a perceptual object, then it cannot be the corresponding property which is associated with a place (and moment). The property thus is severed from the complex; abstraction can no longer be viewed as a matter of paying attention to a part of a complex.[18] Meinong, it is obvious, will eventually have to take another look at his assay of properties, what they are and how we are acquainted with them.

2 *Evidence and Certainty*

Some hallucinations involve existential judgments. But these judgments are false, and nobody, according to Meinong, would call a false judgment a perception.[19] Thus, even though it is true that a perception consists of a perceptual presentation and an existential judgment, these two ingredients do not as yet completely define perception. There are experiences which have these two constituents, but which are not perceptions. The example of hallucination suggests that we characterize perception by adding that the existential judgment must be true. Meinong argues that this simple addition will not do. Someone may be hallucinating and judge, in his hallucination, that the door bell is ringing when it is in fact ringing. His judgment would then be true; yet we would not wish to say that he perceived the ringing of the door bell. One could try to exclude such cases by stipulating that the perceptual judgment must be caused by what is perceived. But Meinong claims that this, too, would not be satisfactory; for one must already know that a thing is there before one can inquire into its causal connections.

From our point of view, the problem is not how to characterize perception, but rather how to distinguish between veridical and non-veridical perception. A perception occurs, I submit, when a perceptual act occurs, that is, when there occurs a seeing, or a hearing, etc. Of course, it is true that such acts only occur, as a matter of fact, accompanied by certain sense-impressions; and there are, undoubtedly, a number of further conditions without which a perceptual act does not occur. However, whether the perceptual act is veridical or not does not affect the question of whether a perception has occurred. Thus we disagree with Meinong when he claims that there are no perceptions during a hallucination. The person who in his hallucination sees a pink rat does indeed *see* something. [20] His experience consists just as much of an act of seeing as the experience of someone who sees a white rat which actually exists. But, of course, what the hallucinating person sees, the pink rat, does not exist. In short, we sharply distinguish two different questions. First, does a perception take place, that is, does a perceptual mental act occur? Second, is the perceptual act veridical or not? This takes care of Meinong's first point.

As to his second point, what are we to make of the 'accidentally true' hallucination? A perception, undoubtedly, takes place, contrary to what Meinong holds. But would we want to call this perception really veridical? Why not? After all, the person presumably perceives a state of affairs which does obtain. What makes this case peculiar is that we ordinarily expect that a veridical perception is, at least in part, caused by the perceived object; just as we ordinarily expect that the perceiver has sense-impressions. One cannot really hear a certain bell, unless the bell is at least a partial cause for the occurrence of the act of hearing. What Meinong's second point stresses is the important fact that we can and must distinguish, not only between veridical and non-veridical perceptual mental acts, but also between acts that are caused, in part, by external objects and acts which are not. Hallucinations, in particular, are not just characterized by the fact that the perceptions which occur are often non-veridical, but also by the fact that these perceptions are not caused in the normal way.

Meinong, it seems clear, would object. He would insist that one cannot distinguish between hallucinatory and ordinary perception in this way by means of causal connections; for, in order to decide whether or not the perceptual act is caused by an 'external' object, one must already assume that one's perceptions are not hallucinatory. Meinong seems to be saying, in effect, that an hallucinatory act of perception must somehow be inherently different from a non-hallucinatory one so that it is possible to distinguish between the two, not just contextually, as it were, but absolutely. The only viable way of meeting Meinong's objection, it seems to me, is to deny that there is such an inherent difference. We must distinguish between two different questions. First, how do hallucinatory acts of perception differ from non-hallucinatory ones? Second, how do we actually distinguish between these two kinds of acts in a given situation? We saw that hallucinatory perceptions, even if they are 'veridical' in the sense explained, differ from non-hallucinatory ones in that the former have different causes from the latter, if I may say so for short. However, in order to decide whether a given act of perception is hallucinatory or not, one must rely, during one's inquiry into its causal origins, upon further mental acts, upon further perceptions, additional memories, etc. And these acts, in turn, may of course be hallucinatory.

In connection with his second point, Meinong invokes the picture of a windowless monad and its 'perceptions.'[21] Such a monad, according to our explication, would perceive things, but its perceptions would be hallucinatory because they are not caused by 'external' objects. Meinong rejects our criterion, as we just saw, on the ground that causal inquiries themselves must ultimately rest on perceptions. He cannot be claiming that our criterion is circular; for it is not. Hallucination is distinguished from ordinary perception partly in terms of its causal origin. There is nothing circular in this characterization. What Meinong seems to attack with his objection is a different kind of 'circularity,' namely, the 'circularity' involved in our claim that one can only decide that a given perception is not hallucinatory on the basis of other mental acts which, in turn, are not inherently distinguishable from hallucinatory ones. This line of reasoning, as we shall see in just a moment is an important motive for the theory of evidence, a theory which looms very large in Meinong's philosophy.[22]

Having rejected a definition of perception in terms of causal connection, Meinong enlarges the topic of the discussion by raising the question: What is truth?[23] A judgment is true, Meinong answers, if and only if its objective subsists. But since mere psychological conviction does not guarantee that the objective subsists, a serious problem arises. How can we ever find out that a given objective, O, subsists? In order to find out whether a given judgment is true, we must find out whether or not its objective subsists. But this seems to mean that we must first find out whether or not another judgment is true, namely, the judgment that the objective O subsists. And in order to find out whether this second judgment is true, we must first determine whether or not a second objective, O', subsists. And so on. Meinong argues as follows:[24]

Of course, there are also enough judgments whose objectives have no being, namely, the false judgments. Everyone knows this; nevertheless, there lies some danger for all of our knowledge in the circumstance that a conviction does not at all guarantee the factuality of the objective which it apprehends. For, how do we know about the factuality of the respective objectives? Obviously, in no other way than through judgments. But of what help are these judgments, if they, in turn, can as easily, perhaps even more easily, be false rather than true? However, this does not, of course, exclude the possibility of making a true judgment. But if it is purely accidental that the right judgment and the right objective once in a while connect, so to speak, then it can in the the end also only be an accident that someone takes a judgment to be true when it is true; for the inclination to take a judgment to be true, which accompanies quite naturally every judgment, is of help to the false judgments no less than to the true ones. Such consequences, which would amount to our abandoning all confidence in our judgments and, hence, to our relinquishing all knowledge, can only be avoided, so far as I can see, under two presuppositions: firstly, that there are judgments whose nature it is to be true; secondly, that we are able to discern this nature of truth of such judgments by means of judgments of the same nature. Experience teaches us that these two requirements are more or less perfectly fulfilled.

This, in a nutshell, is Meinong's argument for evidence. Certain unacceptable consequences can only be avoided, he is arguing, if we assume that there are evident judgments and that we can discern their evidence by means of further evident judgments. Furthermore, it is itself evident, as Meinong later adds, that an evident judgment cannot be false. Knowledge is thus distinguished from other kinds of judgment by this feature of evidence. Evidence is a characteristic of judgments, not of their objectives [25]

Granted that some judgments have this characteristic, the real problem with Meinong's argument, it seems, consists in the requirement that we be able to discern this characteristic in further judgments. [26] Meinong admits that this requirement is fulfilled to a rather imperfect degree; for, 'It is a fact that doubt and error may arise over whether or not one judges in a given case with evidence.' [27] This mental characteristic of judgments is thus not always obvious. According to Meinong, it may even happen that a person who makes an evident judgment overlooks its evidence. On the other hand, it may also happen that a certain objective, which under certain circumstances could be the intention of an evident judgment, is actually judged without evidence. This means that not all true judgments are evident judgments.

It is tempting to interpret Meinong's theory of evidence as a view about certainty. And this, indeed, is how one of his readers understood the matter. In a letter to Meinong, Edith Landmann-Kalischer argues as follows. If judgments may appear to have evidence when they do not have it, and if judgments may seem to lack evidence when they actually have it, and if, furthermore, only additional inquiries can decide which is which, then we seem to be caught in a circle: evidence is presented as the criterion for the subsistence of objectives, but the subsistence of these objectives is also used as the criterion for the evidence-character of judgments. She concludes with the observation that either evidence is such a distinct experience that every possibility of error is excluded, and it is uniquely co-ordinated to truth, or evidence cannot be the ultimate criterion of truth, since it, in turn, requires to be checked by means of other intellectual operations.[28]

Meinong, in several letters, makes quite clear that this interpretation of his theory of evidence is mistaken.[29] Evidence is not conceived of as an infallible criterion of truth. It does not guarantee to us, so to speak, that we cannot be mistaken. It does not yield certainty. It is not an infallible mark of truth or factuality. Rather, it merely distinguishes between certain mental acts, namely, acts of knowing, and others. 'If knowing is that kind of experience,' Meinong says, 'by means of which we apprehend reality, then it seems to me quite natural that this experience must be different from one which is incapable of apprehending reality; for I do not even apprehend red and green through the same experience.'[30] I shall return to this remark in a moment. First, though, let us take a closer look at the earlier quoted argument for evidence.

Without evidence, Meinong is saying, it would be a matter of sheer accident that the right judgment intends the right objective. It is hard to see what Meinong could possibly mean by this assertion. A given judgment has a certain content. This content intends a certain objective. The objective either subsists or it does not subsist. If it subsists, then the judgment is true; if not, then the judgment is false. Whether a judgment is true or not depends, therefore, on two things; first, on its content; second, on the ontological status of its objective. There is simply no room for accidents. But Meinong speaks also in the same context about a guarantee for the factuality of objectives, and perhaps his remark about an accidental connection between judgment and objective must be understood in the light of the first sentences of the passage. In a similar vein, he says a little later: 'What matters to the truth of a judgment is merely the factuality of the objective. But since this factuality appears to us in the end only in the evidence of certain judgments, for us all knowable truth goes back somehow to evidence.'[31] From these remarks, we can reconstruct an argument for evidence. Whether or not a judgment is true, is determined by its objective. If the objective is factual, if it subsists, then the judgment is true; otherwise, the judgment is false. But the factuality of an objective is never directly given to us. Only the corresponding judgments are actually open to our inspection. Hence we could never determine whether an objective is factual or not, unless the corresponding judgment had some characteristic or another which somehow indicates the ontological status of its objective. This characteristic may not stick out like the proverbial sore thumb; we may even make mistakes about whether or not a given judgment has it. But this merely means that truth is not very easy to come by. It merely means that certainty eludes us. If there were no such characteristic at all, however, then it would be not just difficult to discover the truth, it would be impossible. According to this train of thought, the mental feature of evidence must exist because knowledge would otherwise be impossible and it is a fact that there is knowledge.

The crucial assumption, then, in Meinong's argument is that the factuality of objectives is forever hidden from direct inspection. Why would anyone make this assumption? I can think of two very good reasons.

It is part and parcel of the representationalist tradition, at least since Descartes, to restrict what is called 'direct acquaintance' to mental entities. According to this tradition, one is only directly acquainted with the content of one's mind, that is, with one's own ideas, one's mental acts, etc. In regard to judgments, this means that we are only directly acquainted with our mental acts of judging, their contents, and whatever other properties they may have. But we are not directly acquainted with the intentions of judgments, that is, with objectives. Ordinarily, the problem of knowledge for the representationalist is the problem of how we can know of the existence of non-mental (external) things, if it is true that we are only directly acquainted with our own ideas (presentations). But we can quite obviously give it a different twist: How can we ever know a truth, if we are never directly acquainted with the intentions of our judgments, that is, with objectives?

For reasons which I have explained in great detail elsewhere, we must reject the representationalist's identification of inner awareness with direct acquaintance.[32] It is true enough that we are acquainted with our own mental acts in a way quite different from the one in which we are acquainted with 'external' perceptual objects and states of affairs. For example, while we see chairs, mountains, and people, we do not see our mental acts, our sensations, or our emotions; and while we feel pains, we do not, in the same sense of the word, feel perceptual objects. Let me say that we are *aware* of our mental acts and other mental entities, but are not aware of 'external' things.[33] Now, even though there is this difference between awareness and other kinds of mental acts, this difference is not the same as that between direct and indirect acquaintance. Every mental act of whatever kind presents its intention directly or, if you insist, indirectly. There is no difference in this respect between awareness on the one hand and, say, perception and judgment on the other. When we see a table, it is not the case that we are directly acquainted with a mental act of seeing as well as certain visual sense-impressions, and then infer – in some way – from these mental phenomena something about a table. Rather, we are *aware* of these mental phenomena, and we also *see* the table as directly as we are aware of the mental act and the sense-impressions. The identification of awareness with direct acquaintance, and of other mental acts with indirect acquaintance is so pernicious because it inevitably leads to the conclusion that what one is not aware of must be a matter of inference.

Factuality is hidden from us, according to this first reason, because we are not directly acquainted with objectives, but only with judgments. Hence, there must be something in or about certain judgments that allows us to *infer* that their objectives are factual and, therefore, that they are true. Meinong's defense of evidence, seen from this angle, is merely a version of the traditional representationalist move.

But even if one does not make the representationalist's mistake, even if one insists that we are as directly acquainted with perceptual objects and objectives as we are with mental things, there exists still another reason for holding that we are never acquainted with factuality. Factuality, it may be said, is not a discernible feature of objectives. Objectives, it is true, are either factual or they are not factual; put differently, they either subsist or they do not subsist. But the feature of subsistence, unlike any ordinary property, is simply never presented to us. Or, rather, all objectives seem equally well to have it or equally well not to have it. One can inspect a billiard ball and see that it is green, but one cannot inspect an objective and discover that it subsists. Objectives do not wear their ontological status on their sleeves; nor do they hide it any place else where it could be discovered.

If this is so, then it is clear that a criterion for the factuality of objectives is needed. If careful inspection of an objective does not tell us whether it subsists or not, something else must do the trick, since we do, as a matter of fact, distinguish between true and false judgments. Evidence, then, is the feature which, unlike factuality or subsistence, is given to us. From this point of view, Meinong's argument does not rest on the assumption that we are never directly acquainted with objectives, but rather on the assumption that we are never directly acquainted with their ontological status. In either case, a criterion for truth is needed. Evidence is this criterion.

While it is easy to dispose of the first reason for a criterion, the representationalist's fallacy, the same is not true, so far as I can see, for the second reason. States of affairs, it seems to me, are indeed before the mind without any distinguishing quality that would help us to separate fact from fiction. I simply cannot find any feature of objectives that distinguishes factual from non-factual ones, no matter how hard I look and how long I inspect. This is the kind of fact I am willing to accept as a basis for all arguments. By the same token, I also find nothing in or about judgments, no characteristic of evidence, that distinguishes true from false judgments. Must we then accept the dreaded conclusion that knowledge is impossible? Must we concur with the skeptic that the distinction between truth and falsehood, between fact and fiction, must forever elude us? I do not think so. We can and do determine that certain objectives are facts, while others are not. But we do not do so by inspecting a given objective or a certain judgment in isolation, looking, as it were, for a telltale sign of factuality or truth. What we actually do – and cannot help but do – is to compare objectives with each other. There is thus a criterion of truth after all. It consists in the 'coherence,' logical and factual, of objectives. The so-called coherence theory of truth has a point, but it is an epistemological rather than an ontological point. Some states of affairs exist (Meinong would say: they subsist), others do not. This is the ontological part of the story of truth. But the ontological status of a state of affairs is not open to view. Factual and non-factual states of affairs, though they are inherently different, look alike to the mind. Thus, the best we can do in this world is to compare states of affairs with each other, to trust some of them and to eliminate others on the basis of those we trust.

If this account is true, then we are indeed faced with those consequences which, in Meinong's words, amount to our abandoning all confidence in our judgments and, hence, to our relinquishing all knowledge. There is then no solution to the problem of knowledge which would satisfy Meinong. There is then no criterion of knowledge other than one in contextual terms.

To return to the origin of this discourse about evidence, perception, as a form of knowledge, is to be characterized, in part, by evidence.[34] This characteristic it shares with *a priori* knowledge. But it differs from the latter in that it is never necessary. What one perceives does not exist with necessity. What one knows *a priori*, though, subsists with necessity; for example, the inequality between green and red. Meinong can now complete his definition of perception: A perception is an affirmative existential judgment about a present object which is evident and based on a perceptual presentation.

As regards hallucinations and other non-veridical perceptions, they simply turn out to consist of judgments without evidence.

3 *Sensory Qualities*

Armed with a definition of perception, Meinong casts around for experiences that qualify as perceptions. Earlier, we noted that his definition leads to the surprising conclusion that we cannot hear (perceive) melodies. Meinong repeats this claim and explains that it follows from the fact that one cannot hear the difference between two tones. What one can hear is only the two tones; the difference between them is not a matter of perception, but a matter of an *a priori* judgment. Meinong now causes incredulity in additon to our amazement. Applying his definition, he announces that not even such sensory qualities as *instances* of colors and tones can be perceived. [35]

Meinong's view rests on two main ideas. The first is that (instances of) sensory qualities, all appearance to the contrary, do not exist. But since, secondly, perception consists of true existential judgments, its objects must exist. Take (instances of) colors, for example. Meinong argues that one cannot perceive them since perception is of existents and (instances of) colors do not exist. The second idea merely says that one cannot perceive what does not exist; and even though I do not agree with this notion of perception, as I explained above, I shall now accept it for the sake of the argument. What remains, then, is the truly amazing claim that sensory qualities do not exist. Why does Meinong make this claim? He relies, in regard to this issue, on two traditional arguments. I shall call these two arguments the argument from science and the argument from the relativity of sensing, respectively.

The argument from science concludes that science has shown that there are no sensory qualities; that there are no colors, for example, and no tones. Galileo puts it this way: [36]

Hence I think that tastes, odors, colors, and so on are no more than mere names so far as the object in which we place them is concerned, and that they reside only in the consciousness. Hence if the living creatures were removed, all these qualities would be wiped away and annihilated.

And Meinong says quite succinctly: [37]

For if only vibrations occur where we think that we see colors or hear tones, then we have not really perceived colors and tones, but have merely been under the impression that we perceive them; and physics has taught us that the assertion *Something green exists* is, strictly speaking, false. Green simply is no wave motion; what exists, therefore, is not something green, but at best something vibrating.

We are all too familiar with the next few steps of this traditional philosophical journey. First, one distinguishes between primary and secondary qualities. Colors, according to Galileo, Descartes, and Meinong are secondary qualities. Among the primary qualities, Descartes mentions shape and number; Meinong, we just saw, mentions vibrations or wave motions. Second, the secondary qualities are shunted into the mind. This is to mollify the common-sense man who protests that colors do exist, that tones are not just nothing. He is being assured that science does not do away with these qualities altogether; it merely denies their existence in the physical universe. Of course, the tradition usually does not explain any further how, precisely, a color is supposed to be *in* a mind.[38] Third, it is discovered, by some profound philosopher like Berkeley, that all the arguments adduced to prove the secondary status of colors and tones apply with equal force, if they have any force, to primary qualities as well. From this, one may either conclude, with Berkeley, that *all* sensory qualities are 'in the mind,' or else, as I shall, that the original argument was not sound and, hence, that *no* such qualities are.

Meinong is not entirely unaware of the disaster that threatens. His definition of perception, it now seems, must be rejected; for what good is a definition of perception, if nothing whatsoever qualifies as perception? If sensory qualities cannot even be perceived, what remains? Even worse, the acceptance of the argument from science threatens Meinong's theory of evidence. Whether or not colors can be objects of perception should be easily decidable. All we have to do is to inquire whether or not there are existential judgments with evidence about such qualities. However the scientist may have arrived at his conclusion, it can at best be based on indirect evidence, while perception yields direct evidence. Are we, then, to trust the scientist's argument more than our own perceptions?

Let us take our leave from Meinong for a moment. I have already intimated that we must reject the argument from science. There are colors and tones, and these are 'objective entities' in the sense that they do not depend for their existence on there being minds. This is just part of common sense. Why is it then that the argument from science has convinced so many philosophers from Descartes to Sellars? There seem to me to be two main considerations that lend a spurious plausibility to the argument.

What the scientists have shown is, not that, for example, surfaces are not really green, but that a surface is green *if and only if* it has certain 'physical properties.' The scientists discovered, in other words, that a surface is green *if and only if* the atoms of which it consists are in a certain state. One does not have to belittle this discovery in order to maintain that the scientist has not 'reduced' colors to the properties of elementary particles. Assume, now, that someone does not too clearly distinguish between identity on the one hand and equivalence on the other.[39] He may then think that what the scientist has discovered is not just that two different states of affairs are equivalent, as I maintain, but that they are the same. He may then conclude that the scientists have shown that there simply is no such state of affairs as a surface's being green, but only the corresponding state of affairs involving particles and their states. In brief, the argument from science may appear convincing to someone who confuses an equivalence between states of affairs with their identity

But there is also another consideration which may be taken to speak for science and against common sense. If we analyze an ordinary perceptual object far enough into its spatial parts, eventually we get to so-called elementary particles. Physicists tell us that these particles have certain properties and lack others. These particles, for example, are not colored. If we believe the physicists, and there is no reason why we should doubt their theories, then, according to some philosophers, we must conclude that a 'swarm' of particles cannot be the same thing as a perceptual object. This conclusion follows, presumably, from a straightforward application of Leibniz's principle that entities with different properties must be different. Eddington, for instance, expresses this view very aptly in the remark that there are really two tables, with one of which, the perceptual table, he has been familiar from earliest years, with the other of which, the physical table, he has more recently become acquainted.[40]

Other philosophers, loath to accept a duplication for all perceptual objects, felt forced to deny the existence of one of Eddington's two tables. According to some, physics has the last word when it is a question of what there is; and since physics shows that elementary particles have no colors, they conclude – no matter how absurd that may seem – that there are no perceptual objects. There are merely 'swarms' of particles. Perceptual objects, they sometimes add to reassure us, are really appearances to human observers of such 'swarms' of particles. Or one takes the opposite side. Some philosophers insist that common sense has the decisive voice when it comes to what there is. Since there are quite obviously tables, and since these tables are colored, it follows that there are no elementary particles. According to the spirit of this position, elementary particles are merely 'logical constructions,' convenient fictions of the human mind. A third possibility, more sophisticated than the two just considered, has it that there are indeed 'two tables,' but that these two tables are co-ordinated very intimately with each other without being identical.[41]

If one does not like any one of these three views, there is always another way out: one can always contradict the physicists. Since the perceptual table is quite obviously colored, and since it consists of elementary particles, the physicists, one may argue, must be wrong when they tell us that the particles are not colored. Or one may take the opposite way out. The facts of physics show, not that there is no perceptual table, but merely that it is not colored.

But we do not have to choose among these, in my opinion, equally unacceptable alternatives. Here we can have our cake and eat it, too. We can agree with the physicists and, at the same time, live in peace with common sense.[42] Common sense is right: There are perceptual objects and they are colored. But the physicists are also right: a table, for example, consists of elementary particles which are not colored. It does not follow, though, that there must be two tables. There is only one table, and it consists of elementary particles. The table, in other words, is identical with a complicated *structure* of elementary particles. Do we then deny the truth of Leibniz's principle? Are we claiming that one and the same perceptual object is both colored and also not colored? Of course not. We insist that the perceptual table, that is, this complicated structure of elementary particles, is colored. But we also agree with the physicists that the elementary particles of which the table consists are not colored. Why should it surprise anyone that we can make both of these assertions? There seems to exist a more or less implicit assumption to the effect that a structure cannot have any property other than those which are had by (at least one of) its parts. It is the unquestioned acceptance of this assumption which, in my opinion, has led to the fallacious conclusion that perceptual objects, if there are such entities, cannot be colored. But the assumption is false. Imagine a square A whose diagonals have been drawn, so that it consists of four triangles. A is square, but none of its four parts has this property. These parts, on the other hand, are triangular. Of course, there are numerous such cases. Structures have properties which none of their parts have, and parts of structures have properties which the structures themselves do not have[43]. Thus the assumption mentioned earlier is false. And since it is false, we have refuted one of the most pervasive arguments against the existence of perceptual objects, an argument, ultimately, for the pernicious division of properties into primary and secondary properties.

Back to Meinong. He accepts, as I said, the argument from science. But he admits that the conclusion of this argument flies in the face of common sense: 'At first glance, it may well appear paradoxical, if not nonsensical, to deny that the aspects of the sensory realm are perceptual in character, since such a claim must be based, in the end, on other data from the same sensory realm.'[44] Yet he sticks to his guns. He tries to strengthen his case by introducing a second argument for the nonexistence of sensory qualities, namely, what I called the argument from the relativity of sensing. Meinong refers to Locke's experiment with hot and with cold water: first, one hand is put in hot water, the other, in cold water; then both hands are put in lukewarm water. Meinong argues now in the familiar fashion. (1) The first hand will feel cold; the second, hot. (2) If these two experiences are counted as perceptions, then it follows that something cold and something hot must exist. (3) One knows that this something cold and this something hot are one and the same thing, namely, the lukewarm water. (4) However, it is *a priori* certain that the same water cannot be hot and cold at the same time. (5) Thus at least one of the two experiences must be nonveridical. (6) But there is absolutely nothing that speaks for the truth of one experience at the expense of the other. (7) One can, therefore, only treat both experiences alike, and this means that one must reject both of them. (8) Of course, what holds for this particular case holds for other sense-dimensions.

It seems to me that there is quite an obvious response to this kind of argument: Both perceptions are non-veridical. The water is neither hot nor cold, but – as we were told as part of the story – lukewarm. What the experiment proves, if it proves anything, is, not that we cannot perceive sensible qualities, but rather that one's perceptions of such qualities may be wrong. In this case, the temperature of the water is wrongly perceived to be hot and to be cold because the sense-impressions caused by the successive steps of the experiment are indeed hot and cold. This kind of analysis is fortunately so well-known by now that I can here merely allude to it.

Meinong, it must be emphasized, does not feel at ease with where his two arguments have led him. The conclusion that one cannot perceive sensory qualities, since there are none, simply does not jibe with common sense; and common sense, as we know by now, is one of Meinong's most valuable guides through the jungle of metaphysical problems.

4   Phenomenal and Noumenal Objects

What remains of perception, if perception consists solely of evident existential judgments about objects stripped of all sensory properties? This is the question which Meinong has to answer.

Locke's experiment, I said earlier, proves at best that perception is not infallible. For a moment, this seems to be also Meinong's view. But he draws a different conclusion from it. He considers the general alternative: 'either we give up, together with the confidence in our sense, also our natural conviction that an external reality exists, or we try to retain, together with the latter, also the former.' [45] If we conclude, from Locke's experiment, that we cannot trust in our senses, then we can no longer believe in an external world. Meinong, of course, wants to save this belief. The question, then, is how we can reconcile Locke's experiment with a trust in our senses. Evidence for surmise is the answer. If we insist that perceptions must have what Meinong calls *evidence for certainty*, then Locke's experiment presumably shows that no perception has this kind of evidence; hence, that we cannot cling to our conviction of the existence of an external world. What the experiment shows is that even the most obvious, the most clear and distinct, perceptions can be mistaken. But, so Meinong argues now, the same skeptical conclusion does not follow if we conceive of perception as having, at best, a watered-down kind of evidence, namely, *evidence for surmise*.

I shall not go into the matter of the two kinds of evidence.[46] Instead, let us take up the main thread of our investigations: What remains of perception, if sensory qualities are not a matter of perception? Meinong's paradigm is the perception of a piece of chalk on a table. Meinong claims that the perceiver will readily concede that the sensible qualities which he perceives, the color and the shape of the chalk, for example, are subjective. But the perceiver will balk when told that there is really nothing at all on the table in front of him. From this alleged behavior, Meinong concludes two things. First, that the evidence for the existence of the sensible properties of external objects is a rather poor one, if there is one at all. Second, that there is nevertheless a very good evidence of surmise involved in the perception of the piece of chalk, since we are not willing to give up the conviction that *something* is on the table. But this something, obviously, must be something that is stripped of all sensory qualities. Meinong thus holds that the evidence of surmise involved in perception pertains to the existence of a bare 'substance,' a bare object.

But the perceiver, Meinong continues, does not only stubbornly cling to the belief that there is something on the table, he also refuses to give up the belief that this something is not, say, a book or a ruler. Thus the question arises of how the perceiver could possibly believe this, if Meinong is correct in claiming that no sensible property whatsoever is perceived in this case. It seems that Meinong has backed himself into a corner. If it is true that the ordinary perceiver under ordinary circumstances will refuse to be talked out of the belief that what is on the table is a piece of chalk rather than, say, a book, then it is also true that he will not be talked out of such beliefs as that the thing on the table is white, smaller than a book, etc. In other words, he will not easily give up his beliefs about the properties of the thing on the table. Thus Meinong must be wrong in his earlier description of the situation. On the other hand, if it is really true that the perceiver will easily give up all beliefs about the properties of the object in front of him, then there is no reason why he should cling to the belief that it is a piece of chalk rather than a book. It is not hard to guess which one of these two alternatives we accept. Given the case of perception which Meinong has in mind, we agree with his claim that the perceiver will insist that what is before him is a piece of chalk rather than a book. By the same token, contrary to what Meinong asserts, he will also insist that the thing on the table is white, that it is smaller than a book, etc. What may perhaps convince the perceiver that there are no sensory qualities – though it should not, of course – are such arguments as the argument from science and the argument from the relativity of sensing. No inspection of his perceptual experience could convince him. But, then, by the same token, he will also

be convinced, again mistakenly, that he cannot continue to believe
that the thing on the table is a piece of chalk rather than a book. All he
can be sure of, once he accepts those fallacious arguments, is that
something or other, one knows not what, is on the table.

Meinong does not see that or, perhaps better, he is unwilling to
concede that the conviction that the thing on the table is a piece of
chalk stands or falls with the conviction that it has certain sensory
properties. Consequently, he must try to reconcile the irreconcilable:
an alleged belief in the chalk with the absence of all convictions about
sensory qualities. He distinguishes, as a first step, between the mere
something, the 'bare substance,' which he calls 'o,' and the sum of the
sensory qualities which this entity seems to have and which he calls 'o'.'
Then he argues as follows: [47]

Everyone feels justified to believe – put differently: everyone has
evidence – that what looks different, similar, equal also is different,
similar, equal. Insofar as this is correct, it is clear, first of all, that
what appears to us as o'_1, o'_2, etc. is not just the substantial
constituent o of our earlier symbolic notation; for the various
appearing things all agree in that they are things. Rather, there
correspond to the phenomenal determinations o'_1, o'_2, etc. certain
noumenal determinations $\bar{o}_1$, $\bar{o}_2$, etc., for which it is simply evident
that the same relations of comparison hold between them as
between the o'; this implies at the same time the rather obvious
assertion that the substantial moment o, which is secured by the
already claimed good evidence, does not exist in an unnatural or,
really, impossible isolation, but that what exists are in any case
things which have properties.

Thus Meinong argues that there are noumenal properties which
correspond to the phenomenal ones; and he asserts that it is evident
that the same relations hold between these noumenal properties as
between the phenomenal ones. Is this evidence an evidence for certainty
or merely an evidence for surmise? Locke's experiment shows, Meinong
answers, that it can only be evidence for surmise; for, in this particular
case, no noumenal difference corresponds to the felt difference. The
judgment is thus false and, hence, cannot have evidence for certainty.
Granted that we are dealing with evidence for surmise, is this evidence
immediate or mediate and, if it is the latter, what are its foundations?
There are, of course, immediately evident judgments of comparison,
but these are *a priori* and do not concern the existence of what is
compared. In the case under consideration, however, the existence of
the noumenal properties is in question and we are, therefore, not
dealing with one of those *a priori* judgments. It may be tempting,
according to Meinong, to use a causal argument at this point. It may

be tempting to argue that one can infer different, similar, and equal causes from different, similar, and equal effects. But Meinong, as we explained earlier, cannot make use of this kind of argument. We have, therefore, reached an impasse. Since we cannot know that the noumenal properties stand in certain relations of comparison by means of a priori judgments, and since we cannot know that they stand in these relations by means of a causal inference, we do not seem to be able to know it at all.

In order to escape from this predicament, Meinong refers back to one of the assumptions which lead to it. Noumenal properties, he has assumed, are not perceived. Meinong modifies this assumption. It cannot mean, he claims, that the noumenal properties are not given to us at all; for we are justified in making judgments of comparison about noumenal properties, and this could not be the case, as we have just seen, unless these properties are somehow presented to the mind. The question is: Precisely how are noumenal properties given?

Recall Meinong's quite unsatisfactory account of abstraction. Meinong was then faced with the problem of how abstraction is possible from such a simple entity as a certain shade of a certain color. He tried to solve the problem by assuming that one and the same content (idea) can intend different objects with more or less distinctness. He attempts to utilize this same assumption in order to explain how we are acquainted with noumenal objects.[48] He claims that one and the same content can distinctly apprehend phenomenal properties and indistinctly apprehend the underlying noumenal properties. This answer makes little sense, as far as I can see.

But granted, for the sake of the argument, that noumenal properties are in some sense presented, how do the a priori judgments about relations of comparison between phenomenal properties apply to these noumenal properties? Meinong claims that an answer to this question is not very difficult. For example, the difference which holds between two phenomenal properties a priori and with evidence for certainty also holds between the corresponding, indistinctly apprehended, noumenal properties; but it holds for them merely with evidence for surmise. Furthermore, the strength of this latter evidence will depend on the degree of distinctness with which the noumenal properties are presented.

There is an obvious objection – one might say: Berkeley's objection – to Meinong's answer. If the arguments from science and the relativity of sensing really prove that sensory qualities are mere phenomena, do not these same arguments prove that relations of comparison are mere phenomena?

Meinong, we may as well say at the outset, does not give a satisfactory answer to this question. Relations of comparison, he maintains, are not subjective, mental entities, even though their presentations are produced by the mind. Thus while it takes a certain mental activity to create the proper presentation of such a relation, the relation itself is not created by this activity, but subsists independently of all mental activity. Of course, if we could not compare objects, then we could not discern these relations. But the relations would obtain nevertheless. If our intellect were different from what it is, we might not be able to discern these relations, but the subsistence of these relations is not affected by a change in our intellectual ability. 'But the validity of what we are able to know *a priori*,' Meinong sums it up, 'just as we are constituted, is in no sense put in doubt by this subjectivity.'[49]

Meinong thus points out, correctly, that the production of certain presentations is not the same as the production of the relations intended by these presentations. This, of course, is part and parcel of his newly adopted realism in regard to relations. This realism is made possible by his sharp distinction between the presentation and its content, on the one hand, and the intention of the presentation, on the other. But Meinong does not explain why this realism has to be rejected in regard to sensory properties. Just as little as one must confuse the (produced) presentation of a relation of comparison with the relation itself, just as little must one confuse the presentation of a sensory quality with the quality itself. And one may therefore argue, in the same vein as Meinong, that, if our sensory apparatus were different from what it is, this would merely mean that we would not have the presentations of sensory qualities which we now have, but not that the sensory qualities themselves would not exist. If we could not compare, then we could not discern that the object A is different from the object B, but A would still be different from B. Similarly, if we could not see, then we could never make out (by sight) that A is green, but A would nevertheless be green. If what Meinong says about relations of comparison is good enough to establish their independence of mental activity, then it should be good enough to establish the independence of sensory properties as well. On the other hand, if the arguments mentioned earlier really prove the subjectivity of sensory qualities, why do they not also prove the subjectivity of these relations?

But let us assume, if that makes sense at all, that the relations of comparison between sensory qualities are not mind-dependent, what guarantee is there that they are projectible to the noumenal properties? Could it not be the case that any such projection is faulty? For example, how do we really know that to different phenomenal properties there correspond different noumenal properties? Meinong, at the very end of his book, admits that this is an important but dark facet of the theory of knowledge.

Are there features other than relations of comparison which are projectible from the phenomena to the noumena? According to Meinong, there is at least one other kind of object of higher order which is in this sense projectible, namely, number.[50] If we hear two tones or see five people, he maintains, then there are indeed two phenomena or five phenomena, respectively. Moreover, to these phenomena there correspond an equal number of noumena. Be that as it may, why does Meinong add numbers, but reject other objects of higher order, as being projectible? What criterion does he use?[51]

> It is the wide, even unlimited, field of application of those two kinds of ideal objects. One cannot think of a pair of entities which are not different in the extended sense just used; as little [can one think] of objects which do not form a complex with a determinate number of parts. Under such conditions, an application to what is not phenomenally given, that is, to the noumenal objects, is naturally entirely unobjectionable. The situation is quite different for complexes like melodies which are only applicable to tones, or for such complexes as 'Gestalten' in the vulgar sense which are only applicable to spatial entities and, hence, are already not applicable to large fields of phenomena, so that their projectibility beyond the field of phenomena must appear completely inadmissible.

The cat is out of the bag. Projectible are those features of the phenomenal world, it turns out, which are all-pervasive in the phenomenal world. Difference, for example, is a relation that holds between any two entities of the phenomenal world whatsoever, and any type of entity of the phenomenal world whatsoever can be numbered. What is projectible, in other words, are the categorial features of the phenomenal world, features which every possible phenomenal world must possess. This interpretation receives some confirmation from the fact that Meinong speaks of noumenal *objects* and noumenal *properties*. Being a property (or an instance of one) is a categorial feature of the phenomenal world. Hence, it gets projected into the noumenal world. It is clear that this procedure is highly suspect. From the fact that something is a categorial feature of the phenomenal world it simply does not follow that it must be a feature of the noumenal world. That the two worlds share such features must be established on independent grounds. Needless to say, as the problem is set up, no such proof can be forthcoming, Nor should one argue that the categories must be features of the noumenal world since we can neither imagine nor conceive a world without these categories; for it may well be that the noumenal realm is in fact inconceivable.

Let us summarize. Having defined perception in terms of evident existential judgments, Meinong casts about for the proper objects of such judgments. Relying on the traditional arguments from science and from the relativity of sensing, he concludes that sensory qualities cannot be objects of perception. But since perceptual objects are complexes of such qualities (instances), he must also conclude that we do not really perceive such objects. Instead, we perceive, in his opinion, a noumenal object 'behind' the phenomenal one. But we do not just perceive the object, we also perceive certain noumenal properties and relations, though rather indistinctly. These properties and relations are categorial. Meinong's theory, we see, is essentially a Cartesian one. Among objects, we must distinguish between primary and secondary ones. Secondary objects, like colors, tones, etc., have no application to the noumenal world. Primary objects, like relations of comparison, number, etc., have such an application. What distinguishes Meinong's view from Descartes' is, mainly, that the former emphasizes more than the latter the categorial character of the primary qualities and relations. According to Meinong, we perceive the noumenal world since and as far as it shares the same structure with the phenomenal world. That there is a shared structure is the unexamined and unquestioned postulate of Meinong's theory of perception.

5 Introspection

Is there 'inner perception' of mental phenomena? Are judgments about experiences evident? Meinong does not share the view of many philosophers that we are aware of all of our experiences with the evidence of certainty. He insists that one can make mistakes about the contents of one's mind. But he also claims that this is not a matter of either/or. Not all inner experience is evident with certainty, but some is. Hence there is so-called 'inner perception' or, as I shall say from now on, *introspection*. Meinong has not made, at this point, the distinction between evidence for certainty and evidence for surmise. Thus he sets out with the notion that introspection requires evidence for certainty. This notion, however, is later abandoned.

Meinong, in the traditional fashion, considers first the case of sense-impressions.[52] That one now hears a sound or sees a color, he maintains, is as infallible a piece of inner knowledge as one can get. But Meinong runs almost immediately into difficulties which he is unable to overcome.

Assume that I see, as I enter the room, that my neighbor's new dinner table is round. According to the view which I have implicitly adopted and shall continue to use as a foil in order to set off Meinong's position, my conscious state has in this case the following constituents.[53] First of all, there are certain visual sense impressions; among them, there is one that is oval rather than round. This sense-impression is caused by the round table top. That it is oval rather than round is to be explained in the usual way in terms of perspective. Second, my conscious state also contains a mental act of seeing. This act intends the state of affairs: *This dinner table is round*. It has, in brief, a round perceptual object. Thus, though my sense-impression is oval, what I see and as I see it, the table, is round. Of course, on other occasions, the sense-impression which is experienced (but not seen) may have the same shape as the perceptual object which is seen (but not experienced). Third, by experiencing the conscious state, one experiences thus certain sense-impressions as well as a certain mental act of seeing. This experience consists in another mental act, an act which is not a perception and which I shall call an awareness or experience. Fourth, we can then distinguish between the intention of a conscious state and the content of a conscious state, between what is 'before' a mind and what is 'in' it. What one is aware of is one's conscious state, that is, the content of one's mind. In this case, the most important ingredients of this conscious state are certain visual sense-impressions and a mental act of seeing. What is before the mind, in this case, though, is neither the sense-impressions which are experienced nor the act of which one is aware, but the table. The intention of the conscious state is thus the intention of whatever act (or acts) is an ingredient of the conscious state. One's conscious state, on the other hand, is the intention of an act of awareness. When this act occurs, one is not aware of it, but is, by means of it, aware of one's conscious state.

Assume, next, that my attention turns from the shape of the table top to the shape of the sense-impression which is caused in me. Assume, for example, that I wish to paint a picture of the table and that I have to get the correct oval shape on canvas, so that a viewer will also see a round table when he looks at my painting. Now it is no longer the table top which is the intention of my conscious state, but it is the sense-impression. The sense-impression is no longer merely experienced, it is now before my mind. There occurs, as always, an act of awareness which intends the conscious state. But this conscious state contains now, not the visual sense-impression in question, but – among many other things – an act of awareness (sensing). Since this act intends the sense-impression, the sense-impression is 'before' my mind rather than 'in' it.

This account emphasizes the important fact that Meinong's term 'inner perception' is ambiguous. The inspection of a sense-impression may be called 'inner perception' because the entity inspected is a mental entity; it is not an 'external' perceptual object. On the other hand, it may also be called 'outer perception' since the object so perceived is not 'in' the mind, but 'before' the mind; it is not part of the conscious state, but part of the intention of the conscious state. As I said before,

I shall not use the term 'inner perception' at all. To perceive is to see, to hear, etc., and the only entities which can be seen, heard, etc., are perceptual objects. Mental entities, be they sense-impressions or mental acts, cannot be perceived. But one can be aware of them (experience them) as well as inspect them.

Assume that you are seeing something green and that you experience a green sense-impression. How does Meinong analyze this situation? Let us first recall his general view, leaving aside all complications in regard to the distinction between phenomenal and noumenal entities: there occurs a perceptual presentation and, based on this presentation, a judgment. The presentation intends the perceptual object (the phenomenal object) and, hence, the color ingredient of it. If we impose our schema on Meinong's view, the presentation would be part of the conscious state, what it presents would be the perceptual object. The most important difference, for the present purpose, between Meinong's account and our analysis is that there are no sense-impressions according to the former.

I am ready to explain Meinong's problem with 'inner perception.' 'Outer perception,' we just saw, aims at the colored object by means of a perceptual presentation. What 'inner perception' thus intends must be that presentation itself. More accurately, since what matters is not the presentation as such, but the presentation of this object, 'inner perception' must be 'perception' of the *content* of the perceptual presentation. In other words, while 'outer perception' intends the color green (the object with this color), 'inner perception' intends the idea of this color (the idea of this colored object). Perception thus tells us something about perceptual objects, while introspection tells us something about our ideas. But Meinong now remarks that this conclusion does not seem to hold. It looks as if introspection concerns once more the perceptual object: 'Not what the content, but what the object of my presentation of red is like, inner perception tells me.'[54] If this is so, then Meinong is faced with the paradoxical situation that 'inner perception' is really 'outer perception,' that introspection tells us something about perceptual objects.

Why does Meinong, even for a moment, believe that introspection tells us something about the object of the perceptual presentation rather than its content? At this point, he does not give any reasons whatsoever. It seems to me that there may lurk in the background Brentano's doctrine of '*eigentümliche Verflechtung*.'[55] Introspection, according to Meinong, aims at the content of the perceptual presentation. Is there, then, another presentation which intends this content – an 'inner presentation,' so to speak – just as the perceptual presentation intends the green object? Meinong denies that there is such a second presentation. No further mental act is necessary in order to be aware of the content of the perceptual presentation. It is this assumption, I submit, which contributes to the puzzling view that introspection tells us something about the 'outer objects.' Recall our analysis of perception. What would an inspection of the act of presentation look like in our view? There would occur, first, an awareness of a conscious state. There would occur, second, as part of this conscious state, another act of awareness. Third, this second act would intend the act of presentation. The act of presentation would thus be the intention of the conscious state; this act would be 'before' the mind, in the sense explained, rather than *its* intention (the perceptual object). According to this analysis, introspection differs radically from perception. When one inspects a mental act or, more accurately, its content, one does not merely experience this act, but has it 'before' one's mind. When one inspects a perceptual object, on the other hand, one experiences certain perceptual acts, but does not have them 'before' one's mind. In brief, inspection of the presentation differs from perception in that in the former case the presentation becomes the intention of a new act. But assume now, as Meinong does, that no such new act occurs. Then it is hard to see how introspection could aim at anything but what the presentation itself aims at, namely, the perceptual object.

Be that as it may, why does Meinong follow his teacher in maintaining that introspection does not require mental acts which intend other mental acts? We may speculate that the reason is the traditional argument against the existence of mental acts.[56] This argument runs, roughly, as follows. Suppose that a mental act A occurs. In order to know that A occurs, another act, B, is required. B is an awareness of A. But if B occurs, we must be aware of it, too. Hence, there must occur still another mental act C which is an awareness of B. And so on. The occurrence of A would thus involve the occurrence of an infinite number of further mental acts. But such an infinite series of mental acts never occurs. Therefore, there are no mental acts.

This argument rests on two crucial assumptions: (1) the assumption that if there are mental acts, one is aware of every single one that occurs, and (2) the assumption that such an awareness always consists of another mental act. The conclusion that there are no mental acts can be avoided if we reject either one of these two assumptions. Brentano, to make a long story short, thinks we must accept (1); he argues that there are no 'unconscious' mental acts.[57] He therefore rejects (2); one can be aware of a mental act, he claims, without there being another act by means of which one is aware of it.[58] How, then is one aware of a mental act? How, for example, is one aware of the perceptual presentation which intends the green object? According to Brentano, every act has two intentions, a primary object as well as a secondary object. In our example, the primary object of the presentation is the green object; its secondary object, the presentation itself. This is called the '*eigentümliche Verflechtung*' of an act with its own awareness.

Whatever the reason, Meinong adopts Brentano's view that acts intend themselves:[59]

> What, then, is the mental situation when inner perception aims at this content of the perceptual presentations? If I am correct, it does not require a new content, to which the first content would then belong as object just like red belongs to the first content. Rather, the experience of the content suffices for inner perception in order to turn it into an object for the perceptual judgment. Of course, to this end, a different activity must occur in connection with the content than when, starting with it and by means of it, red is to be apprehended. The same content can therefore be used in principle in two ways, so to speak; it can serve for the perception of the co-ordinated outer objects or it can serve for the perception of itself.

The same idea, according to Meinong, is both an idea of red and also of the idea red. Put this way, Brentano's and Meinong's view seems rather absurd. Even if we admit that one and the same idea may intend different objects, it seems hard to believe that the idea of red is the same as the idea of the idea of red.

For the time being, though, let us set aside any misgivings we may have about ideas which are ideas of themselves and return to the original problem created by the impression that 'inner perception' seems to aim at the perceptual object. Meinong now claims that this is mere appearance: 'inner perception' aims here really at the content of the presentation, not at its object.[60] He explains this appearance in terms of another misapprehension of ours. Even in 'outer perception,' he says, we are prone to project characteristics of the content into the object. Hence we are even more liable to do so when it is a matter of 'inner perception.' Meinong's argument at this point is rather unconvincing, to say the least. But I shall not harp on it, since he himself admits that his analysis may have to be improved on. Of greater interest, at any rate, is the peculiar doctrine of '*eigentümliche Verflechtung*' and its consequences for the knowledge of our own minds.

So much about Meinong's analysis of introspection. It is clear that it leaves many questions unanswered. Its greatest liability, as I see it, is the dogma of '*eigentümliche Verflechtung*,' the notion that in 'inner perception' the act of perceiving and its object must be somehow identical. Meinong's view shows, as I see it, that even a very complex and thorough analysis can make no sense out of this dogma. Let us look at some of the main critical points.

Take first the case where a content becomes its own object. The presentation of the object green has a certain content *C*. Meinong, accepting the dogma of '*eigentümliche Verflechtung*,' denies that we may inspect this content by means of another mental act whose object it would be. But he sees that the mental state of a person who perceives green on the basis of the presentation is different from the mental state of a person who inspects the content *C*. Thus there must be a difference somewhere. In both cases, there occurs, at first, nothing but the presentation with the content *C*. Later, a judgment about an external entity occurs in the first case, a judgment about the content occurs in the second case. But the original situation is exactly the same. At this point, Meinong introduces two mysterious activities of the mind, called 'turning outward' and 'turning inward.' What distinguishes the first case from the second, is, in his view, that the mind turns outward in the first case, inward in the second. The different judgments result then from the different turns of the mind. Clearly, we are offered a mystery instead of an analysis. What determines the particular turn of mind? Meinong does not tell us. In what does this activity consist – another mental act? Again, Meinong does not tell us. It is clear that there are only two possibilities. Either mental acts are all there is to a mind or they are not. In the first case, the activities of 'turning inward' and 'turning outward' must themselves consist of mental acts, and Meinong's analysis is incomplete as long as he does not tell us whether these acts are, say, presentations, or judgments, or something else. On the other hand, if this activity does not consist of mental acts, Meinong must list it as a separate mental category and explain just how it differs from mental acts. Needless to say, he never does so.

Mysterious mental activities aside, the notion that one and the same idea is an idea of green as well as of the idea of green seems to be mistaken. An idea, as I said in an earlier context, can only have one object, one intention. Moreover, even if it could have more than one intention, how could it intend itself in addition to something else? I must confess that I simply do not know what to make of the assertion that an idea is an idea of, say, green and also an idea of the idea of green. But the mystery darkens even more when we turn to other mental entities. Contents have objects. Thus it may be thought intelligible that a content may intend itself as its object. But what about a total mental act, how does it intend itself? Up to now we have always assumed that contents and only contents stand in the intentional relation to other entities. Are we now to abandon this view? Can a complex consisting of a mental act intend the whole mental act? An affirmative answer to the first two questions necessitates a complete revision of Meinong's analysis of mental acts; a revision, in particular, of the alleged function of contents as giving direction to mental acts. An affirmative answer to the third question assigns one more function to the already over-burdened content. The idea of green, say, must not only be capable of intending green and itself, it must now also be able to intend the whole mental act consisting of the idea and the kind. And similar considerations apply when we turn to our introspection of kinds. Either kinds can intend themselves or they must be intended by contents. The first alternative is really absurd within the framework of Meinong's analysis of mental acts. But the second alternative is also hard to accept.

To sum up, Meinong holds, for reasons not further explained, that the introspection of mental acts and their parts does not consist in the occurrence of further mental acts. We speculated that his reasons may have been the same as those which led Brentano to formulate his doctrine of the '*eigentümliche Verflechtung*' of mental acts with their objects. As a result, Meinong holds that in introspection mental acts are somehow turned upon themselves and become their own intentions.

Let us review, in conclusion, the most important ingredients of Meinong's theory of empirical knowledge. (1) Perception is analyzed into perceptual presentations and existential judgments. (2) No predicative judgment is a perceptual judgment since all such judgments are judgments *a priori*. (3) Perception is distinguished from non-veridical experiences by the fact that the perceptual judgment has evidence. (4) But this evidence, as Locke's experiment shows, is not evidence for certainty, but merely evidence for surmise. (5) The true objects of perceptions are, not phenomenal instances of properties and complexes composed of them, but noumenal objects. We know, by means of perception, that there are such noumenal objects and that they stand in certain relations to each other. (6) Introspection has, for the most part, only evidence for surmise. (7) In introspection, a certain mental activity turns a mental act unto itself so that it becomes its own object.

VIII

Rational Knowledge: The Theory of Entities

Empirical knowledge, as we have seen, occurs only in the form of existential judgments. All other knowledge, in Meinong's opinion, must be rational knowledge.[1] When we contemplate how impoverished the field of empirical knowledge is, compared with the richness and vastness of the realm of rational knowledge, then there can be no doubt as to the side of the traditional controversy on which Meinong belongs.

Empirical knowledge, according to Meinong, is confined to existential judgments. This means, first, that all judgments about the subsistence of entities constitute rational knowledge. It means, second, that all predicative judgments whatsoever are rational in kind. Among predicative judgments, we can distinguish three kinds. There are predicative judgments about existents, predicative judgments about subsistents, and predicative judgments about objects which have no being. No matter how we may think about Meinong's division of knowledge into empirical and rational knowledge, we may be able to agree that we have knowledge about entities which have some sort of being. Knowledge, we may agree with Meinong, reaches at least as far as being. But Meinong, as we know, claims more. Knowledge, in his view, even embraces predicative judgments of the third kind, that is, predicative judgments about entities without being. It is this part of his theory of entities which I find most problematic. But before we can discuss it, we shall have to gather a first impression of the vast scope of the theory of entities.

1   Homeless Entities

Sensory qualities, we saw, do not, in Meinong's view, exist. They are not ingredients of the physical world. Traditionally, these qualities are shunted into the mind. Secondary qualities are said to be mental entities. But this gambit leads to quite a number of difficulties. In the last chapter, I referred to a passage from Berkeley in which he claims that these qualities are not modifications of the mind; they are not 'in' the mind in the same way in which a modification is 'in' a substance. Berkeley, undoubtedly, wanted to avoid the corollary that a mind turns out to be, for example, green and square. But if secondary qualities are neither mental substances nor modifications of such substances, what are they? According to one contemporary view, which goes back to Brentano, secondary qualities are properties of mental acts of sensing. [2] According to this view, one does not have a green sense-impression, but, rather, one 'senses greenly.' I find this view extremely implausible. If it amounts to the claim that green is quite literally a property of my sensing, then I reply that this is as unsatisfactory a view as the older view that green is a property of my mind: neither mental acts nor minds are the kinds of things which are colored. On the other hand, if it is maintained that to 'sense greenly' is, not to have a green act of sensing, but to have an act of sensing of a certain kind, then I can only wonder where the color went. Nothing seems now to be left of the color; and nobody can convince me that the philosophical dialectic of the problems of perception requires that we deny the existence of colors.

Meinong steers clear of these and other problems by denying that secondary properties are mental entities. [3] Thus they are, in his view, entities which are neither physical nor mental. The Cartesian distinction is therefore not exhaustive; there must be entities which are neither physical nor mental. Sensory qualities are such entities. We see now why Meinong calls these qualities 'homeless.' They are neither at home in the physical sciences nor are they at home in psychology. In other words, the laws that govern, say, colors belong neither to physics nor to psychology. But these qualities do find a home, at long last, in the theory of entities.

Why does Meinong deny that sensory qualities are mental? It seems that he follows in Brentano's footsteps. Brentano, as is well known, tried to define mental entities in terms of intentionality. A mental entity, as distinguished from a physical entity, is characterized by the fact that it is directed toward an object. According to this characterization, mental acts and only mental acts turn out to be mental entities. Sensory qualities, it follows, are not mental. Since they are also not physical entities, according to Brentano, Brentano subscribes to the same rejection of the Cartesian dichotomy as Meinong. [4] Meinong, at any rate, seems to assume that all mental entities are mental acts, that is more exactly, either mental acts or their parts (kinds and contents). Compare this with our view. We agree, of course, that mental acts are mental entities; they are mental entities *par excellence*, so to speak. But we also hold that, in addition to these mental entities, there are others, namely, mental entities which are not intentional. For example, there are such mental entities as visual sense-impressions, images, and pains.[5] As to sensory qualities, it just happens that we come to the same conclusion as Meinong and Brentano, namely, that they are neither mental entities nor 'physical' (perceptual) entities; but we arrive at this conclusion for entirely different reasons. Sensory qualities, in our view, are properties both of mental individuals and of perceptual individuals, and this is the reason why they can be classified neither as mental nor as perceptual. For example, the color green (more precisely: a particular shade of green) may be exemplified both by certain perceptual objects, say, by a billiard ball, and also by certain visual sense-impressions, say, the sense-impressions which are now caused in me by that billiard ball.

Sensory qualities, though, are not the only homeless entities. Meinong mentions next so-called impossible entities, entities like the round square.[6] These entities, too, find a home in the theory of entities. In this context, Meinong answers the objections which Russell had raised in a review of Meinong's earlier work.[7] Russell there objects, first, that impossible objects violate the law of contradiction. Meinong readily admits that this is the case, but he remarks that nobody has ever tried to apply this law to anything else but the actual or possible anyway. Contradictory entities, in other words, quite obviously must violate the law of contradiction or they would not be what they are. Perhaps, Russell felt that his objection had more of a thrust because he thought of logic, not as applying solely to what there is, but as encompassing everything. Impossible entities show that this conception of logic is mistaken.

Russell's second objection is more to the point, and Meinong devotes several paragraphs to it.[8] If the round square is really round, as Meinong claims, then the existing round square must also exist. But this is absurd. Hence, the round square cannot have any properties. The principle of the independence of so-being from being is false. There can be no knowledge about impossible entities. Here is Meinong's reply to Russell's criticism:[9]

> One can therefore add such existential determinations to other
> determinations, speak just as much of an 'existing golden
> mountain' as of a 'high golden mountain,' and then assert of the
> former as clearly the predicate 'existing' as of the latter the 'high.'
> Nevertheless, the former mountain exists just as little as the
> latter: 'to be existing' in the sense of that existential determination
> and 'to exist' in the ordinary sense of 'being there' (*Dasein*) are
> not at all the same thing.

Meinong thus distinguishes between existence and something else, an existential determination, called 'to be existing.' The latter, he claims, behaves like an ordinary property in that just as the golden mountain has the ordinary property of being golden, so the existing golden mountain has the existential determination of being existing. Existence, though, does not behave in this fashion. What follows from the principle of the independence of so-being from being is, not that the existing golden mountain exists, but only that it is existing. Thus it is no contradiction to assert that the existing golden mountain does not exist, even though it is existing. To all of this, Russell simply replies that he 'cannot see how one can distinguish between "to exist" and "to be existing".'[10] And I must confess that my sympathies lie with Russell. But I also think that more can be said about Meinong's view.

Meinong, you will have noticed, speaks of existential determinations in the plural. What he has in mind are properties which correspond to such characteristics as the characteristic of being localized in space and/or time, but which, in distinction to such characteristics, do not imply existence. For example, the golden mountain which is now located at the end of the rainbow over there is located at that place, but only in the same figurative sense in which the existing golden mountain *is existing* without being an existent.[11]

What about existence itself? It seems that Meinong could have turned back Russell's criticism without making the dubious distinction between to be existing and to exist. Existence, he could have said, is not a property. The principle of the independence of so-being from being specifically refers to so-being: properties are said to be independent of the being of their subjects. Here nothing is said about existence. Thus, while it is true that the golden mountain is golden and the round square is round, it simply does not follow that the existing golden mountain exists, since existence is not a property like being golden and being round. Existence, according to the doctrine of the *Aussersein* of the pure object, is not a part of the pure object, and only a part of the pure object can be truly attributed to it.

In a way, Meinong does make this move in response to Russell. He does say that, while the golden mountain is golden, the existing golden mountain does not exist. But then he adds the 'existential determination' *'to be existing,'* and this addition merely seems to cloud the issue. Why does Meinong think that he has to bring this existential determination into the picture? Why does he add it to the entity *existence*? Why does he think that there is a property which somehow corresponds to existence without being existence? To grasp a possible answer to these questions, we have to consider a later remark:[12]

> In regard to every genuine or, so to speak, ordinary
> determination of so-being, it is in my power, according to the
> principle of unlimited freedom of assumption, to pick out – by
> means of adequate intention – an entity which in fact has the
> determination of so-being.

In order to conceive of, say, the round square, one must pick out this nature from the boundless realm of *Aussersein*. That one can fasten on this entity is guaranteed by the principle of unlimited freedom of assumption. But this same principle also guarantees that one can think of an existing round square. Clearly, to think of an existing round square is not the same thing as to think just of a round square. Thus the objects before the mind must be different in these two cases. We can now understand why Meinong has to introduce 'existential determinations.' It is such a determination that distinguishes the one intention from the other. This determination is required for epistemological reasons. Existence may not be part of an object, but it can be thought of as belonging to something. Hence it can be before the mind just as well as an ordinary property. Meinong, having reasoned like this, saves his principle of the independence of so-being from being by claiming that it is not full-fledged existence, but merely an existential determination, that is before the mind in such a case. But can one not think of a round square which *exists* just as easily as of an *existing* round square? And is not existence, rather than the existential determination, in such a case before the mind? Meinong returns to this problem in his book on possibility and probability. Later, in the last chapter of this book, we shall see what he has to say there.

In addition to sensory qualities and impossible objects, Meinong mentions objectives as a third kind of homeless entity.[13] And he adds that objectives are responsible for such modalities as necessity and possibility.

2   *Predication without Being*

As I said in the last section, of all the kinds of rational knowledge the most problematic kind consists of predication without being. We may agree that there are subsistents in addition to existents, and we may even agree that all predication involving existents and subsistents proceeds *a priori*, but our robust sense of reality rebels when we are invited to believe that the golden mountain is golden and that the round square is both round as well as square. Meinong, as we have seen, appeals in this connection to the principle of the independence of so-being from being. But why should we accept this principle? So-being, we could insist, depends on being. Only entities which are there have properties. What are Meinong's arguments for accepting the principle?

Recall Descartes' famous passage about the properties of a triangle in the fifth *Meditation*. Descartes quite clearly subscribes to Meinong's principle: this triangle, he claims, has properties irrespective of whether or not it exists in reality. And this is so, it appears, because there is the immutable nature of this figure or, in Meinong's words, because there is the pure object. In order to understand the dialectic of the situation, let us contrast Descartes' view with another position, a position which I shall try to defend. We must distinguish between individual triangles, on the one hand, and the property of being a triangle, on the other. This property, we shall assume for the sake of the argument, is a complex property; a property which includes such properties as having three sides, having three angles, etc. Let the following class of properties constitute this property (nature) T: F, G, H, etc. Now, it is true that, say, G 'belongs' to T irrespective of whether or not there is any individual thing which has the property T. But it is, of course, not true that T, or G, 'belongs,' therefore, also to some individual thing. Let T_1 be an existing triangle. We must distinguish now between two quite different assertions: (1) the assertion that G is *a part of* the complex property T; (2) the assertion that T_1 *is* G. We deal here with two quite different relations: on the one hand, there is the relation which holds between a property and the complex property of which it is a part; on the other hand, there is the relation between a property and the thing of which it is a property. When we reject the principle of the independence of so-being from being, we do not reject assertions of type (1), but only assertions of type (2). In other words, we do not wish to deny that a given complex property may consist of such-and-such other properties, even though the complex property is not exemplified.[14] What we deny is that an *individual thing* can have properties even if it does not exist. While it is true that the property of having a fishtail is part of the property of being a mermaid, it is not true that *the Lorelei* (an individual thing) has a fishtail. Similarly, while it is true that a part of the complex property of being both round and square is the property of being round, it is not true that the round square is round.

This consideration sheds some light on Meinong's notion of such complex objects as the golden mountain and the round square. On the one hand, Meinong argues that these entities have the properties which we mention when we describe them. This indicates that he conceives of them in analogy to complex properties. On the other hand, it is also quite clear that he thinks of them as individual things on the same level as ordinary perceptual objects. Obviously, the principle of the independence of so-being from being rests on the first of these two ways of looking at these entities.

In the spirit of Descartes, Meinong, in order to defend his view, turns to mathematics and geometry and argues in the rationalistic spirit, that since there is geometry and since there are no circles, triangles, etc., we must not insist that geometrical truths are about real circles, triangles, etc. [15] But we do persist in our view that geometry is about the circles and triangles which we draw on a piece of paper and on a blackboard. Can we reconcile this insistence with the fact, if it is a fact, that the figures we draw are not 'really' circular, are not really bounded by completely straight lines? [16] It seems that we can; for, as Mach objected to the rationalists in geometry, one could use the same argument to prove that physics cannot be about real physical objects; surely, an absurd conclusion. [17] Just as little as there is in nature the 'perfect' circle, just as little is there in nature a pure case of uniform motion. Put differently, geometry is about real figures in the same sense in which physics is about real bodies; and insofar as almost everyone admits that physics is a matter of empirical observation, so must one also admit that geometry is empirical rather than rational.

Meinong concedes that Mach's counter-argument is justified. Thus we cannot prove, along Cartesian lines, that there are true predications without being. But what arguments do we have against this position, Meinong wants to know. He says that he knows of no authentic argument against it, so that he has to fall back on the arguments which he himself can make up. And the basic objection to his view, as he sees it, is contained in the question: What sense could it possibly make to predicate a color or a shape of a desk, unless that desk has at some time existed? Similarly, when we assert that equilateral triangles have equal angles, with what else could the occurrence of equal angles be connected but with the real occurrence of equal sides? [18] How, then, can we reconcile the fact that there are no geometric figures in nature with the fact that geometric laws seem to be about such figures? Meinong sees two possibilities.

First, one could hold that the assertion (1) *All equilateral triangles have equal angles* is really of the form: (2) *An equilateral triangle which is not also equiangular does not exist.* What Meinong has in mind is, of course, Brentano's transformation. Meinong rejects this way out on the ground that (2) is not the same objective as (1). In most cases, he claims, it is quite obvious whether a given judgment has a positive or a negative objective; and if there seems to be some doubt in some cases, then this may be due to the fact that equivalence is often mistaken for identity, especially in connection with matters of logic.

Second, one could give an interpretation of (1) that turns it into the hypothetical judgment: (3) *If there exists an equilateral triangle, then it is also equiangular.* This is, indeed, today the most widely accepted rendition of (1). (3), it is clear, does not imply that there are 'perfect' triangles. Nor, of course, is it about a nonexistent triangle. But Mei-nong does not think that (3) will do either. He raises the question: 'But what happens if the equilateral triangle does not exist? Is it then not equiangular?'[19] And then he argues that if the equilateral triangle is not equiangular in case it does not exist, then the law (1) turns out to be false, since there are no equilateral triangles (in nature).

But, quite obviously, this would not be our answer to his question. If there are no equilateral triangles, then they are neither equiangular nor not equiangular. It is the very point of our view that nothing whatsoever can be predicated of entities which do not exist (or have no being). The law (3) does not turn out to be false, if there are no equilateral triangles; as a matter of fact, it turns out to be true in such a case. Of course, it is a further and important question whether or not one wants to call a hypothetical state of affairs of the form (3) a law, even if the property in the antecedent is not instantiated. Be that as it may, though, Meinong is quite aware of our insistence that non-existent triangles are neither equilateral nor not equilateral. But he persists in his questions:

> In this case, one could of course still try to insist that the very point of the position in question is that one cannot attribute anything to a triangle which does not exist. But would not someone who asserts this be in a position similar to that of the absolute skeptic? Would he not have attributed to the non-existent triangle at least this much, namely, that nothing can be attributed to it? Furthermore, can one really deny that the non-existent triangle is triangular? And who could then draw more than an arbitrary line in regard to the possibility of further justified attributions?

Let us take up Meinong's points one by one. First, there is the objec-tion that we are asserting something about the nonexistent triangle when we say that nothing can be asserted about it. But, obviously, our view does not have to be put in this contradictory manner. When we say that entities which do not exist have no properties, we do not attribute to these entities the property of having no properties; for there is simply no such property.[21] The state of affairs which we have in mind is not of the form: *For all individuals, if these individuals do not exist, then they have the property P*, where *P* is the property of having no properties. Rather, it is of the form: *For all individuals, if these individuals do not exist, then there is no property which they exemplify*. As to Meinong's second question, we can only reiterate what we have said before: the nonexistent triangle is neither triangular nor not triangular. Third, the last question does therefore not really arise for us: we do not have to draw a line between the properties which the nonexistent triangle has and those which it does not have, since it has no properties what-soever.

But we can turn the table on Meinong in regard to this last question. How does he distinguish between the properties which a nonexistent object has and those that it does not have? Meinong admits that a desk which he makes up in his imagination has only those properties which he himself imagines it to have.[22] From our point of view, this is the most revealing admission which Meinong could possibly make. The imagined desk has, presumably, all the properties which I include in my thinking of it; and, we may perhaps assume, all those further properties which it must have – by virtue of logical laws or scientific laws – if it has the former properties.[23] But the desk does not have any other properties.[24] However, what we conclude from Meinong's distinction between the two kinds of properties – those which I do include in my thinking and those which I do not – is, not that the desk *has* the former but not the latter properties, but rather that it is imagined to have the former but not the latter properties. What is true of the imagined desk is, not that it has certain properties, but merely that it is imagined to have certain properties.[25] Our objection to Meinong's principle of the independence of so-being from being is just as vehement as our insistence that the common-sensical distinction be preserved between what a thing is and what it is imagined to be. Here we have reached the deepest reason for our resistance to Meinong's arguments, no matter how plausible some of them may sound. The round square is neither round nor square, it is merely thought of as round and square or, perhaps better, we conceive there to be something which we conceive to be both round and square. In a nutshell, while Meinong holds that imagined entities have properties, we maintain that imagined entities are imagined to have properties.

The desk which I imagine does not have the properties which I imagine it to have. But what about Hamlet? If I think of Hamlet as being indecisive and you think of him as being decisive, then we do not settle the dispute by simply appealing to our respective conceptions of Hamlet. Rather, we turn to Shakespeare's text. And since we can turn to the text and settle the issue, so to speak, objectively, it may appear that it is really either true of Hamlet that he is decisive or true of him that he is indecisive. But, of course, this appearance is quite misleading. It just so happens that Hamlet was not created by me – like the marvelous desk – or by you, but by someone else. Thus he was imagined to have properties by someone else, and what we can settle in an 'objective' way is, not whether Hamlet is decisive or indecisive, but whether Shakespeare thought of him as being decisive or indecisive, whether Shakespeare depicted him to be decisive or indecisive, whether Shakespeare implied him to be decisive or indecisive, and the like. Our distinction between what a thing is and what it is thought to be remains thus in full force.

Meinong cannot help but notice that we do indeed turn to the text when confronted with a question like the one about Hamlet. Since he holds that Hamlet is, say, decisive, he must explain why the text becomes important. He must explain, in other words, why we cannot just inspect Hamlet, as he appears before our minds, in order to solve the dispute. Meinong discusses this problem in the article '*Über Urteilsgefühle: was sie sind und was sie nicht sind.*'[26] He starts with a quotation from Lipps which I shall translate, since it reflects so well much of of what recently has been written about the matter:[27]

> I know that the Mephisto of Goethe is a purely fictional
> character, that there never existed a Mephisto, and hence that he
> never spoke the words which Goethe puts into his mouth. Yet I
> can argue about how Mephisto answers Faust or the Lord at a
> particular place. I can say that he answers 'in fact' in this way and
> not in that. And it is to be noticed that thereby I do not intend
> to make a judgment about my activity or Goethe's activity of the
> imagination, but that I make it about the person Mephisto. . . .
> On the other hand, I do indeed not talk of the historical
> Mephisto, but of Goethe's or, more accurately, of the Mephisto
> of fiction. But the latter has a peculiar kind of being. No doubt,
> he has been called into being some time ago by Goethe. But
> after he has been called into being and has achieved artistic
> representation in fiction, he has a kind of reality.

Fictional characters, according to Lipps, have a special kind of reality, a peculiar sort of being; they do not exist in actual reality, but they exist nevertheless, namely, in fiction. Meinong remarks, just like Russell in a famous passage, that there is only one kind of reality, empirical reality, and that so-called fictional reality is no reality at all. But Meinong also thinks that Lipps' view contains a kernel of truth, namely, that what is given to us in the case of Mephisto is not only the imaginings and conceptions of Goethe, but also, and most importantly, the nonexistent creation of Goethe's imagination, that is, Mephisto. When we think about Mephisto, what is before our minds is, not Goethe's mental activity, but the fictional character himself. From this, Meinong draws the conclusion that Mephisto has properties, even though he has no being.[28]

But he also admits that we ascribe these properties to Mephisto neither with an eye on empirical reality nor with an eye on *a priori* necessities, but rather with reference to the creator of this character. The author, according to Meinong, creates a piece of reality, in this case the manuscript, which has a meaning to other people. An aesthetic object is thus picked out of the infinite totality of entities with *Aussersein* by the person who understands that piece of reality; and this object may appropriately be called a *predetermined* object as far as that person is concerned. Furthermore, the predetermined object, according to Meinong, as such remains beyond being, that is, whether it is or is not, is inessential as far as its predetermination is concerned. But knowledge about this object has empirical character insofar as it is based on knowledge about the predetermining piece of reality.

It seems to me that we must distinguish between two different questions. First, do we think of Goethe's imagination, whenever we think of Mephisto as having this or that property? Second, does Mephisto have any properties? It is true, I think, as both Lipps and Meinong emphasize, that we may think of Mephisto without thinking of anyone's mental processes. To think of a fictional character is not necessarily to think of someone else who thinks about it or invents it. Just as Mephisto can be before Goethe's mind when he creates this character without there being at the same time before his mind someone's imagination, especially not his own, so Goethe's Mephisto can also be before my mind without any thought of Goethe's imagination. This answers the first question negatively. Assume, then, that I conceive of Mephisto as being sly. From this conception, I have stressed earlier, it does not follow that Mephisto is sly. But we must now face the really important question, namely, what precisely happens when I conceive of Mephisto as being sly? What precisely is it that is before my mind in this case? Meinong's view, we must realize, constitutes an attempt to answer these questions. In the process, though, Meinong eradicates, as I have pointed out, the important distinction between what a thing is and what it is thought to be.

To be specific, consider a case where I assume that there is a certain (fictional) person *M* whom I imagine to be very sly. What I assume (to be the case), we may say, is the state of affairs (proposition, circumstance, etc.): *M is very sly*. According to Meinong, I have then picked out of the infinite totality of entities beyond being a certain entity *M*, and I am attributing to this entity (analytically, as it were) the property of being sly. Which entity I pick out, may be predetermined or not. If I think of Goethe's Mephisto, then it is; if I make up my own devil, then it is not. In either case, though, all that is in my power to do is to pick out an entity which is already 'there' in that totality of entities beyond being. If I think of Faust, on the other hand, I pick out a different entity. Now, how could these two entities possibly differ, unless they have properties? The first entity must differ from the second by being sly, for example, and the second entity, in turn, must have properties which the first one does not have. In short, these entities could not be what they are, unless they had the properties of being sly, of being learned, etc.

Let us look at the matter from a purely ontological point of view in order to shed further light on Meinong's position. Consider a class of properties F, G, H, etc. According to Meinong, 'there are,' in the realm of *Aussersein*, a group of complex *objects*: $<F, G>$, $<F, H>$ $<F, G, H>$, etc., which correspond to all the possible combinations of those properties. [29] Any two of these complexes are distinguished from each other only in regard to some part or parts, since the relationship that makes complexes (structures) out of classes of properties is the same for all complexes. Consider now a particular one of these objects, say, the object $<$Round, Square$>$. To think something about the round square involves, according to Meinong, having that object before the mind. Is this object round? Is it square? Of course, it is both, since round as well as square are parts of the complex. Compare this complex with another which consists of certain instances of the properties round, red, etc., and which happens to be a particular billiard ball. Is this object round? Is it red? Again, it is both, and it has further properties as well. There is no difference between the round square and the billiard ball, if I may put it so, so far as predication is concerned, even though the billiard ball exists, while the round square has no ontological status whatsoever. [30] Where, then, does the difference in ontological status appear? It never appears in the realm of pure objects, but only in the realm of objectives. Neither existence nor subsistence ever occurs as a part of a complex object. The difference between the round square and the billiard ball does not consist in the fact that the latter contains existence as a part, while the former does not. Rather, since the billiard ball exists, there subsists a certain objective O; since the round square does not exist, there subsists for it no corresponding objective. Among the complexes in the realm of *Aussersein*, there are thus some that consist of properties, others that consist of instances. Only those complexes which consist of instances have being, however. Take the round square. This pure object consists (at least) of the two properties *round* and *square*. But this does not mean, we must emphasize, that it is just a complex property. For *the* round square is an object, something 'individual.' We now understand Meinong's strange habits of speaking of *the* round square and of *the* golden mountain and of also talking about these objects as '*a* round square' and '*a* golden mountain.' Meinong assumes that, for every subset of properties, there is in the realm of *Aussersein* precisely one pure object. The definite (or indefinite) article maps classes of properties onto complexes in such a way that to each such class there corresponds precisely one complex, namely, the 'individual' which has those properties.

It is clear, furthermore, that all predications turn out to be *a priori* and necessary. At least, this is true when we think of predication as the relationship between complex and part and leave psychological matters aside.[31] Finally, notice that I had to add 'etc.' when I listed the properties of the billiard ball. I assumed, of course, that the billiard ball has many properties which I might not even know. The same cannot be said about the round square. Entities which have ontological status seem to be much more complex than entities which do not have being. Whether such a 'complete' entity can ever be before my mind is an entirely different and, I might add, fascinating question, a question which the astute Meinong soon discovered.

The golden mountain, we insisted, is not golden. It is merely thought to be golden, imagined to be golden, conceived of as golden, etc. Now, if I assume that there is a golden mountain which is finally discovered by the prince, then there is a state of affairs before my mind which is represented by some such sentence as: 'There is something (an individual) which is a mountain and which is golden (which has these properties) and which is finally discovered by the prince.' Let us assume that I think that there is precisely one such mountain. In this case, what is before my mind is a state of affairs of the following kind: The (precisely one) thing which is a mountain and golden is finally discovered by the prince. Now, there is, of course, a great difference between Meinong's analysis of this state of affairs and our analysis. Individual things are, on our view, not complexes of properties (instances). But this difference, so far as I can see, makes no difference for what we are about at the present. According to Meinong, what is before my mind is a complex object; according to our view, it is an individual thing. According to Meinong, this object is before my mind *as* having the properties of being a mountain and being golden (it has these properties as parts); according to our view, the individual is before my mind *as* exemplifying the properties of being a mountain and being golden. In either case, what is before my mind would not be what it is, unless it is before my mind *as* what it is before my mind. Thus we must agree with Meinong that the golden mountain, *as it is before my mind*, is golden and a mountain. There is no way around that insight.

Let us look at the same point from a different angle. When I assume that there exists a golden mountain and when I merely believe it, in both cases precisely the same state of affairs is before my mind. In both cases, what is before my mind is the state of affairs: There exists something which *is* a golden mountain. *As it is before my mind*, we may say, the something *is* a golden mountain. To talk about things *as they are before my mind*, we see, is to talk about states of affairs, irrespective of whether they are facts or not. But we also want to insist that what is before my mind neither exists nor is a golden mountain. By that we cannot mean to say, and this is the lesson of the last paragraph, that a different state of affairs is really before my mind. Rather, what we must mean is that the state of affairs before my mind is not a fact. Thus, although it is true that what is before my mind is golden, *as it is before my mind*, it is not true that it is golden. We continue to insist on a distinction between what things are and what they are thought to be.

We see now more clearly where we have to look for the real difference between Meinong's view and our alternative. This difference must appear in connection with the factuality of objectives. After everything is said and done, Meinong, it turns out, asserts that, since one thinks of the golden mountain as being golden, the objective *The golden mountain is golden* is factual. While we agree that one thinks of the golden mountain as being golden, we do not draw Meinong's conclusion.

3   *An Explication of Necessity*

Rational knowledge, as we briefly mentioned in the last chapter, is supposedly characterized by four features: (1) It is said to be founded on objects, (2) it is necessary, (3) it is certain with evidence, and (4) it is independent of existence. We have just considered a part of this last feature. Evidence for certainty and evidence for surmise were discussed in the last chapter. Meinong also explains in greater detail what the first two features are. His point of departure is Russell's criticism of necessity.[32] Russell, in his article 'Meinong's Theory of Complexes and Assumptions,' had rejected Meinong's notion of necessity, referring in this connection to Moore's article 'Necessity.'[33] In this latter article, Moore argues in effect that a proposition is necessary relative to other propositions from which it follows logically. Moore thus embraces, as far as the essentials are concerned, our earlier explication of necessity which, as we pointed out, is due to Frege.

Meinong starts his defense of the notion of necessity with an explanation of the terms 'reason' (*Grund*) and 'consequence' (*Folge*) as applied to objectives. He says that just as an objective is called 'true' with respect to the kind of judgment which is possibly directed toward it, in a similar fashion an objective is called 'a reason' in regard to the fact that a judgment which apprehends it may confer evidence upon another judgment which apprehends the 'consequence.'[34] This relationship between objectives can also be characterized without reference to judgments, that is, without reference to mental entities: 'This happens when one says of an objective that it is "necessary" relative to another one: the necessary coincides with the consequence; that relative to which the necessity holds, with the reason.'[35]

Meinong holds that there is a connection between objectives such that an objective is necessary if and only if it has that connection to certain other objectives. He seems to be embracing Moore's and, hence, our view; especially, when he adds that this connection holds between the premises and the conclusion of a syllogism. But this appearance is deceptive. Meinong wants to hold also that some objectives are 'inherently' necessary. He says, for example, that the fact that 2 is smaller than 3 has no reason which lies outside of this objective, but most certainly one within it. This reason consists in the nature or kind, for short, the so-being, of the objects 2 and 3, so that the earlier assertion that only an objective can be a reason proves itself here, too.

Meinong thus envisages an 'entailment' between certain objectives about the natures of 2 and 3 on the one hand and the objective that 2 is smaller than 3 on the other. Necessity is therefore reduced to 'entailment.' But we must distinguish between two quite different cases. An object may be necessary simply because it follows from other objectives, but it may also be necessary because it follows from objectives which state the nature of the objects involved. An ordinary syllogism is an example of the first kind; the objective that midnight blue is darker than canary yellow, an example of the second kind. But it is clear that this explication of 'inherent' necessity raises a question: What, precisely, are the objectives concerning natures from which the inherently necessary objective follows logically? What, for example, is there in or about the two numbers 2 and 3 such that it follows that 2 is smaller than 3? Meinong never answers these questions. As a matter of fact, he seems to imply that there is no answer to them; for he says that the only thing one can say is that 2 is smaller than 3 'because 2 and 3 simply are what they are.'[36] Meinong's explication implies that the numbers 2 and 3 are 'defined' in such a fashion that it follows logically from these definitions that 2 is smaller than 3. Yet he does not even hint at these possible 'definitions.' Nor, in the end, would it really matter whether he could give such 'definitions'; for he would want to hold, I presume, that there are necessary objectives involving 'undefined' objects.

4 Arithmetic, Geometry, and Logic

Mathematics and logic, in Meinong's view, consist of *a priori* knowledge. But this does not mean, as he repeatedly emphasizes, that these disciplines deal with entities which are not given in experience. Only through experience do we know what black and white are, but that these entities are different we know *a priori*.[37] Similarly for geometric truths. Our geometric concepts are derived from experience; nevertheless, geometric truths are known *a priori* rather than *a posteriori*. Thus we must distinguish between empirical concepts on the one hand and empirical knowledge on the other. Furthermore, we must realize, according to Meinong, that rational knowledge which involves empirical concepts is possible.

But if one cannot argue against Meinong that mathematical knowledge is empirical knowledge, since mathematical concepts are derived from experience, how can one show that mathematical knowledge is not rational knowledge? Meinong suggests that one may try to show that mathematical truths are arrived at by induction. But he claims that inductive truths do not measure up to what we actually find in mathematics, and they do not do so in two respects: they do not have the certainty of mathematical truths and they do not yield their kind of insight. That a stone will fall when it is dropped, of that we are, of course, certain under ordinary circumstances. But if we think a little bit about this fact and, especially, about how we first discovered it, then we see quite clearly that we have no right to be so certain; we realize that there is the theoretical possibility that things may happen differently. The same cannot be said about such an arithmetic fact as that 2 is smaller than 3. Here we have a right to be certain, and this right derives from an insight into the nature of the entities involved. Meinong sums up: 'Mathematical knowledge is not arrived at by induction because induction, by its very nature, is incapable of yielding results of such high quality (*Erkenntnisdignität*).'[38]

Nor are arithmetic truths a matter of experience, Meinong adds. That 12 is divisable by 3 is not, unlike that fire burns, an 'experience,' but can be known *a priori*. One cannot experience how often 3 is contained in 12, but, at most, into how many complexes of three things (*Dreierkomplexe*) 12 apples, 12 nuts, etc. can be divided; and again, not just 12 apples in general, but only these or those 12 apples. Thus the instances of induction would have to be themselves arrived at by induction. But, so Meinong asks rhetorically, who has experienced that such inductions have taken place for apples and nuts, or who would be inclined to expect them from himself or others.[39]

Recall our earlier discussion of induction and *a priori* knowledge.[40] We can agree with Meinong that the arithmetic statement in question is not known *a posteriori* in the sense that it is not known by induction.[41] But there are many truths which are not known by induction and which would, nevertheless, ordinarily be classified as empirical truths. For example, that a certain book is now on my desk is a fact which I do not know by induction and yet it is also a fact which is ordinarily considered to be known *a posteriori* rather than *a priori*. Meinong, as we saw earlier, would have to say that even this fact is known *a priori*. This is a measure of his extreme rationalism, according to which only existential judgments are empirical. But even if he had not held this extreme view, he would probably have objected to our form of 'empiricism' in regard to arithmetic. His probable objection is suggested in the just mentioned passage where Meinong claims that one could not possibly experience how often 3 is contained in 12, but at best how often 3 nuts are contained in these particular 12 nuts. If we have further experiences of this kind, we may inductively arrive at the general statement that any 3 nuts are contained four times in any 12 nuts. And if we branch out to observe apples and other things as well, we may even come to the inductive conclusion that any 3 things are contained four times in any 12 things. But be that as it may, we cannot experience that 3 is contained four times in 12.

The question, then, comes down to this: Can we or can we not experience that 3 is contained four times in 12 or that, to take another example, 2 plus 2 is 4? I think that we can, while Meinong holds that we cannot. But this is not the place to explain my view in great detail. [42] A few hints must suffice. First of all, we must be clear about what we mean in this context by 'experience.' I shall take it that we may have perception in mind; for example, the 'empiricist' of my conviction may claim that we can *see* – quite literally with our eyes – that 2 plus 2 equals 4. In order to defend this claim, one must explain quite carefully what it does not imply. It does not imply, for example, that numbers ever appear in isolation, so to speak. When I *see* that 2 plus 2 equals 4, there must be in front of me, say, 4 apples. The case is not at all different for colors. When I see that midnight blue is darker than canary yellow, then there must be before me, not two colors all by themselves, but two colored objects of a certain kind; and, in all likelihood, I will have seen these colored objects before I see that the one color is darker than the other. Numbers, just like colors, do not occur in the world divorced from all other entities, in splendid isolation, as it were: rather, what there is in front of us are always numbered *objects*, just as there are in front of us colored *things*. But notice that I wish to distinguish between what there is in front of me on the one hand and what I see (at a given moment) on the other. I go so far as to grant that I cannot possibly see that midnight blue is darker than canary yellow, unless I have first seen – in another mental act of perception – that there is, for example, a midnight blue sweater and a canary yellow blouse in front of me. But I shall insist that one can also see – through another mental act of perception – that the two colors stand in that relation to each other. This leads us back to Meinong's objection. Meinong claims, as we saw, that we cannot see that 2 plus 2 equals 4, but at best that 2 nuts plus 2 nuts equal those nuts right here on the table. He would also maintain that we cannot see that midnight blue is darker than canary yellow, but at best that this midnight blue sweater is darker than that canary yellow blouse. Assertion stands against assertion. What are we to do? I appeal to my experience: it seems to me that the very same kind of mental act of seeing is involved when I see, say, that there is a midnight blue sweater before me and when I see that midnight blue is darker than canary yellow. I do not conclude this somehow from something else, as Meinong wants to have it, but see it with my very eyes. And there I shall let the matter rest.

Having defended the rational character of arithmetic, Meinong turns to geometry. His task here is much more formidable. What is at stake is the significance of non-Euclidian geometry for a rationalistic conception of knowledge. Meinong sets out to show that the discovery of non-Euclidian geometries does not imply that Euclidian geometry is empirical rather than rational in character. The broad story of the intellectual impact of the discovery of non-Euclidian geometries, especially on certain Kantian theses, is so well known that I can be brief in setting the stage for Meinong's rather long discussion. [43]

That the assertions of Euclidian geometry are true may be shown in either one of two ways, as far as the traditional dialectic is concerned. One may maintain, first, that the axioms are immediately self-evident, that they constitute a piece of rational' knowledge. Or one may claim, second, that these axioms can be shown to be true by experience and experiments with actual triangles, circles, etc. In short, there is the traditionally rationalistic and the empiricistic approach to Euclidian geometry. But there are also objections to these two interpretations. In regard to the rationalistic interpretation, it was argued that certain axioms simply do not seem to be self-evident; for example, the parallels axiom. The empiricists on the other hand, were unable to make measurements precise enough to verify the Euclidian theorems. When Lobatchewski and Bolyai developed their non-Euclidian systems, it could be shown that axioms other than Euclid's could lead to results which are empirically indistinguishable from the ones derived from the Euclidian axioms. Faced with the two horns of this dilemma, one tried to avoid taking a stand in regard to the rationalism-empiricism issue by treating geometries as deductive systems, that is, one looked upon the assertions of geometry as consisting of hypothetical statements with the axioms as antecedents and the theorems as consequents. [44]

Meinong, it is clear, has to defend the rationalistic interpretation of Euclidian geometry. In the end, this comes down to a defense of the claim that the parallels axiom is known *a priori*. As Meinong sees it, the discovery of non-Euclidian geometries may invite the following argument against his position. [45] This discovery, it may be said, has shown that one can give up the parallels axiom and still get a geometric theory. Thus the axiom does not seem to have the kind of necessity which Meinong attributes to rational knowledge. But nobody really doubts that the axiom is true. Hence, if someone decides for Euclidian geometry and against non-Euclidian geometries, then this decision can rest on nothing but the fact that the former has all experience on its side. And this means that geometry can after all be nothing but an empirical matter.

Meinong, first of all, explains why a non-Euclidian geometry is possible, even upon his own view that, for example, the negation of the parallels axiom is an impossible objective. He simply reminds us that upon his view even impossible objects have properties and that even impossible objectives entail other equally impossible objectives. This, as he also reminds us, is shown by every indirect argument in which we conclude from the impossibility of the consequences the impossibility of an assumption. Parallels which intersect are thus equated to other kinds of impossible objects. Meinong says that two parallels which intersect seem to him to constitute, speaking precisely, just as impossible an object as the round square, and that the insight into this impossibility has for him there the very same character as here.[46]

In what sense is the round square an impossible entity? Assuming that we are dealing with two simple properties, it is clear that the round square is not a contradictory entity, unless there is a law to the effect that, say, everything that is square is not round. Since there is such a law, it follows that the round square would have to be both round and not round. Thus the round square is an 'impossible' entity only in virtue of the law. Compare this case with the one of parallel lines which intersect. We assume that to speak of parallel lines is not just another way of speaking about lines which do not intersect. We assume, in other words, that we are dealing with two simple properties, the property of being a parallel and the property of intersecting. Intersecting parallels, from this point of view, are impossible entities in the very same sense in which the round square is an impossible entity. Intersecting parallels are contradictory entities in the sense that such parallels would have to intersect and also not to intersect, since there is a law that says that no parallels ever intersect.

The question, then, is how we know that squares are not round and parallels do not intersect We know by now what Meinong would say. These are *a priori* truths, founded on the natures of the objects involved. These truths are *necessary*, *evident*, and *independent of existence*. They are known by rational insight rather than experience. Of course, Meinong would not 'define' these objects in terms of empirical operations. The notion of a straight line, for example, is not derived from the notion of a light ray or from what a measurement would show about two points. Rather, the notion of a straight line – being an object of higher order – is an ideal object.

The discovery of non-Euclidian geometry, we see, does not affect Meinong's rationalistic interpretation of geometry. The basic issue between an empiricist and Meinong cannot be settled by an appeal to the fact that consistent geometries are possible without the parallels axiom. The issue revolves ultimately around the question of whether or not certain truths – like the truth that parallels do not intersect – are necessary or, as Meinong puts it, whether or not certain truths are axioms for which a proof is either impossible or can be dispensed with since they are immediately guaranteed by rational evidence.

What Meinong says in the articles here surveyed about the relationship between logic and the theory of entities shows a sophistication which is not apparent at earlier stages of his philosophical development. Logic, according to this new view, is a practical discipline which deals with concepts, judgments, and inferences. [47] It teaches us how to gain knowledge. Logic must not be confused either with psychology or with the theory of entities. Although logic deals with inferences, it does not study inferences as mental phenomena. Rather, it inquires into what kinds of inferences are *valid*. In doing so, it must turn to the theory of entities; for it is the theory of entities which studies those relationships between objectives which are characteristic of valid arguments. Logic, in other words, does not describe how we actually argue, but how we should argue in accordance with the objective relations among objectives. Logic rests on the theory of entities, but it is not a part of it.

5 The Emergence of Incomplete Objects

One of the most interesting and important conceptions of Meinong's ontology is that of an incomplete object. Incomplete objects come up in connection with the discussion of the relationship between logic and the theory of entities. Logic, he believes, deals with concepts, judgments, and inferences. This raises the question as to what concepts are. Meinong is no longer quite satisfied with his very early characterization contained in the *Hume Studies*. He now argues that concepts are incomplete presentations (ideas). But the notion of an incomplete object – then called an indeterminate object – occurs for the first time in a different context in his article '*Abstrahieren und Vergleichen.*' [48]

What is at stake in the earlier paper is the apprehension of universals. Meinong, as we saw, defends a theory of abstraction: we presumably apprehend a property when we pay attention to the corresponding instances in a complex; that is, when we pay attention to it and it alone, divorcing it from a certain place and time. Meinong contrasts this view with another one defended by, among others, Cornelius. According to this view, we apprehend a universal when we compare an object with other objects in regard to similarity. The objects are here supposed to be 'simple.' They do not 'contain' the respects in which they are similar to other objects. According to Cornelius' view, the compared objects are in regard to their natures *indeterminate*. Their characteristics are determinations which are only gotten through apprehensions of similarities. According to Meinong's view, on the other hand, the universal is, so to speak, a part of the complex object; it is already somehow contained in it, although not as a universal, but merely as an instance. According to the 'Humean' view defended by Cornelius, the universal is 'created' by the mind by means of acts of comparison involving similarity. The object is by nature 'simple'; and this means that it is by its nature indeterminate in regard to properties. We create the determinations by acts of comparison.

Meinong attacks the 'Humean' view in several ways. One of these ways revolves around the notion of an indeterminate object. Meinong asks whether or not there really are indeterminate objects as Cornelius' view presupposes. And he starts out with an explication of the notion of an indeterminate object, making quite clear that he is only interested in 'objective' rather than 'subjective' indeterminateness. [49] Meinong considers the two basic objectives (1) A is (has being) and (2) A is B. An object would be indeterminate in regard to being, according to Meinong's explication, if it would neither be the case that A is nor that A is not. An object would be indeterminate in regard to the property B if the object would neither have B nor not have B. Are there indeterminate objects in this sense? Meinong asserts quite emphatically that every object that has being – that either exists or subsists – is determinate.

But, he adds, 'there are' also such objects as the round square and the golden mountain; and he thinks that these entities constitute exceptions to the rule. The round square, for example, is neither blue nor is it not blue. The golden mountain, as he also claims, is neither a thousand yards high nor is it not a thousand yards high. But Meinong does not feel quite at ease with this view. He seems to have discovered an exciting new category of objects, namely, indeterminate objects, but he cannot get used to his discovery.

Yet, warming to the topic, Meinong goes on to discover another notion of indeterminateness, what he calls 'relative indeterminateness.' That 2 is smaller than 3, Meinong reminds us, is determined by the nature of 2. On the other hand, the nature of 2 does not determine whether among tones the octave is closer or farther from the prime than a seventh or a sixth. Similarly, the nature of the triangle determines that it cannot contain more than one right angle. But this nature leaves indeterminate whether or not its angles are equal. I think we can generalize Meinong's examples and extract the following view. Properties (natures) stand in certain relations of inclusion and exclusion to each other. For example, the property of being a triangle includes the property of not having more than one right angle; the property of being (a certain shade of) red excludes the property of being (a certain shade of) green (at the same time, all over). Now, an object (a nature) F is undetermined in regard to some other object (nature) G if and only if G neither includes not excludes F.

Meinong calls our attention to the indeterminateness of what he calls general ideas. If we think of *a horse* or *a triangle*, Meinong says, then it is obvious that the listener cannot possibly know whether we mean, say, a white horse or a black horse, an equilateral or non-equilateral triangle. Meinong seems to be saying – revealing an often noted confusion – that since a white as well as a black horse may 'fall under' the idea of a horse, the idea itself is undetermined. But this kind of indeterminateness seems to be reducible to the kind just mentioned in the last paragraph. The idea is undetermined, we may say, because its intention is undetermined; and its intention is undetermined because it is the complex object (nature) *horse* which neither includes nor excludes the properties *white* or *black*. But notice that this reduction rests on the view that the intention of a general idea is a 'general object' (a nature) rather than one or several particular objects. Meinong himself notices the force of the dialectic. He is disturbed about two things. First, he wonders about the intention of the general idea *a horse*: does this idea intend indefinitely a particular horse or does it intend definitely an indeterminate object, namely, the object <Horse>? He is inclined to admit that the latter is the case. But this raises then a second question for him: how can he reconcile his earlier assertion that there are no indeterminate objects with the conclusion that there is such an entity as the indeterminate object *a horse*? That this second question arises in the wake of his tentative answer to the first shows that the reduction attempt of the last paragraph is really misguided. The general idea in question is not really the idea *horse*, but the idea *a horse*. The expression 'a horse' describes an individual thing; it is not a word for a property in particular, it is not a word for the property of being a horse. What Meinong wonders, we see, is not whether or not properties correspond to what he here calls general ideas, but rather whether or not one or the other of two kinds of individual entities corresponds to such expressions (and hence ideas) as 'a horse', 'a triangle,' etc. It now becomes apparent why Meinong's second worry arises. If indefinite descriptions do not describe particular objects, then the entities which they describe would have to be indeterminate in the first of the two senses listed above. A horse for example, would have to be indeterminate in regard to the color white in the sense that it would neither be white nor not white.

The indefinite description expression 'a horse' ('an individual thing which is a horse') describes an individual thing. Hence Meinong is justifiedly worried about how the assumption of the being of such an indeterminate object agrees with his earlier assertion that all existents and subsistents are completely determinate. He tries to assuage his worry by claiming at first that the indeterminate object of a general idea would merely be an 'immanent' object and would, therefore, at best 'pseudo-exist.' But he realizes almost immediately that this is a paltry evasion. And he rejects undetermined objects by asserting once more that every being either has a given property F or does not have it.

Let us summarize the highlights of Meinong's first encounter with indeterminate objects. Every entity which either exists or subsists is fully determined, according to Meinong's early view, in regard to being and to properties. But there are entities which neither exist nor subsist and which are undetermined. The round square and the golden mountain are examples. It may seem that the idea of *a horse* has as its intention an indeterminate object rather than, depending on the occasion, this or that individual, fully determined, object. But this is mere appearance: such indeterminate objects must be rejected since their being would violate the principle of the excluded middle. Meinong also mentions a different kind of determinateness, the relative kind, where natures are determinate relative to each other. But this is a side issue.

Let us now return to the main point. Meinong, as I said, is trying to clarify the relationship between logic and the theory of entities. In the process, he stumbles upon the question of what concepts are. In the tradition of Twardowski, there is an obvious answer to this question: A concept is the content of a general presentation, that is, it is a general idea. But Meinong does not give this answer straightforwardly, although what he says in the end comes very close to it. He starts with an example of thinking of a tone without being concerned with its loudness, namely, the tone the great C. The object of the C-presentation, Meinong says, is, of course, a tone of a certain pitch, but does it also have loudness? Then he argues:[50]

> We are now not talking about whether the tone of the cello has loudness; nor whether the object of the sensation of the person who hears the tone has loudness; not even about whether loudness belongs to the object of that presentation by means of which someone understands the expression 'tone C.' In none of these cases is the datum of loudness missing; but it is without doubt, not included in what is meant when one talks about the

'tone C' in regard to its characteristic pitch, when the pitch, for example, is predicated. The object of the abstract C-presentation, therefore, has no loudness. Does one therefore think in truth of a C without loudness? One can reject this perhaps even more certainly than that the thought of the C already contains a datum of loudness. This 'abstract' C has the very peculiar property that loudness neither belongs to it nor is missing from it.

Meinong then continues to say that one should not call this kind of object simply 'undetermined,' but rather incompletely determined or, for short, *incomplete*. He remarks that incomplete objects have some- thing to do with the old controversy about universals and that they may show that there is more to that controversy than may often be admitted. As far as concepts are concerned, Meinong's explication of this notion is now obvious: a concept is a presentation (an idea) with an incomplete object (intention).

Meinong's incomplete objects seem to be nothing else than what we have called properties. And yet this explication does not fit; for pro- perties are not in any plain sense incomplete. Consider a certain shade of a color, say, midnight blue. In what sense is this color incomplete? Of course, this property is not, say, round; as a matter of fact, it has no shape at all. But since it is *not* round, it is determined in respect to round- ness. Nor does the question of its shape really arise: for we all know, of course, that it has no shape. In terms of Meinong's example, it is simply not true, as Meinong asserts, that the great C is undetermined in regard to loudness. The great C, most certainly, has no loudness, just as midnight blue has no shape. But if the incomplete objects midnight blue and the great C are not properties, what are they? A few pages back, we gave a different interpretation of Meinong's notion of an incomplete object, and this interpretation may also be applicable here. We must distinguish between the property midnight blue and the individual *a midnight blue thing* (something midnight blue). While it is obvious that the property does not have a shape, this is not quite so obvious for this object. And it may perhaps be equally sensible to claim that it has a certain shape. There is some *prima facie* plausibility in claiming that this individual is undetermined in regard to being round. When we apply this interpretation to the present case, we have to say that Meinong means to talk, even though this does not come out too clearly, about an individual tone rather than the property great C. He means to talk about *a tone with the pitch great C*, rather than about the pitch itself. Incomplete objects, in short, are the referents of indefinite descriptions. Meinong here answers the question of what an expression like 'a man' or 'a tone of pitch great C' represents.

Nevertheless, there remains the fact that Meinong connects the topic of incomplete objects with the controversy about the existence of universals. And he also uses the notion of an incomplete object in order to explicate the notion of a concept. Both of these facts indicate that Meinong himself must have thought of incomplete objects as being akin to properties. There is some similarity, of course. Just think how little difference there is, purely verbally, between, say, 'man' and 'a man,' between 'blue' and 'something blue.' Yet there is all the difference in the world between the referents of these expressions. 'Man' represents the property of being a man, while 'a man' describes an individual in terms of having this property.[51] Assuming that Meinong does indeed tend to confuse these two different entities with each other, is there any explanation for this confusion? It seems to me that the confusion goes back to another mistake of Meinong's. Meinong, we saw in the very first chapter, conceives of a concept (a general idea) as intending, not the corresponding property, but as intending ('indefinitely,' one is compelled to add) the individual things which 'fall under' the concept. For example, the concept *man* is supposed to intend, not the property man, but individual men (though not the class of all men). With this view in the background, his notion of an incomplete object becomes intelligible. The concept great *C*, for example, is said to intend the incomplete object *a tone with the pitch great C*. Incomplete objects are intimately associated with properties in that the concepts which intend incomplete objects are really, in our view, concepts of properties.

From our point of view, then, Meinong makes the following mistakes. First, he continues to hold that concepts intend, not properties, but the entities which, as one usually says, fall under the concepts. Thus he continues to hold that there are general ideas but no properties. But he improves on the traditional nominalistic doctrine by the introduction of a new kind of individual, namely, the incomplete object. What a concept intends is thus, in his view, neither a property, nor a class, nor (indefinitely) a particular individual (which would have to be completely determined). Rather, it intends an entity which belongs to the category of individual thing, but which differs from other individual things in being incomplete. Meinong introduces here a new subcategory of the category of individual things. This subcategory does the duty, in his system, of properties. Second, he confuses, in the process, the concept great *C* with the concept *tone with the pitch great C* or, to use a more obvious example, the concept *man* with the concept *a man*. From our point of view, we must insist that the concept *man*, this mental general idea, is not the same entity as the concept *a man*. Nor, of course, are the respective intentions of these two mental concepts the same, as we have repeatedly emphasized. But notice also that Meinong raises an important question and gives an ingenious answer while bolstering his nominalistic view. Forget about the concept *man* and the universal *man*. Forget about the whole nominalism-realism controversy for a moment. There remains the question of what an indefinite description like 'a man' describes; there is still the question of what the idea of *a man* intends. And one may think of Meinong's introduction of incomplete objects, not as a nominalistic gambit, but as an answer to these important and almost universally neglected questions. Let us take another look, then, at incomplete objects from this ontological position.

Assume again that we have a class of properties: *F*, *G*, *H*, etc. Then there is, in the sense of *Aussersein*, for every class of these properties a certain nature. These natures are described by such expressions as 'the round square' or 'a man.' Furthermore, these individuals are incomplete in regard to every property which is not contained in the class from which they spring. For example, the round square is round and it is square, but it is neither red nor is it not red; it is incomplete in regard to this property. Meinong now simply identifies the nature described by the expression 'the golden mountain' with the intention of the concept *a golden mountain*. Meinong identifies *the golden mountain* with *a golden mountain*, *the horse* with *a horse*.[52] Concepts, in short, intend natures. They neither intend properties nor do they intend, indifferently, particular things. Meinong's newly discovered incomplete objects are nothing else but his old natures.

IX

The Apprehension of Objects

We saw how tortuous Meinong's discussion of the problem of non-existent objects is in the first edition of *Über Annahmen*. Clinging to the notion that an idea can have an intention only if that intention has being, he nevertheless tries to convince us and himself that even the idea of the golden mountain *has* an object in some sense, since it *could have* one. He even claims that the idea of the round square *has* an object, although it *cannot have* one. In the second edition of this work, he returns to this topic of nonexistent intentions.[1] He reprints, without any changes, the relevant chapters of the first edition. But then he adds a new section under the title: 'Self-Criticism: The View of *Aussersein*.' In this section, he criticizes his earlier view, and proceeds to diagnose the reason for his mistake. The postulate that ideas can be intentional only if their objects have being, he says, rests on a prejudice in favor of the real or, at least, in favor of what has being. This prejudice in favor of being, Meinong argues, is associated with a prejudice in favor of knowledge.[2] If we overcome the first prejudice, then we realize that the characteristic relationship between a mind and its objects is, not that of knowledge, but that of apprehension. Intentionality, then, is not to be explicated in terms of the relationship between the knower and the known, but in terms of the relationship between a mind and what it apprehends from the limitless realm of *Aussersein*. Before something can be known about an object, the object must first be apprehended; it must be picked out from the realm of *Aussersein*. Thus Meinong is faced with the question of what kind of experience the apprehension of a pure object is.

1   *Apprehension and Objectives of Being*

There is the traditional answer: Presentations bring things before the mind, so that there is no mental act which is not either a presentation

182

or somehow based on a presentation. But Meinong now rejects this view of Brentano's. He marshals two arguments against it. Presentations, he argues, are necessary for the apprehension of objects, but they are not sufficient.

His first argument rests on the assertion that apprehension is an activity, while presentation is a purely passive experience.[3] Hence some activity must be added to a presentation before the apprehension of an object can take place. Meinong claims that there are many cases where a presentation does not lead to the apprehension of 'its' object. For example, every sense-impression (*Empfindung*) has the capacity to apprehend its object, but the respective objects, which really cause our sense-impressions, do often not appear in our mental life as objects.[4] Furthermore, we often understand the speech we hear, according to Meinong, even though the experienced sounds and what is built upon them, is not an object to consciousness.

What these examples show, from our point of view, is that the experiencing of sense-impressions is not the same as the perceptions of objects and that the hearing of words is not the same as the understanding of their meaning. It is indeed true, as Meinong claims, that we experience many sense-impressions without perceiving the corresponding perceptual objects that cause these sense-impressions. Perception, as we explained earlier, requires, not only the experiencing of certain sense-impressions, but also the experiencing of certain mental acts of perceiving, for example, the experiencing of a mental act of seeing. When we have a visual sense impression which is caused by a certain perceptual object, we do not as yet see that object; there must also occur a mental act of seeing. But notice that our view differs from Meinong's in at least two important respects. First, we do not claim that the distinction between having a sense-impression and seeing a perceptual object is a distinction between passivity and activity. Second, we do not try to reduce perceptual acts to other kinds of acts like judgments or assumptions.

Meinong's second objection to the view that mere presentation constitutes the apprehension of objects rests on the assertion that different contents of presentations may intend the same object and, conversely, that different objects may be intended by the same content.[5] Meinong reminds us of his view that the very same content may be 'turned outward' to intend an external object as well as 'turned inward' to apprehend itself. He also mentions his conclusion that one and the same content may apprehend a phenomenal object and, less distinctly, a noumenal object. It is clear, Meinong now argues, that such differences in objects cannot be a function of the unchanging content. Something else, added activities, must account for the fact that the content can occur in connection with different objects.

Granted, for the sake of the argument, that the apprehension of objects does not consist solely in presentations, what is it that constitutes such an apprehension? At this point, Meinong makes a most interesting preliminary move. He suddenly switches to what seems to be an entirely different matter, and identifies apprehension with meaning (reference): 'It is therefore at least an admissible analogy when one now says of presentations, through which an object is actually apprehended, that something is meant by them.'[6] According to Meinong, only those presentations actually apprehend an object by means of which something is meant, by means of which one refers to something. Thus the question about the nature of apprehension becomes *ipso facto* a question about the nature of meaning and referring.[7]

We still have the question: What is apprehension? Meinong considers, very briefly, the possibility that apprehension constitutes an irreducible kind of mental act. In addition to such kinds of mental acts as presentations, assumptions, and judgments, there would then exist another kind, variously called 'apprehension of an object,' 'reference to an object' and 'meaning an object.' But he rejects this possibility on the ground that it would be advantageous if one could explain the occurrence of apprehension in terms of customary mental activities; and he claims that one can indeed explain apprehension in these familiar terms. To this purpose, he starts once more with the paradigmatic case of knowledge as the apprehension of a piece of reality. To mean one's friend John, Meinong says, is to be cognizant of the fact that he exists.[8] To refer to an equilateral triangle – to apprehend it – is to be cognizant that it subsists. In either case, the object is apprehended (meant, referred to) by means of an objective of being, which itself is judged. Put differently, the object is indirectly apprehended through the direct apprehension of an objective of being.

In order to apprehend an object, therefore, an objective of being must be apprehended. The object is apprehended indirectly by means of a direct apprehension of a certain objective of being. What one means or refers to, though, is not the apprehended objective, but the object in it. In order to mean or refer to the objective itself, Meinong explains, one must apprehend it, in turn, through another objective. For example, in order to mean the friend John, one must apprehend the objective of his existence. But in order to mean or refer to his existence, one must apprehend a different objective, an objective to the effect that the first objective is factual.

We must, quite obviously, distinguish between three different relationships between acts and intentions in order to make Meinong's view clear. First of all, there is the relation between a presentation and its object. This, we have seen, is not as yet an apprehension of an object. Let us call it the relationship of *presenting* an object (to the mind). Then there is, secondly, apprehension of an object. Such apprehension consists of (a) the *presentation* of an object and (b) the making of a judgment (or assumption). The question now arises as to how we may describe the relationship, this third one, between a judgment or assumption and its objective of being. Meinong, we saw, speaks here, too, of apprehension. But this is only possible because, at this point, apprehension no longer signifies the same as meaning something or referring to something. Since we wish to retain the original synonymy, we must look for a different expression. Let us say that a judgment intends an objective. Using this, somewhat artificial, terminology, we can describe Meinong's view as follows. The apprehension of an entity (meaning the entity, referring to it) takes place through an objective of being which is intended by a judgment or assumption. If the entity is an object, then this object is judged to have being, and the object is first presented to the mind by a presentation. If the entity is itself an objective, then this objective is judged to have being (to be factual), and it is brought before the mind by the very same act of judging which intends the objective of its being. It is clear why the situation for objectives must be different from the situation for objects. If the objective to be meant has to be brought before the mind first by another judgment before one can judge that it subsists, then an infinite regress occurs. On the other hand, the question arises why Meinong denies that objects can be brought before the mind through the very act of judging by means of which they are apprehended. Why, in other words, does he still cling to the view that a judgment about an object must be based on a presentation of the object? Put more radically, why does he hold on to the notion that there must be presentations? It is obvious that presentations have lost most of their importance in Meinong's latest system. The theory of apprehension relegates presentations once and for all to a rather insignificant role. They are the mere 'stuff,' the 'raw material,' which supplies the mind with something to work on. But all the interesting work is done by judgment and assumption.

So far, we have only considered cases where the objects in question existed and subsisted, respectively. What happens, Meinong asks, if someone refers to an object which has no being, but which is believed to have being? In this case, the situation is presumably the same as before: the object is apprehended through an objective of being, but this objective does not subsist. However, in case someone means an object of which he denies that it has being, judgment is supplanted by assumption. Meinong cannot simply maintain that in this case there occurs a judgment to the effect that the object in question has no being and that this judgment apprehends the object; for, we must recall that he also holds that all negative judgments of this sort rest on assumptions. Finally, the situation is again clear if someone means an object without raising the question of its being. In this case the object is apprehended by means of an objective of being which is merely assumed. In short, every object is apprehended by means of an objective of being, but this objective may be intended either by a judgment or an assumption.[9]

Meinong's theory of apprehension has two important parts. There is, on the one hand, his amended answer to the problem of objects without being and, on the other, his new explication of meaning and referring. As far as the first part is concerned, he simply affirms that presentations can present pure objects irrespective of whether these objects have being or not. The relation of presentation, in other words, can connect an existent mental act of presentation with an object which has no being. But a similar problem also arises on the level of objectives: Since there are objectives which do not subsist, some judgments and assumptions intend objectives which have no being. Again, Meinong seems to hold that the intentional relation between a judgment or assumption and its objective can hold even if the latter has no being whatsoever.

In regard to the second part of the theory, Meinong holds that the realm of pure objects can only be reached by the mind through the realm of objectives. Presentations, as I mentioned before, play a subordinate role in this new theory. Objectives, on the other hand, can be reached directly, either through judgment or through assumption. Meinong considers briefly the possibility that all objects are apprehended by means of objectives which are intended by judgments; assumptions, in other words, would not be involved in apprehension. This possibility is suggested, he points out, if we think of *Aussersein* as a third kind of being. If *Aussersein* is a third kind of being, then there would be certain judgments which would intend objectives of *Aussersein*. For example, if someone denies of an object that it has being, that it either exists or subsists, he would then apprehend the object by means of a judgment rather than an assumption, but this judgment would intend an objective of *Aussersein*. In general, if *Aussersein* were a third kind of being, then one could hold that the apprehension of all objects consists in judgments which intend objectives of *Aussersein*. But Meinong does not accept this possibility. He remarks that everything speaks for an important role of assumptions in the apprehension of objects and that, at any rate, the notion of *Aussersein* is too obscure to decide in favor of the view that it constitutes a third kind of being.[10]

Meinong claims that objectives of so-being may also be involved in the apprehension of objects.[11] Assume that you believe that this rose is red. According to Meinong's view, the rose is meant in this belief;

an objective of being, in this case an objective of existence, is judged. But what about the object *red*? Is not this color meant, too? And if it is meant, must there not also occur a judgment which intends an objective of being about the color? Meinong maintains that his experience shows no such additional judgment. The judgment (belief) to the effect that this rose is red suffices, he claims further, in order to apprehend the color. Thus while the rose must be brought before the mind through an objective of existence before something can be predicated of it, the color can be brought before the mind in the very judgment of predication. Why is there this asymmetry? Meinong does not seem to realize the urgency of this question at this point. Surely, the theory of apprehension would be greatly simplified if we reduce it to the view that all objects are apprehended by means of objectives, namely, by whatever objectives are before the mind, be they objectives of being or objectives of so-being. If one judges that this rose exists, for example, the rose would be apprehended by means of an objective of being; if one judges that this rose is red, the rose as well as its color would be apprehended by means of an objective of so-being. And so on. This alternative differs from Meinong's view in that it allows the rose to be apprehended by means of an objective of so-being which is not first preceded by an objective of being; and it also differs from Meinong's view in that it allows for properties (and relations) to be apprehended be means of objectives in which they occur in a predicative position. We shall see in a moment that Meinong will indeed allow for the apprehension of objects through certain predicative objectives. But at this moment, he still clings to the 'doctrine of presentation' or, rather, to a version of this doctrine, according to which every mental act rests ultimately on an assumption (or judgment) which brings the object before the mind by means of an objective of being.

2 *Apprehension and Objectives of So-Being*

The example of the rose suggests that an object may be apprehended by means of an objective of so-being. Meinong takes up this suggestion, but changes the example to the objective: My desk is square. He remarks that the desk is here apprehended by means of an objective of existence which is based on a certain presentation. Then he continues:[12]

> But one notices easily that here in order to mean the subject, N [square] can also be used. For such a different kind of meaning, however, the categorical sentence is not the adequate expression so long as it remains the principal clause. The situation changes when we turn it into a relative clause. If I say: 'My desk which is square,' then in this way (as distinguished, for example, from my

round table), an apprehension can clearly have taken place in which the predicative determination, which now occurs in the dependent clause, plays an essential role. The circumstance that the N, too, can be used to mean something becomes even more obvious if we see to it that this function is not obscured by the participation of the M [my desk], as happens in the phrase 'M, which is N.' If we take away from the M all determinations, so that in their place there remains, as it were, only the space for determination – saying, for example, 'Something which is N' or 'That which is N' – then all determining is done solely by the N. The N-presentation has now completely taken the place of the M-presentation in regard to the function of being the presentational basis for the meaning.

Meinong adds that the determination N in the objective *Something which is N* retains its predicative position, so that it is not it which is apprehended here by means of an objective of being. He also adds, most interestingly, that the subject M can be used to apprehend a determination as, for example, in the objective: *Something which M has* (Something exemplified by M). Thus we may apprehend the object N by means of the objective: Something which my desk has.

Meinong, it is clear, has backed into the problem of descriptions or, more succinctly, into Russell's distinction between knowledge by acquaintance and knowledge by description. An object like my desk may be apprehended 'directly' through an objective of existence, or it may be apprehended indirectly through a predicative objective which is expressed by a description expression. To draw the parallel more clearly, acquaintance with an object consists of the apprehension of the object by means of an objective of being; knowledge by description consists of the apprehension of the object by means of a certain objective of so-being. There is one feature of Meinong's view which I cannot stress too emphatically. According to Meinong, a description expression like 'Something which is square' *represents* an *objective*, although it *describes* an object. A description expression, in other words, represents something and describes something; it has, in Frege's famous terminology, a sense and a reference.[13] But, and this is what I want to stress, what it represents, in distinction to what it describes, is always an objective, always a state of affairs. Meinong thus holds a view which I have outlined elsewhere.[14] And this view differs markedly both from Frege's as well as Russell's.

Where do we find apprehension by means of predicative objectives? As we would expect, Meinong denies that this kind of apprehension occurs in perception. Perception is the province of apprehension by means of objectives of being: 'The object of the perceptual presentation is the genuine concretum, which can only be apprehended through an objective of being (*Seinsmeinen*), more precisely, through an existential judgment.'[15] Apprehension by means of so-being, Meinong continues, takes place 'wherever we apprehend objects by means of their more or less abstractly presented properties, which is the rule.'[16] We are tempted to infer that perception and only perception ('inner as well as outer') constitutes apprehension by means of being, while any other apprehension proceeds by means of objectives of so-being. But Meinong does not say so unequivocally. Yet this inference is plausible and it leads to a rather profound characterization of perception as compared to all other kinds of mental acts: perceptual acts would be the only ones which present the mind with an object directly as a part of an objective of being. Furthermore, what would also follow is that perception and only perception presents the mind with a *complete* object. Reference by means of objectives of so-being, it is obvious, always involves an *incomplete* object. I think, as may have transpired in the course of earlier arguments, that this characterization is essentially correct. Perceptual acts, and only perceptual acts, intend states of affairs of which such objects as chairs, tables, and mountains are literally constituents. When you think of a certain mountain, rather than see it, then the state of affairs before your mind does not literally contain the mountain. Rather, it contains instead a description of the mountain, that is, a certain property F (or a certain relation R) which the mountain has. The state of affairs before your mind is then quantified and not of the simple subject-predicate form.

Notice that the notion of an objective of being is no longer ambiguous. We must distinguish between objectives of the form (1) *This has being* from objectives of the form (2) *Something which is F has being*. Only perception would ever apprehend an object by means of an objective of kind (1). When we merely pick out, in thought, an object from the realm of *Aussersein* by means of an objective of being, this objective would have to be of the form (2).

Be that as it may, Meinong runs into two important difficulties as he tries to elaborate on his theory of apprehension by means of so-being. The first difficulty appears when he asks what kinds of mental acts intend the objectives of so-being which are characteristic of reference by means of so-being. The obvious answer seems to be: either judgments or assumptions. But Meinong thinks that judgments cannot be involved. He argues as follows. Consider the cases where someone refers to the *inventor of the typewriter*. It seems as if he apprehends this person by means of a judgment which intends an objective of so-being. But this conception runs into trouble. The object in question can undoubtedly be judged to be the inventor of the typewriter *after* it has been apprehended. But when it is a matter of apprehending the object by means of a certain objective of so-being, how could a judgment about its characteristics *precede* the apprehension of the object? Whenever we have a presentation as the basis for an apprehension of being, there is no difficulty; for the presentation presents us with the object directly, so to speak. But when the presentation is missing, and we have to depend solely on an objective of so-being, a judgment cannot be involved. Meinong concludes that in all these cases assumptions occur. But if it is true that the mountain which is made of gold is really golden, Meinong muses, is it not then also true that we judge it to be golden when we apprehend the golden mountain through an objective of so-being? Meinong merely repeats his earlier argument: 'The so-being through which I apprehend an object in the first place, I cannot attribute to it since to this end I must already have apprehended it.'[17]

It seems clear enough that one cannot judge in regard to a certain object that it has a certain property, unless that object is before the mind. Thus one cannot attribute the property of the description in question to a *certain, definite,* object, unless that object is before the mind in some other way. But how does assumption here accomplish what judgment fails to achieve? It seems equally clear that one cannot assume in regard to a *certain definite,* object that it has a certain property, unless that object is before the mind. Hence, one cannot assume in regard to a certain object that it has the property of the description in question, unless the object is brought before the mind in a way other than by the description itself. But when we mean an object by means of a description, we do not mean a *certain* object at all. In the objective: *Something is the inventor of the typewriter,* the property of being the inventor of the typewriter is not attributed to some definite object at all. The very meaning of the statement in question is that some object or another has this property. By means of a description, we pick *an* object out of the realm of *Aussersein,* but we do not pick out a definite, specific, object. I see no reason why one may not judge, as distinct from assuming, that something is the inventor of the typewriter, even though the object to which one attributes the property of being the inventor of the typewriter is in this case not further specified. But Meinong, of course, looks at the matter in a different way. The nature which we pick out, according to him, from the realm of *Aussersein* is indeed a certain, definite, entity. Hence he faces a problem.

The second difficulty arises from Meinong's analysis of objects as complexes of properties (instances):[18]

For example, if I perceive the door to my room, then I experience, without doubt, primarily an apprehension by means of being. But nobody will deny that this experience implies determinations of so-being like being brown, being rectangular, etc.; nay, that the whole object, which is meant by means of being through the perception, must be analyzable into objectives of so-being like *something that is brown, something that is rectangular*, etc.; perhaps with the exception of a remainder which has to be investigated further and which seems to hide behind the 'something' which is here perhaps not used in the fullest generality.

Call the door to Meinong's room 'A.' Assume that A is a complex consisting of the properties F, G, H, *etc.,* so that $A = <F, G, H, etc.>$. What Meinong is puzzled about is the view that one can apprehend A through an objective of being without apprehending, in the same act, that A consists of F, G, H, etc. Put more succinctly, Meinong seems to wonder how one could apprehend A without properties, since A is a complex of properties. But if one apprehends these properties, then one does not intend a mere objective of being, but an objective (or several objectives) of so-being. If A is nothing but a complex of properties, how could one possibly be said to have apprehended that A exists, unless one has first apprehended all of these properties? Does not the apprehension of A consist in the apprehension of these properties?

Meinong's puzzle is an old one. Alas, it is also a difficult one. It has the same source as the problem which confronts Moore and Husserl, among other philosophers, when they argue that we can never perceive a whole perceptual object. Recall Husserl's theory of *noemata* as profiles or aspects of perceptual objects.[19] According to this kind of theory, when Meinong apprehends his door by means of the objective *This exists*, what he really apprehends is merely an aspect of the door, a spatial part of the door, namely, its front. The back side and inside of the door are, at that moment, hidden from Meinong's view. By walking around the door, though, he would be able to see other parts of the door. Thus, even though he would be seeing the same door, from the front and from the back, as we ordinarily say, he would in reality only see two aspects of that door. No single perceptual act would present Meinong with the door as a whole. Moore expresses the same view in these words:[20]

> Nobody will suppose, for a moment, that when he judges such things as 'This is a sofa,' or 'This is a tree,' he is judging with regard to the presented object, about which his judgment plainly is, that it is a *whole* sofa or a *whole* tree: he can, at most, suppose that he is judging it to be *a part of the surface* of a sofa or *a part of the surface* of a tree.

Husserl's and Moore's view involves three main assertions. First, when we perceive that this is a door, we really perceive that this is a part of something which is a door. Second, we never, therefore, perceive the door as such, but merely perceive parts of it. Third, what we perceive, the *this*, is never the door, but only part of the door. If we substitute for the *spatial* analysis of the door an analysis in terms of properties, we get a similar view about Meinong's complexes. Just as one can never apprehend the *whole* door as a spatial structure, according to Husserl and Moore, so one can presumably never apprehend the *whole* door as a structure of properties; for, just as one cannot see, from one point of view, all the spatial parts of the door, so one cannot apprehend, from one point of view, all the properties of which the door consists.

All three assertions, I believe, are false. Let me try to show this first for the spatial case. Concerning the third assertion, it is absurd to maintain, as Husserl and Moore do, that we are literally mistaken when we see and say that *this* is a door. All of us do not, as they want to have it, mistake the front of the door for the door. We know very well the difference between the door and its front, and we do not judge that the front is a door when we judge that this is a door. When we really see that this is the front of the door, we see something quite different from what we see when we see that this is a door. A quite different state of affairs is before our minds, if I may put it so; and to see the one state of affairs is not to see the other. Hence the first assertion is false, too. Finally, since to perceive that this is a door is not the same as to perceive that this is part of a door, and since we are not mistaken in thinking that this is a door, we do really and truly perceive doors, not just parts of doors. Similarly for the case where we conceive of the door, not as a spatial structure, but as a structure of properties. When we apprehend that the door exists by means of the objective *This exists*, we do not apprehend the existence of something brown or of something rectangular. What is before our minds is the objective *This exists*, not an objective of the form *Something brown exists* or of the form *This brown (the instance) exists*.

Granted that Husserl and Moore are wrong when they claim that we cannot apprehend the whole complex, but only a part of it, how can we reconcile our bold assertion that we see the whole door with the plain fact that we cannot see, from one point of view, the back side of it or that we cannot see other properties of it? The view that we cannot see the whole complex may have its shortcomings, but our view appears to be outright absurd; for it seems to imply that, when we see the door, we see all of its spatial parts or all of its properties at once. But it is precisely our point that there is no such implication. We must distinguish between two ways in which one may be said to have seen the (whole) door. One may either have seen it by seeing that *this* is a door or one may have seen it by seeing that this is the front side of the door, this its back side, etc. In the first case, if I may again put it this way, what is before the mind is the state of affairs *This is a door*; in the second case, what is before the mind are, successively, the states of affairs: *This is the front side of the door, This is the back side of the door*, etc. We admit, even insist, that having seen the door in the first sense does not imply that one has seen the door in the second sense. Furthermore, we also insist that, unless one starts to walk around the door, one cannot see that this is the back side of the door, even though one has seen that this is a door.

Can we put our finger precisely on the point where Husserl and Moore go wrong? With this question we return to Meinong's puzzlement. The door A, we assumed, is the structure $<F, G, H, \text{etc.}>$. This is to say that A is the same as *the structure consisting of F_i, G_i, H_i, etc.* We have here an identity statement involving the description expression 'the structure consisting of F_i, G_i, H_i, etc.' To apprehend that A is a door (that *this* is a door), Husserl and Moore may have reasoned, is to apprehend, therefore, that a structure which consists of F_i, G_i, H_i, etc., is a door. But it seems clear that we apprehend no such thing when we apprehend that this is a door, since it seems obvious that not all of these parts F_i, G_i, H_i, etc., are at once before the mind. Hence, we cannot really apprehend that A is a door, they concluded, but must apprehend something else, namely, that something else, not A, is part of a door. Similarly, in the other case. To apprehend that A exists, one may think, is to apprehend that a structure which consists of F_i, G_i, H_i, etc., exists. But this means, Meinong seems to be arguing, that one cannot really apprehend the existence of A without intending an objective of so-being, namely, the objective involved in the description: *the complex consisting of F_i, G_i, H_i, etc.* It also means, as Meinong later realized, that one cannot really apprehend the *complete* complex A at all. Meinong concludes then that a complete object can only be apprehended through an incomplete one. He goes wrong, just as do Husserl and Moore, in stepping from the fact that A is the same as the structure consisting of F_i, G_i, H_i, etc., to the alleged conclusion that, therefore, the apprehension which intends the objective that A *is a door* (or that A *exists*) is an apprehension which intends the objective that the structure consisting of F_i, G_i, H_i, *etc.*, is a door (or that the structure consisting of F_i, G_i, H_i, *etc.*, exists). Although it may be true that a certain entity has the properties F_i, G_i, H_i, etc., it simply does not follow that to see A is to see it as having all these properties. In a nutshell, what Husserl's, Moore's, and Meinong's mistake reminds us of is the fact that perception (apprehension) is 'intentional.' Or, to put it more illuminatingly, what it reminds us of is the fact that the state of affairs A *exists* is not the same as the state of affairs A *structure consisting of F_i, G_i, H_i, etc., exists*, so that the first of these two may be before a mind without the second being before that same mind, and conversely.

I think that an assay of individual things as complexes (collections) of instances (or of properties) – an approach which Meinong shares with Husserl and Moore – almost inevitably leads to the mistaken view that 'complete' individual things cannot be presented to a mind. If a door is (identical with) an infinite bundle of instances (or of properties), then it seems to stand to reason, since we can never perceive infinitely many instances (or properties) in one act of perception, that we cannot perceive the whole door. On the other hand, if we conceive of the door – following my suggestion – not as a complex of instances (or properties), but as an individual thing which exemplifies numerous properties, but does not consist of them, then there is no strong reason to believe that we cannot perceive this individual thing (together with a few of its properties) in one act of perception. According to my ontological analysis, it is one thing to perceive the individual with some of its properties, quite another thing to perceive the sum total of all of its numerous properties; and while the latter may be impossible, the former is not.

Meinong, at any rate, vacillates as to whether or not there can be any apprehension by means of a pure objective of being. In regard to another point, however, he does not waver. His new view on apprehension shows, he declares, that the connection between an idea and its object is not one-one: 'The situation is different when I apprehend first the color black through an objective of being, and then use the same content to think of something which is black or, more briefly, of something black.'[21] What Meinong seems to have in mind is that the very same content of a certain presentation can be the foundation for two different judgments (or assumptions) and, hence, for two different apprehensions. This content may lead to the judgment that *this* exists, where the *this* is a color (an instance), or it may lead to a judgment to the effect that something is black. Meinong's analysis, of course, raises all the problems which we mentioned earlier concerning the connection between a presentation, more precisely, its content, and the judgment or assumption built upon it. In particular, it raises the question of whether a judgment has no other content than what the underlying presentation provides for it.

Having argued that one and the same content can function in the apprehension of different objects, he argues also that the same object can be apprehended by means of different contents. A blackboard, for example, can be apprehended by means of the content of the presentation 'black' as well as by means of the presentation 'square,' since it is something black as well as something square. But this, Meinong stresses, does not prevent black and square from being two different objects; even though something black and something square, both taken as closed off, are different.[22] Meinong's point here is straightforward and very important. He realizes now that his earlier view, taken over from Twardowski, was mistaken. According to this view, as I explained in the third chapter, two definite descriptions like 'the site of the Roman Juvavum' and 'the birthplace of Mozart' were said to intend the same object by means of two different ideas. No distinction was then made between the intention of an idea and its object. I argued that these two different ideas do not intend the same object in the sense of the same intention. Meinong, we also recall, simply repeated Twardowski's argument. But now, as we see, he realizes his mistake. He does now distinguish between the object of two descriptions and the intentions of the respective apprehensions. The blackboard is the object which can be apprehended by means of the two 'indefinite' objectives *Something is black* and *Something is square*. But these two objectives have also more 'immediate' objects – what I call their intentions here – namely, the different objects *something black* and *something square*. Meinong's indeterminate objects correspond here to our intentions; the determinate objects which are somehow also intended, correspond to the objects in the sense in which Salzburg is the object of the two definite descriptions mentioned above.

But Meinong's new view is still not correct. It now has one entity too many; for we must keep in mind that Meinong has in the meantime – since the *Hume Studies* – also discovered objectives. To see this clearly, consider the description 'the birthplace of Mozart.' According to Meinong, there are three non-mental entities connected with this description: (1) the determinate object which is (the city of) *Salzburg*, (2) the indeterminate object *the birthplace of Mozart*, and (3) the objective *the entity which is the birthplace of Mozart*. By means of (3) we are said to apprehend directly, so to speak, (2), and by means of (2), indirectly, (1). The one entity too many is (2). According to our view of descriptions (2) and (3) are really the same. The complex part of a state of affairs which a description represents and which is the entity (3) describes the city of Salzburg which is the entity (1); in addition to the part of the state of affairs and what it describes, there is no further entity involved. Here, then, is our criticism of Meinong's introduction of indeterminate objects. By means of certain objectives of so-being we do not apprehend indeterminate objects in Meinong's sense, but determinate objects. But these determinate objects must be distinguished from the objectives through which they are apprehended. Definite and indefinite descriptions are thus connected with only two kinds of entities, namely, with certain objects which are described and with certain parts of objectives by means of which these objects are described. Meinong, we may surmise, was misled by the grammatical form of description expressions. Although he saw quite clearly, in distinction to Frege and Russell and to his lasting credit, that descriptions involve objectives of so-being (predicative parts of states of affairs), he also thought mistakenly that they must involve certain indeterminate objects, since they behave, grammatically speaking, like terms. The description 'something (which is) black,' for example, describes quite clearly the blackboard in question, and it also involves quite obviously a predication and, hence, an objective of so-being. But this is all that is involved: the blackboard and the objective. 'Something black' is not a name (term) for an object, the indeterminate object *something black*.

But Meinong, as I said, does at least rectify the earlier mistake of the *Hume Studies*: the difference between two descriptions of the same thing is no longer accounted for solely in mental terms, in terms of ideas, but has now its objective counterpart in the form of a difference between indeterminate objects. In this connection, Meinong criticizes his own earlier view by citing Husserl's example of the victor of Jena and the vanquished of Waterloo. His complaints are that the terms 'content' and 'object' have, as a consequence of that mistaken view, not been clearly separated and that the notion of an object has not been seen in its full generality. It is clear, though, from Husserl's *Logical Investigations* that Husserl, too, realized Twardowski's earlier mistake and tried to avoid it. [23]

The very fact that Meinong now distinguishes between the two indeterminate objects *something black* and *something square* proves how misleading his contention is that the connection between content and object is many-many rather than one-one. This contention, we must realize, rests entirely on the assumption that the contents in question are the contents of presentations, that is, that they are ideas. As soon as we turn to the contents of judgments and assumptions, contents which may differ from the underlying ideas and which are coordinated to objectives rather than objects, we notice that the intentional connection is one-one after all. One content of a judgment or assumption intends precisely one of these indefinite objects by means of precisely one objective of so-being. For example, the judgment that something is black has a content – different from the idea of black – which intends one and only one objective, namely, the state of affairs that something is black; and by means of this state of affairs one and only one indeterminate object is meant, namely, the object *something black*. Similarly, the judgment that something is square has a content which intends precisely one objective and, by means of it, precisely one indeterminate object. Furthermore, this latter state of affairs and this latter object are not the same as the state of affairs that something is black and the object something black. Conversely, one and the same content cannot be said to be associated with different intentions, as soon as we are talking, as we should, about the content of a judgment or assumption.

Therefore, if we sharply distinguish between an idea and the content of a judgment or assumption which is built upon that idea, then we are not tempted to assert that the relationship between a content and its intention is many-many rather than one-one. Does Meinong distinguish between ideas and the contents of judgments and assumptions? There are some brief passages in the second edition of *Über Annahmen* where he does.[24] But he is not too explicit on the matter, not as explicit, say, as Husserl in his magnificent analysis of the many meanings of Brentano's dogma that every mental act either is a presentation or rests on one.[25] The fact that Meinong argues for a many-many relationship seems to indicate that he sometimes inadvertently slides back to his earlier view, according to which the content of every act is an idea.

Meinong discovers apprehension by means of so-being in connection with an old problem of his philosophy. Let me remind you of this problem. Consider the presentation with the object: *relation R holding between A and B* ([A, B]). Meinong believes that there are only two things that could happen to the ideas of R, A, and B so that the idea of this complex object is formed. First, a new idea of another relation, R', may be added. R' is the relation that connects R, A, and B, into the complex object *relation R between A and B*. Meinong rejects this possibility because it leads to an infinite regress. The second possibility is that the three ideas enter into a real relation so that they form a complex idea. It is this complex idea, then, which intends the complex object. But Meinong has to reject this alternative as well; for he holds that the intentional relation is an ideal relation. He argues that the intentional relation between the idea of R and R, between the idea of A and A, and between the idea of B and B can in no way be altered when these three ideas enter into some kind of real relationship with each other. This means that the idea of R will continue to intend R, no matter what happens to it; no matter how it may get related to other ideas. The connection between the idea of R and R, in other words, is fixed once and for all.

In the first edition of *Über Annahmen*, Meinong admitted, therefore, that he cannot explain how ideas of complex entities are possible at all. He never seriously considered an alternative which we advocated, namely, the view that the ideas of complex objects are not themselves complex. Even in the second edition, he really sees no way out of the problem.[26] But he thinks that he can shed some light on the problem by talking about the function of assumptions and judgments in the apprehension of objects. A complex object like [A, B], he asserts, can only be apprehended by means of the corresponding objective, namely, the objective: R *holds between A and B*. In general: 'Where there is a complex entity, there is also an objective as an integral feature of it, and if one wants to apprehend the complex, one can do that in no other way than by apprehending also the objective.'[27] Now, this principle shows, according to Meinong, that presentations cannot possibly suffice for the apprehension of complex objects, that is, of objects of higher order. As far as objectives are concerned, we already know that they can only be apprehended by judgments and assumptions. Thus we arrive at the conclusion that no complex entity can be apprehended merely by means of a presentation.

Meinong's line of reasoning at this point is not too clear. What he has shown is, at best, something which we already know from an earlier argument, namely, that a mere presentation never suffices for the apprehension of an object. The real problem about the apprehension of complex entities remains completely untouched by Meinong's consideration. This problem concerns the nature of those contents which intend complex objects. Is such a content an idea, namely, the idea of the underlying presentation which leads to an assumption or judgment? If so, is it complex or simple? If it is complex, how can we get around the conclusion stated in the last paragraph to the effect that a single idea can never be made to change its intention, no matter how it is combined with other ideas? Or is this content not an idea; is it, perhaps, the content of an assumption or judgment? If so, how does it differ from the underlying idea? Or is there, perhaps, no underlying idea at all? In addition, we have the questions: if the content is the content of an assumption or judgment, is it complex or simple? If it is complex, how are we to avoid the conclusion of the last paragraph which we just repeated? Meinong does not answer any of these questions. The apprehension of complex entities remains a mystery as far as the nature of the contents is concerned which are involved in this kind of apprehension.

X

Modalities

The discovery of objectives leads Meinong gradually away from a psychological characterization of modalities.[1] Or rather, to certain mental characteristics, Meinong gradually adds non-mental counterparts, and the latter become more and more important. Instead of evidence, necessity becomes the center of discussion; instead of truth, factuality is now being considered; and instead of probability, Meinong now is talking about possibility. These objective modalities are not characteristics of mental acts, but are characteristics of objectives. Meinong's analysis of these characteristics is one of his greatest ontological achievements. But this very analysis brings also a number of problems into sharp focus, problems which have accumulated in Meinong's ontology and which still await some kind of a solution.

Foremost among these problems are some that center around the notion of factuality. What distinguishes a factual from a non-factual objective? Are there, in the sense of *Aussersein*, pure objectives just as there are pure objects? And how are factual objectives apprehended? Is their factuality given to the mind in the same way in which they themselves are presented? These are just a few of the many questions that arise in regard to Meinong's view on one kind of being.

An objective may be either factual or unfactual (actual or not actual). Is there any other possibility? Meinong clings tenaciously to the view that there is. To say of an objective that it is (merely) possible, he maintains, is to say that it is neither factual nor not factual. Thus there is a third alternative between factuality and unfactuality. There is, if you wish, a third truth value. Meinong's book on possibility and probability is, to a very large extent, an attempt to make sense of a 'many-valued logic.' That this attempt encounters considerable difficulties goes without saying.

Possible objectives, Meinong believes, involve incomplete objects.

This idea raises a whole series of urgent questions about the nature of incomplete objects. What kinds of incomplete objects are there? How are incomplete objects related to complete ones? And how are complete objects apprehended, if only incomplete ones can, strictly speaking, be before the mind?

In the following sections, I shall take up these three main clusters of problems.

1 A List of Modal Properties

Meinong proposes a tentative list of modalities. [2] He mentions actuality (factuality), possibility, necessity, truth and falsehood, probability, certainty, and evidence. As we shall see, only the first three characteristics (and their opposites) turn out to be properties of objectives. An objective may either be actual or it may not be actual. To this distinction on the side of the objectives, there corresponds on the side of the mental acts the distinction between truth and falsehood. An objective may be possible (to a certain degree) or it may be impossible. On the mental side, we find, correspondingly, the distinction between probability (to a certain degree) and impossibility, in the sense of 'not even probable to any degree.' Finally, to the characteristics of necessity and impossibility, there corresponds the mental feature of rational evidence; an objective is necessary if and only if its factuality can be judged with rational evidence; it is impossible if and only if its unfactuality can be judged with rational evidence.

Meinong takes a closer look at factuality. A factual objective, as is obvious, has the ontological status of subsistence. Meinong reminds us of the way in which factual objectives can also be characterized by means of a certain kind of judgment: an objective is factual if and only if it can, under favorable circumstances, be apprehended with evidence and certainty. But this does not mean, as he stresses, that to think of a factual objective is to think of evidence and certainty. [3] The factuality of an objective, Meinong seems to be saying in this context, is not inferred from the evidence and certainty of the judgment which intends the objective. Thus he now rejects his earlier view. According to that view, evidence is the only feature accessible to us which guarantees that our judgments are not merely accidentally true. Meinong, we recall, argued that we can only escape from complete skepticism if we admit that judgments may have the characteristic of evidence. According to his new view, though, factuality is not merely inferred, but apprehended. And this raises the important question as to how precisely it is apprehended.

Meinong reminds us of the fact that judgments, just like presentations, have contents. And just as there correspond, in general, to different objects different ideas, so there correspond to different objectives, different contents of judgments:[4]

> In order to judge being on one occasion, non-being on another, on one occasion subsistence, on another so-being, there must occur judgments with different contents, while differences in regard to the acts seem here to play no important role. And just as one has sufficiently justified the intellectual possession, if one may put it so, of an object if one can refer to the possession of a presentation with the appropriate content, so everything necessary has been accomplished in regard to our acquaintance with the basic features of objectives, if one has judgments with the appropriate contents. What existence and subsistence is, what positive and negative being is, that I apprehend by means of the corresponding affirmative and negative judgments, respectively; and this as immediately as the color by means of the color-sensation: as little as there occurs here a 'reflection' on the sensing, so little occurs there a reflection on the judgment. But now the same would have to be said in regard to factuality, if one could point at some content-like feature of judgments which corresponds to factuality as its natural means of apprehension.

The problem is clear: Meinong must search for a 'content-like feature' of judgments by means of which we apprehend the factuality of objectives. This search proves to be in vain, even though it looks at first glance rather promising. After all, we have already discovered that certainty and evidence are those features of judgments which correspond to factuality. What could be more natural, therefore, than to assume that evidence and certainty simply constitute that 'content-like feature' for which we are looking? But Meinong notices immediately that our first impression is deceptive; for we are faced with another difficulty: 'May we conceive of evidence and certainty as determinations of the content of judgments, although it is so much more natural, on first glance, to ascribe them to the act of judgment?'[5] Certainty, Meinong claims without hesitation, is indeed a feature of the act rather than the content. The very same proposition may be believed, for example, with different degrees of certainty. But the situation is not equally clear in regard to evidence.

On the one hand, there is the fact that while there are no judgments without some degree of certainty, there are judgments which have no evidence whatsoever. And this fact seems to speak, so Meinong argues, for the view that evidence is a matter of the content rather than of the quality of the act. On the other hand, it seems to be the case that the presence or absence of evidence does not influence the objective apprehended in the slightest. And this seems to speak against the view that evidence is a feature of the content. Meinong is facing a dilemma: factuality, as a property of objectives, must be brought before the mind by means of a content-like feature; this feature, most naturally, is thought of as evidence; yet, whether a judgment has or does not have evidence makes absolutely no difference to what it intends. This dilemma springs from an even deeper problem. By considering the nature of evidence, Meinong slowly comes to grips with this problem. Factual objectives, as they are presented to the mind, simply do not seem to differ from unfactual ones; and how can one possibly reconcile this fact with one's conviction that an inspection of objectives can reveal which objectives are factual and which ones are not?

Meinong, groping for a way out, concentrates on the question: Does a judgment with evidence have the same intention as one without evidence? It may seem that it does; for whether or not the judgment has evidence, the state of affairs judged is the same. But if this is so, then evidence cannot possibly be that content-like feature which supposedly apprehends the factuality of objectives. Meinong asserts that the presence of evidence does make a difference to what is judged, all appearance to the contrary. This becomes clear, he argues, if one turns from the judgment of an objective to a judgment about it. 'When one says, for example, "That the angle in the half-circle is a right angle, that is a fact," then the factuality as a property of the previously judged objective is impressed upon us with such an immediacy that there can be no doubt that this property of the objective must have been apprehended from the very beginning.'[6] Meinong thus maintains that an evident judgment differs from one without evidence in that the former apprehends a certain feature of its objective, factuality, while the latter does not.

His way out, though, is rather unsatisfactory. First of all, his view clashes with the phenomena. No objective ever appears before the mind wearing its factuality on its sleeve. When I judge with certainty and evidence, whatever that may mean, that $2+2=4$, I judge this particular state of affairs and no other. And when I merely believe, without certainty and evidence, that $2+2=4$, I believe exactly the same state of affairs. Meinong himself has to admit, as we saw, that the factuality which is presumably involved appears only when we turn from the first-level judgment to a second-level judgment about the factuality of an object. But even in this regard his argument is fallacious. What appears, we must counter his assertion, is not at all the factuality of a factual objective. When we turn to the second-level judgment O is factual, factuality appears before the mind, irrespective of whether or not O itself is factual. Thus we cannot possibly argue, as Meinong does, that what appears on the second level is what was already contained in the objective of the first-level judgment. Even if factuality does not pertain to an objective, it can occur before the mind as soon as we turn to the corresponding judgment of the second level.

Furthermore, what precisely could it mean to claim that factuality was already *contained* in the original objective? Put differently, what precisely was the original objective apprehended by the evident judgment? We can distinguish between the two objectives (1) $2+2=4$ and (2) $2+2=4$ *is factual*, but neither one of these two can be the original objective of the evident judgment. The original objective cannot be of type (1) because an objective of this type can presumably be before the mind, even if the act involved is without evidence. This is particularly obvious when we switch examples and consider an unfactual objective like $2+2=5$. But the original objective cannot be of type (2) either; for this kind of objective is before the mind if and only if a judgment of the second level occurs. According to Meinong's view, the objective apprehended by the evident judgment is thus neither of form (1) nor of form (2). But Meinong does not tell us what structure it has. Nor is there any plausible candidate for the role of this objective.

It is clear that the objective apprehended by the evident judgment cannot be a first-level objective; for such objectives can be before the mind even when they are not factual. Nor does this result change when we turn to second-level objectives: they, too, can be before the mind, irrespective of whether they are factual or not. Hence, Meinong would not be better off, as one might suspect for a moment, if he coordinated to evident judgments, not objectives of the first level, but objectives of the second level. He could have held, one might think, that judgments without evidence apprehend the 'pure objective,' the objective of first level, while evident judgments apprehend objectives of the second level. This view is excluded, as we just saw, by the fact that such second-level objectives can be apprehended, not only by judgments without evidence, but even by false judgments.

Finally, consider what happens when someone judges without evidence that $2+2=4$. This judgment differs, presumably, in regard to its content from the corresponding evident one. But if there is a difference in content, then there is a difference in intention, that is, in the objective apprehended. Hence it follows that one cannot really judge the very same objective once with evidence and once without evidence, as Meinong claims.

From factuality, Meinong turns to possibility.[7] Factuality, he says, constitutes one end of a line which contains various degrees of possibility. The other end consists of unfactuality. Since possibility allows for degrees, it makes sense to say of objectives that they are very possible, slightly possible, hardly possible, etc. Possibility is thus conceived of as reduced factuality.

And here, too, the question arises as to how possibility, as a property of objectives, can be apprehended. A possible objective, Meinong answers, is apprehended if (a) certainty is replaced by mere surmise, and (b) some evidence nevertheless remains in the judgment: 'If I have the right, based on evidence, to surmise that, say, a certain result in a game will occur, then there exists, of course, not the factuality but the possibility of this result; and this possibility is the greater, the stronger the justified surmise is.'[8]

But this answer will do not do, as he himself immediately notices. What distinguishes the apprehension of factuality from the apprehension of possibility cannot simply be a certain degree of certainty; for it is evidence, not certainty, that is supposed to apprehend factuality. Hence it cannot be the case that this same sort of evidence is present when a merely possible objective is apprehended. It is obvious what Meinong will say next. He distinguishes simply between two kinds of evidence: evidence for certainty and evidence for surmise. The former is the content-like feature which apprehends factuality; the latter, the content-like feature which apprehends possibilities. Evidence for surmise, unlike evidence for certainty, allows of degrees. By means of these degrees, one apprehends the various degrees of objective possibility.

A third kind of evidence, as is to be expected, is then assigned to the task of apprehending necessity.[9] This kind is called rational evidence. An objective is necessary if and only if it can be apprehended by an *a priori* judgment, that is, by a judgment which has rational evidence. Impossibility, the opposite of necessity, is explicated in terms of necessity: An objective is impossible, in this particular sense, if and only if it is necessary that it is unfactual. We must therefore distinguish between impossibility as the opposite of necessity and impossibility as the negation of possibility. In the latter sense, an objective is impossible if and only if it is not possible, that is, if it is unfactual. Ultimately, therefore, Meinong has three 'rational modalities' and three 'empirical modalities.' The three rational modalities are: necessity, rational impossibility (explained as the necessity of unfactuality), and rational possibility (explained as the negation of rational impossibility). The three empirical modalities are: factuality, unfactuality, and possibility. Truth and falsehood, Meinong remarks in conclusion, are not properties of objectives. He does not say in so many words that they are nothing, but one can infer from his remarks that to say of a judgment that it is true or that it is false is to say of it nothing more nor less than that it intends a factual or that it intends an unfactual objective. Thus while there corresponds some feature or another of mental acts to such terms as 'rational evidence,' 'evidence for certainty,' and 'evidence for surmise,' no such mental feature is connected with the terms 'true' and 'false.' Degrees of probability, be it noted, are identified with degrees of evidence for surmise. Probability, as distinguished from possibility, is thus a feature of mental acts.

2 *Incomplete Objects*

According to Meinong's general view of possibility, an objective may be neither factual nor unfactual, but may be something in between, so to speak, namely, possible (to a certain degree). But this notion of possibility clashes with the Principle of the Excluded Middle, according to which every objective is either factual or not factual (unfactual). There is simply no room for merely possible objectives. Nor does Meinong's earlier paradigm of a possible objective make his case any stronger. He claimed, as we just saw, that an objective concerning a certain future result of a game of chance is neither factual nor unfactual, but is merely possible. But is it really true that an objective like *The next throw with this die will show a six* is neither factual nor unfactual? Obviously not. Of course, the die has not as yet been thrown, and we do not as yet know what the result will be, but all of this has absolutely no bearing on the factuality or unfactuality of the objective in question.[10] The factuality (or unfactuality) of this objective, contrary to Meinong's assertion, 'exists' even before the die has been cast. Here, too, there is no room for possibility as envisaged by Meinong.

Meinong becomes aware of this objection against his conception of possibility and takes the bull by the horns.[11] It may be true, he admits, that a great number of objectives do not allow for a degree of possibility. They are either factual or unfactual. For these objectives, the Principle of Excluded Middle holds. But may there not be, in addition, other kinds of objectives, objectives which do not obey the Principle and which constitute the realm where possibility dwells? If there are such objectives, then we can divide all objectives into two groups. One group comprises objectives which do not have any degrees of possibility, but which are either factual or unfactual. The second group consists of objectives which are neither factual nor unfactual, but which are possible to some degree. For this group the Principle of the Excluded Middle would obviously not hold. Is there such a second group?

Meinong sets out in search of this second kind of objectives. If the search is successful, then his notion of possibility is vindicated, and so as he sees the situation, is his explication of the objective basis for probability. In modern terms, nothing less is at stake than the possibility of making sense of so-called many-valued logics. Whatever we may think of the occasion for Meinong's search or of its eventual result, one praise he undoubtedly deserves: Unlike so many contemporary philosophers who discuss the same topic, Meinong never confuses sentences with what they are about, namely, objectives. His search never veers from the straight and narrow path of ontology. Nor does he ever confuse epistemological or even linguistic considerations with ontological ones. The object of his search is as simple as it is, in the view of many, unattainable: a kind of objective which is neither factual nor unfactual, which neither subsists nor does not subsist, which neither is actual nor not actual, but which is possible.

This search is guided by the idea that just as there are incomplete objects, there may be incomplete objectives. Meinong, first, explains in great detail the distinction between complete and incomplete objects. Then, second, he claims that objectives which contain incomplete objects are themselves incomplete. Third and finally, he maintains that incomplete objectives are neither factual nor unfactual, but have the ontological status of possibilities.

Meinong begins his long journey into the land of incomplete objects with the declaration that the nature of every object can be analyzed into a collection of 'determinations of so-being.' It is clear, he continues, that the determinations of every existent are rather large in number; and if we count, not only the properties which a thing has, but also those which it does not have, then their number must be infinitely large. [12] For, as Meinong argues, there is no object, no existing or nonexisting object, no object beyond being even, which can be excluded from the 'determinations' of an existing object. This is the very meaning of the Principle of the Excluded Middle. Similar results hold, according to Meinong, for 'attributes which, since they belong to a concrete object, have themselves been made concrete.' [13] In other words, instances, too, have infinitely many determinations. Notice, first, that Meinong here once more reverts to his earliest view that a property can become an instance by becoming part of an existent complex, a view which we discussed in the very first chapter. Notice, second, that instances are here explicitly counted among the complete objects. They are complete in regard to being, since they exist; and they are complete in regard to every property, since the Principle of Excluded Middle holds for them.

But compare now an existent complex or an instance with an entity like the object *something blue*, and ask yourself whether or not this object is extended. Of course, we know that blue things are extended. But we are not here concerned with blue existents. Rather, we are talking about the object *something blue*. Meinong claims, as we saw in the last chapter, that this object is not extended; it does not have this determination. But he also maintains that it is not true that this object does not have this determination. Similarly, the incomplete object *something extended* is neither blue, nor is it not blue. [14]

If we accept that *something blue* as such is not extended, does it not follow that it must therefore have the 'property' of not being extended? Meinong argues that this inference would be wrong. He considers a different example and asks: Is the triangle, *in abstracto*, isosceles? Obviously not. Does it then follow that the triangle is not isosceles? Meinong argues as follows. Every particular triangle has all the properties which the triangle *in abstracto* has. Now assume that a particular triangle is isosceles. If *the triangle* as such is non-isosceles, then this particular triangle has to be isosceles, but this is, of course, impossible.

Meinong points out that the two sentences (1) 'It is false that A is F' and (2) 'A is not F' (A is non-F') do not mean the same thing, if his view on incomplete objects is correct. Nor, of course, are these two sentences equivalent. Meinong tries to explain the non-equivalence by claiming that (1) represents an objective of second level, while (2) represents an objective of first level. Since we deal here with very different objectives, Meinong seems to be saying, it is not surprising that, say, an objective presented by a sentence of form (1) should subsist, while the corresponding objective represented by a sentence of form (2) does not exist. Needless to say, I do not see the force of this argument.

The Principle of Excluded Middle supposedly does not only hold for properties, but is alleged to hold for being as well: An entity either has being (it exists or subsists) or it does not; there is no third possibility. Meinong, we saw, claims that all entities with being are completely determined. Do, conversely, all complete entities have being? Meinong does not think so: 'Nothing is easier than to conceive of objects which do not exist or which, since they contain an inner contradiction, do not even subsist, without its being the case that, for this reason, it could be claimed that any one of their determinations has to be left open.'[15] But at this point Meinong does not give an example of such an object.

Granted that there are such objects, what about incomplete objects? It is clear that they cannot have being; for Meinong has asserted, as we just noted, that all objects with being are also complete. Meinong concludes, therefore, that *the triangle* is incomplete in regard to being as well. *The triangle* thus is neither isosceles nor is it not isosceles; and it neither has being nor does it not have being. In general, objects which are incomplete in regard to their properties are also incomplete in regard to being, unless their particular nature excludes their being.

Meinong turns to the familiar topic of the apprehension of objects. He wishes to show that incomplete objects play an essential role in all such apprehension. Assume that there is a brown door before you, Meinong says, so that presentation will present you with the data

Brown, Square, etc. Then there may also occur the corresponding existential judgments concerning these data. So far, Meinong just calls our attention to the familiar first steps of his theory of perception. But now a thought occurs to him which threatens to destroy this theory. What kind of objects are these so-called immediate data of presentation to which Meinong refers by words beginning with capital letters? What kind of an object, say, is Brown? Meinong thinks he has found another kind of incomplete object. The question of whether Brown is square, he claims, makes no sense.[16] Not only is it obvious that Brown cannot be square, the very nature of the object Brown prohibits any kind of determination, either positive or negative, by means of the property square. Thus Brown is incomplete in regard to being square; it is also incomplete in regard to being brown and in regard to many other properties. And similar considerations hold for the object Square, as distinguished from the property of being square.

Meinong's view is extremely puzzling. The main puzzle, of course, is to what kind of objects these data Brown, Square, etc., belong. One may be tempted to think of them as instances; for they are presumably the immediate intentions of acts of presentation. A process of abstraction, as Meinong might put it, has not as yet taken place, so that the property has not as yet appeared before the mind. But this interpretation cannot possibly be correct. Instances, Meinong told us just a few pages ago, are existents just like the complexes of which they are parts. Thus instances cannot possibly be incomplete objects. On the other hand, it is also clear that the object Brown, for example, must be distinguished, according to Meinong, from the incomplete object *something brown*. I must confess that I have no consistent interpretation of what Meinong means when he talks of the object Brown. But I shall assume that Brown is, roughly, a property which, as it appears before the mind, is not individuated.[17]

Whatever kind of object Brown is, it is to be distinguished from *something brown*. According to Meinong, the object *something brown* is incomplete in regard to the property of being heavy; but this does not mean that something brown may not also be heavy. Brown is also incomplete in regard to the property of being heavy, but in this case the very nature of the object Brown prohibits it from ever being heavy or not being heavy. Brown is by necessity incomplete in regard to being heavy, while something brown is only accidentally incomplete in regard to this property. This distinction makes some sense if we think of Brown as an instance. That instance, one may argue, cannot possibly be heavy; nor can it possibly be not heavy. Instances are simply not the kind of things that are or are not heavy. Something brown, on the other hand, belongs to the category of complexes, and complexes are the kind of things which can be heavy or not heavy.

But Meinong's distinction also makes sense if we think of Brown, not as an instance, but as a property; for then we can appeal to a similar kind of consideration. Properties, in distinction to complexes, are simply not the kind of entities which can be heavy or not heavy. Recall also that Meinong claims that Brown is not brown. Once more, this makes sense if Brown is an instance and also if it is a property. If it is an instance, then we could argue that an instance of brown is not brown because for something to be brown is to *contain* an instance of brown, but an instance of brown does not contain an instance of brown.[18] If it is a property, then it is clear that one may deny that the property brown is itself brown.[19]

The puzzle that surrounds the mysterious entity Brown does not completely elude Meinong's attention. He notices it when he suddenly realizes that his theory of perception must be changed if Brown is an incomplete object.[20] According to that theory, as he had just reaffirmed it, the rudimentary first steps of perception consist of experiencing an idea which presents the object Brown and of an existential judgment about this object. But if Brown is an incomplete object, then it is indeterminate in regard to being. Hence all such perceptual judgments would turn out to be false. Meinong concludes that there must exist another kind of apprehension which makes the very first contact with reality. The original theory of perception must be amended. He tries to get around the difficulty by appealing to apprehension by means of so-being. But it is not clear at all how an appeal to apprehension by means of so-being is supposed to prevent the unacceptable consequence that all perceptual judgments turn out to be false.

Nor is this the end of Meinong's troubles. When the content of the presentation is used to apprehend *something brown* rather than Brown, then this apprehension supposedly intends every object which is brown, while the same content may also be used, on another occasion, to apprehend the unique object Brown. Thus Meinong tries to underline the difference between Brown and something brown in terms of a difference between idea and intention: The relation between idea and Brown is one-one, while the relation between idea and the things which are brown is one-many. This fact explains, according to Meinong, why apprehension by means of so-being is not, like apprehension by means of being, restricted to incomplete objects:[21]

In this case [of reference by means of being] content and object are so close, as it were, that for the apprehension of a complete object a complete content would be required or, more precisely, a complex of contents such that each one [of the contents] would be adequate to one of the determinations of the object, a possibility which is already excluded by the infinitely large number of parts of such a complex. On the other hand, in the case of reference by means of so-being, it suffices if the content merely points at, as it were, the object to be apprehended. This is the case for every object which has that determination or complex of determinations which the content, which is the basis for the reference by means of so-being, can present in the primary sense (hence, for simple reference by means of being).

The idea of Brown, we saw, may give rise to an apprehension of the incomplete object *something brown*. How can it lead to an apprehension of a complete brown object? Meinong's answer is extremely simple: 'If I want to refer by means of the thought *a brown square* to a particular thing, without having to know of determinations which distinguish it from other things, then I merely have to think of *a particular brown square*.'[22]
Meinong considers two objections to this view. It may be argued that the simple addition of the determination of being particular could not possibly turn an incomplete object into a complete one. For example, by adding the determination heavy to the properties brown and square, we still get an incomplete object and not a complete one, namely, the incomplete object *something which is square, brown, and heavy*. It seems that we would have to add infinitely many further properties before we would get a complete object, since the complete object is supposed to consist of infinitely many properties (instances). Meinong replies that this objection equates constituent with non-constituent determinations. While it is indeed true that the addition of a single constituent property does not complete our incomplete object, the same does not hold when we add the non-constitutent property of being a particular thing. But is it really true, one may also object, that whenever we mean complete objects, their completeness is explicitly included in our meaning? Meinong replies that this is indeed the case. When we think of a triangle or an airplane, we would not hesitate to say that we are thinking of a particular triangle or a particular airplane.
In the last chapter, we saw that, according to Meinong, two different incomplete objects may aim at the same complete object. For example, the door in Meinong's room may be apprehended by the incomplete object *something brown* as well as by the incomplete object *something square*. It is clear that we are here dealing with a 'mediated' apprehension. What is apprehended directly, if I may put it so, is the incomplete object. By means of it, though, another object is also apprehended. Meinong tries to shed some light on this situation by making a number of important distinctions.
First, he distinguishes between the immediate object of an idea,

say, the object Brown, and what he calls an auxiliary object, namely, the object *something brown*. [23] For every immediate object, there is precisely one such auxiliary object. If you conceive of the immediate object as a property (simple or complex), then the auxiliary object is simply the object of the notion of something which has this property. All auxiliary objects, Meinong remarks, are incomplete. Second, he distinguishes between auxiliary objects and intended objects. The auxiliary object *something brown*, for example which is directly apprehended, also apprehends those complete objects which form the extension of the property brown. What makes this second distinction interesting is a third one. Meinong thinks that there are also incomplete objects which are somewhat more nearly complete than the incomplete auxiliary objects. Consider, for example, the auxiliary object *something bounded by three straight lines*. Meinong argues that since we attribute to the triangle not only this property of being enclosed by three straight lines, but also many other essential properties, the incomplete object *the triangle* cannot just have the properties of the auxiliary object. The triangle, he therefore says, is a *completed* object, but not a *complete* object. We must distinguish, then, between the auxiliary object, the completed object, and the complete object.

Meinong uses these distinctions to explicate two notions, namely, the notion of an analytic judgment and the notion of a concept. Every concept, he says, as it is given by its definition, has first of all the incomplete object which is constituted by that definition. [24] This is the auxiliary object. Next, Meinong turns to the distinction between analytic and synthetic judgments. He takes it that this distinction is not to be explicated in mental, but rather in nonmental, terms. And then he formulates the traditional problem: 'But how could one correctly ascribe something to the object in the subject place which does not belong to it? Hence every true affirmative judgment would have to be analytic.' He solves the problem by saying that a judgment is analytic if and only if the predicate property is a part of the completed object which functions as the subject of the judgment.

For our purposes, Meinong's second explication is more important. Meinong starts with the relationship between a concept and its extension. The concept *triangle*, he maintains, is first of all a concept of individuals. By means of this concept, we apprehend individual triangles. Furthermore, some concepts have more than one object, others have precisely one object. But even concepts of the first kind can be used to intend just one object. Or they can be used to mean several objects, but not all of the objects which fall under the concept. In this fashion, Meinong gets the concepts: *all triangles, some (but not all) triangles*, and *any triangle* from the concept *triangle*. How does the concept *triangle* differ from the concept *all triangles*? Meinong thinks that there may be a difference in the immediate objects of these two concepts. He surmises that concepts like *all triangles, some triangles,* and *any triangle* intend as their immediate objects classes, so that their ultimate objects are apprehended by means of an object which is a class.

The concept *triangle* is, according to Meinong, the content of a certain presentation. This content has an auxiliary object. Let us assume this object is represented by the expression 'something bounded by three straight lines.' But the content has also a completed object. This object would be represented by an expression of the form 'something bounded by three straight lines whose angles are equal to two right angles, and which, furthermore, has the properties *F, G,* etc.'; the properties *F, G,* etc., are properties which belong necessarily to all triangles. Neither one of these two incomplete objects, however, is as yet the ultimate object of the concept. Rather, the ultimate objects of this concept are completed objects, namely, individual triangles. By comparison, consider the concept *President of the United States in 1972.* This concept has just one ultimate object, namely, a complete object, a certain person. But it, too, has an auxiliary object as well as a completed object; and the ultimate object is apprehended by means of these incomplete objects. Similarly, for the concept *all triangles.* The auxiliary object, in this case, would be a class, say, the class represented by the expression 'things which are bounded by three straight lines.' Then there would also be a completed object of the type: *things which are bounded by three straight lines and whose inner angles are equal to two right angles, etc.* Finally, the ultimate objects of these concepts would again be complete objects, namely, individual triangles.

But not only complete objects can be ultimate objects. We may have occasion to concern ourselves with *the* triangle or with *the* (kinds of) triangles. In these cases, the ultimate objects are completed incomplete objects; the immediate objects are also incomplete objects, either auxiliary objects or, at least, even less nearly completed objects than the respective ultimate objects. *Genera* and *species* are thus identified with completed objects.

Let us sum up Meinong's distinctions, this time with reference to the idea brown. In addition to this idea, there is the strange entity Brown, which is most easily identified with an instance, but which cannot be an instance, since it is said to be incomplete. Then there is the auxiliary object *something brown.* Furthermore, there is the completed object which is constituted by all the other properties which necessarily belong to brown things. And, finally, there are the individual brown things. Thus we have three incomplete objects and one kind of complete object. The incomplete objects are: (1) the strange entity Brown, (2) the auxiliary object *something brown,* and (3) the species 'the brown thing.' The complete objects are the individual things which are brown, that is, all complexes which contain an instance of brown. By means of the concept, either Brown or the object *something brown* can be before the mind. If the latter is before the mind, then by means of it, in turn, either a completed object or complete objects are before the mind. Thus, *the triangle* is before the mind if the auxiliary object *something bounded by three straight lines* is before the mind; triangles are before the mind, if the auxiliary object *particular (complete) objects bounded by three straight lines* is before the mind.

Meinong's theory of incomplete objects, as here outlined, has two important features. First, there is the claim that Brown is an incomplete object. Meinong's argument for this contention, as we have seen, is of quite a different sort from the argument which he presented earlier for the incompleteness of the object *something brown*. The latter argument rested on the indubitable fact that the object *something brown*, as it is before the mind, is thought of neither as, say, square nor as being not square. The argument that the entity Brown is incomplete, on the other hand, was based on the fact that it makes no sense to say of such an entity that it is square or that it is not square. Brown, we might say, belongs to a category such that it is nonsense to say that entities of this category are square or to say that they are not square.

The second important feature consists in Meinong's explanation of why we cannot be acquainted with complete objects directly. In the last chapter, we compared Meinong's view with the views of Husserl and Moore. Now, we have encountered another argument for the conclusion which is reached by all three of these philosophers, namely, the conclusion that we are never acquainted with a complete object. Such acquaintance, Meinong claims, would presuppose the presence of a content of infinite complexity. For each of the infinitely many properties of which the complex object consists, there would have to be an idea, so that the idea of the whole object would have to consist of these infinitely many partial ideas. Of course, this argument rests on the assumption that the idea of a very complex object must itself be very complex. Moreover, it is only plausible if we think of individual things as complexes of properties. If we distinguish sharply between an individual and the properties which it *has*, but of which it does not *consist*, then there is no reason to assume that the idea of the individual is the complex idea of all its properties. Rather, we can then distinguish between the idea of the individual and the various ideas of its properties. The former would be different from the latter and from any combination of the latter.

Having distinguished between various incomplete objects on the one hand and complete objects on the other, Meinong considers the relationship between these two kinds of objects. Incomplete objects, we saw, are incomplete in regard to being. But is it not the case,

Meinong asks, that *the sphere*, for example, is part of the existing billiard balls which belong to my friend? And if it is a part of these complete objects, must it not partake in their existence? Thus we are led to conclude that *the sphere* cannot really be incomplete in regard to being. Meinong defends his view that incomplete objects are incomplete in regard to being by claiming that *the sphere* is not a part of any existing billiard ball.[26]

But if incomplete objects are not literally parts of complete objects, what is the relationship between them? After all, it must make a difference to *the sphere*, as Meinong puts it, if there actually exists a spherical object. Meinong, therefore, claims that there is a special relationship between the incomplete object *the sphere* and any one of the complete spherical objects. He expresses this fact by saying that the former is *'implektiert'* in the latter. I shall translate this rather outlandish term by the more familiar 'involved.' In general, then, an incomplete object is involved in all those complete objects which have the properties of the incomplete object. Meinong then argues:[27]

> More important than the name is, of course, the fact that the
> incomplete object, as pointed out, does not really exist or subsist
> in the object in which it is involved, but that through the
> existence or subsistence of the latter the involved incomplete
> object is somehow determined, not in regard to its so-being,
> but in regard to its being, so that one can, accordingly, form the
> concept of implexive being, that is, of implexive existence and
> implexive subsistence.

Instead of 'implexive beings,' 'implexive existence,' and similar expressions, I shall use the terms 'pseudo-being,' 'pseudo-existence,' etc.

One may be tempted to think that an incomplete object has pseudo-being if and only if there is an object in which it is involved. But Meinong rejects this explication. He claims that we would then also have to say that an object has pseudo-non-being if and only if an object in which it is involved has non-being. And he claims, second, that such incomplete objects as *the sphere* would therefore have to have both pseudo-being as well as pseudo-non-being; for just as the sphere is involved in the billiard ball which belongs to my friend, so it is involved in the nonexistent ball of ivory which is two miles in diameter. The situation is different for the incomplete object *plane figure bounded by two straight lines*. This object is involved only in objects which have no being. We could therefore say that it has pseudo-non-being. There exists thus a curious asymmetry between incomplete objects which are involved in objects with being and those that are involved only in objects with non-being. The former are always also involved in objects which have no being.

Let us assume, though Meinong, as we saw, would not agree with us, that all complete objects have being. The following partial picture of Meinong's ontology then unfolds. We start once again with a group of properties: F, G, H, etc. There is then a relation of association which combines these properties into complex objects: $<F, G>$, $<F, H>$, etc. If these properties are associated with a moment and/ or place, they form a complete existent object. Such a complete object is infinitely complex. Through some mysterious process the association with moments and/or places also turns the original properties into instances. An instance is said to be a part of the complete object to which it belongs. There is, therefore, a second important relation, in addition to the relation of association. Next, we must ask how, say, $<F>$ is related to the incomplete but completed object $<F, G>$ and to the complete object $<F_1, G_1, etc.>$.[28] There is an obvious answer but it is not Meinong's. F, one could say, is in both cases a part of the more complex object; in the first case, a part in a straightforward way, in the second, a part in the sense that an instance of F is a part of the complete object. Meinong holds instead that a relation holds directly between the object $<F>$ and the other two complex objects. He says that $<F>$ is *involved* in these other two objects. Thus he avoids, once again, having to talk about properties. But $<F>$, as we have seen, plays in Meinong's ontology the role of a property. The relation of involvement, correspondingly, plays the role of exemplification. When we predicate the property of being spherical of a certain billiard ball, we are saying, according to Meinong's ontology, that a certain incomplete object, the sphere, is involved in a certain complete object, the billiard ball.

Since complete objects can only be apprehended by means of incomplete ones, there must occur still another relation between, say, $<F, G>$ and $<F_1, G_1, etc.>$. The object $<F, G>$, we assume, is intended through an (ideal) intentional relation which connects the object with a certain (complex) idea. This relation thus holds always between an idea and an incomplete object. But what can presumably be also intended, at least in some cases, is the complete object which involves the incomplete object $<F, G>$. This further relation between $<F, G>$ and $<F_1, G_1, etc.>$ remains a mystery in Meinong's later philosophy. Nor is there any easy explanation. The specter of representationalism hovers in the background. Some entity has once again been interposed between the mind and its (complete) object. While this entity is traditionally an idea, in Meinong's later philosophy it is the incomplete object by means of which we are said to apprehend a complete object, that is, by means of which we are acquainted with such things as ordinary perceptual objects. And just as traditional presentationalism had to face up to the problem of how ideas are related to what they are ideas of, Meinong has to explain what relationship there is between an incomplete object and its complete counterpart, since only contents can intend anything. Representationalism, we all know from the history of philosophy, eventually leads to idealism. In Meinong's case, this fatal mistake is never made. But Husserl's later philosophy shows how easily the dialectic of incomplete object and complete object, of noema and real thing, invites idealism.

3 *Possibility*

The pseudo-being of an incomplete object depends somehow on the being of a complete object. An incomplete object has pseudo-non-being if and only if it is not invovled in a single object with being. Similarly, an incomplete object would have pseudo-being if and only if it is not involved in a single object without being. We saw that there are no incomplete objects of the latter kind. An incomplete object which is involved in an object with being will always be also involved in some object without being. We find, therefore, that a great many incomplete objects have neither pseudo-being nor pseudo-non-being. They fall somewhere in the middle between these two extremes. Possibility, too, was explicated as lying somewhere in the middle between actuality and its opposite. Meinong now combines these two notions, the notion of pseudo-being and the notion of possibility. Or rather, he uses the former in order to explicate the latter. According to Meinong, 'incomplete objects, insofar as they have pseudo-being to any degree, have the ability to function as subjects in merely possible objectives of being, an ability which, as we saw, complete objects lack.'[29]

What Meinong is driving at is the following view. The sphere, as we have seen, has pseudo-being to a certain degree; it does not have full pseudo-being, since it is also involved in some objects without being. The degree to which an incomplete object has pseudo-being depends somehow on the number of objects with being in which it is involved. Meinong says, for example, that the type of personality which Goethe has or Beethoven has is less possible (*weniger möglich*) than the type of personality of an ordinary person. But by identifying degree of pseudo-being with degree of possibility of being, Meinong completely repudiates his original idea that possibility is something between actuality and its opposite. The sphere either is or it is not involved in an object with being; there is no room for *mere* possibility. Meinong creates the illusion of dealing with three alternatives by postulating the case of full pseudo-being, a case for which there simply are no examples. He pretends that there are three alternatives: an object may have (full) pseudo-being (this is made to correspond to the actuality of an objective), an object may have (full) pseudo-non-being (this is correlated to the opposite of actuality), or an object may have a degree of pseudo-being (this corresponds presumably to possibility). But the first alternative is really no alternative at all. Every object either has pseudo-non-being or it has (some degree of) pseudo-being. And this means that the objectives in question are either not actual or are actual.

From the possibility of being, Meinong turns to the possibility of so-being. An incomplete object, Meinong holds, has certain properties just as a complete object has properties. The round square is round just as an existing billiard ball is round. But a completed incomplete object has the properties which complete it only by virtue of another fact. The triangle, for example, has the property of having inner angles equal to two right angles only by virtue of the fact that every individual triangle has this property. This means, according to Meinong, that the triangle has this property only insofar as it is involved in all individual triangles. Notice that Meinong here speaks of a property as being involved in a complete object. This shows how easy it is to confuse an incomplete object with the property from whence it is born. At any rate, the so-being which we encounter in connection with incomplete completed objects is now called 'implexive so-being.' I shall talk instead of 'pseudo-so-being.'

In regard to pseudo-so-being we can again distinguish between three cases. First, as in the example about triangles just mentioned, the relevant property may be involved in every object with being of the relevant kind. Every triangle, in our example, has the property of having inner angles equal to two right angles. Second, the property may not be involved in any of the objects with being. For example, the triangle does not have a pitch - in the sense of pseudo-non-so-being – since no complete triangle has a pitch. Third, the property may be involved in some objects but not in others: 'It cannot be said, for example, that the triangle is actually isosceles or actually non-isosceles; but it does have the possibility of being isosceles as well as the possibility of being non-isosceles, and the second of these possibilities is obviously greater.'[30]

Let us take another look at the triangle and its relationship to the Principle of the Excluded Middle. The triangle, as an incomplete object, neither has being nor does it not have being. This means that there subsists for it neither an objective of being nor an objective of non-being. But it has possible being; and this means that it has a degree of pseudo-being. It has this degree of pseudo-being because it is involved in objects which have being. I noted a moment ago that that explication of possible being leaves much to be desired. The situation is somewhat better in regard to pseudo-so-being. The triangle does have three sides, if we assume that by 'triangle' we mean something like 'three-sided plane figure.' This is a case of straightforward so-being. But now there is also pseudo-so-being. This kind of predication belongs to completed incomplete objects only in virtue of the fact that certain of their parts (properties) are involved or are not involved in complete objects. Consider the property of having a certain pitch. This property neither belongs to the triangle, nor does it not belong to the triangle. But if we go from so-being to pseudo-so-being, then we can say that in the pseudo-sense, the triangle does not have this pitch, since this property is not involved in a single actual triangle.

Consider the property of having inner angles equal to two right angles. Starting with the earlier mentioned definition of *triangle*, we get a completed incomplete object, if we add this further property. The triangle neither has this property, hor does it not have this property. There is again a violation of the Principle of the Excluded Middle. But if we turn to pseudo-so-being, then we can say that the triangle has this property, since this property is involved in all complete triangles. Finally, consider the property of being isosceles. In a straightforward way the triangle is neither isosceles nor is it not isosceles. And the same is also true when we consider its pseudo-so-being. But here we find a third possibility, namely, that the triangle is possibly isosceles.

Let us try to give the gist of Meinong's explication of possibility, but entirely in our own terminology. As long as we talk about complete objects, the Principle of Excluded Middle holds for their being as well as their so-being. Sentences of the form '*CO* has being' and '*CO* has property *P*' either represent factual objectives or they represent unfactual objectives. There is no third possibility. But this picture changes when we consider sentences about incomplete objects. Consider the case of predication. The sentence '*IO* has the property *P*' has a factual objective if and only if *P* belongs to the incomplete object *IO* 'by definition,' or 'analytically.' If *P* does not belong in this trivial fashion to *IO*, then we cannot conclude that there is a factual objective to the effect that *IO* does not have *P*. In this case we have to switch to pseudo-so-being, that is, to pseudo-predication. Consider, then, the sentence '*IO* pseudo-has the property *P*.' This sentence may have a factual objective, it may have an unfactual objective, or it may even have a merely possible objective. The sentence 'The triangle is isosceles,' for example, represents neither a factual nor an unfactual objective, but represents a possible objective. From our point of view, however, this sentence merely says that all triangles are isosceles. If so, then it is clearly false. It has quite obviously an unfactual objective. But be that as it may, we now have the key to Meinong's explication. Meinong assigns possibility to those objectives which are represented by sentences of the form 'All *F* are *G*' if and only if some *F* are *G* and some F are not G. If all F are G, then this sentence is said to have a factual objective; if no F is G, the sentence has an unfactual objective.

The objective *All F are G* is unfactual, we said, if some F are G and others are not. Meinong can hold that this is not the case, only because he distinguishes between *all F* and *the F*. But *the F* does not really mean here what, more often than not, it means in ordinary discourse either; it does not mean: the one and only one individual thing which is F. Rather, it is supposed to refer to a genus, to an abstract entity. The sentence 'The F is G' is thus really short for: 'F pseudo-has G.' And this, in turn, is short for: 'All complete objects (individuals) which involve the incomplete object $<F>$ also involve the incomplete object $<G>$'. If we neglect for a moment the distinction between a property and the corresponding object, then the sentence simply comes down to one we mentioned earlier: 'All complete objects which have the property F also have the property G.' But this sentence is surely false if some F are not G. Meinong's explication of what it means for the incomplete object $<F>$ to pseudo-have the property G, robs his claim that such a state of affairs may be neither factual nor unfactual of all plausibility; for the explication shows that this state of affairs is none other than the one which is more perspicuously represented by the sentence: '*All* complete objects involving the incomplete object $<F>$ also involve the incomplete object (or the property) $<G>$.' Meinong's view is only plausible as long as the role of the universal quantifier is obscured by the use of the definite article in such expressions as 'the triangle,' 'the whale,' etc. In short, while one may perhaps be inclined to believe that the sentence 'The triangle is isosceles' is neither true nor false, there is no inclination to believe this about the sentence 'All triangles are isosceles.' In order to save Meinong's view, it is not enough to claim that these last two sentences represent different though equivalent objectives. Since the first sentence is supposed to represent a possible objective, while the second is supposed to represent an unfactual objective, the two objectives in question cannot even be equivalent.

Thus we see that the real problem with Meinong's explication of possibility is whether or not there are such objectives as *The triangle is isosceles* (as distinguished, of course, from the quite different objective: *All triangles are isosceles*). And this question, in turn, depends on the problem of whether there really are such incomplete objects as *the triangle*. Meinong's claim that in addition to factuality and unfactuality there is also possibility in the world stands or falls with his claim that there are such incomplete objects. From this point of view, Meinong's later view combines a thoroughly Aristotelian theme with Meinong's own, highly idiosyncratic, version of nominalism. There is the Aristotelian theme of possibility as lying somehow outside of the dichotomy of factuality and unfactuality, truth and falsehood. And there is also Meinong's very own invention, the incomplete object. *The triangle*, for example, is neither the property of being a triangle nor is it a particular individual thing which has the property of being a triangle. It cannot be the former, for the property of being a triangle simply does not have such properties as that of having three sides. It cannot be the latter, for a particular triangle is a complete entity. Yet, *the triangle* has features of both, of properties as well as of individuals. It resembles an individual in that it is said to have such properties as that of having three sides. It is like a (complex) property in that it consists entirely of properties and is involved in all individual things which are triangles. Incomplete objects are queer entities indeed.

The notion that *the triangle*, although it behaves in many respects like a property, has properties just like an individual triangle, is crucial for Meinong's Aristotelian explication of possibility. It allows Meinong to treat the sentence 'The triangle is isosceles' as if it were of the subject-predicate form, while being, at the same time, about some entity other than the property of being a triangle. Hence, the negation of this sentence becomes 'The triangle is not isosceles,' and this latter sentence is just as false as the former. Meinong concludes, therefore, that we have here an exception to the Principle of Excluded Middle.

In conclusion a brief word about probability.[31] Probability, according to Meinong's general plan, is reducible to objective degrees of possibility. How does this reduction proceed in a particular case? Consider the statement that the next throw with this particular die will result in a five with a probability of 1/6. Now, this particular die is, of course, a completely determined object. How can we apply to a complete object what Meinong says about the possibilities attached to incomplete objects? Meinong replies that we ascribe a probability to the complete object on the basis of the probability for the incomplete object which is involved in the complete object. The incomplete object, in our case, is *the die*. This object has the property of showing a five with the next throw with only a certain degree of possibility (probability). Since it has this degree of possibility for the property in question, we also attribute this degree to the particular die which involves the incomplete object *the die*.

4 *The Apprehension of Factuality*

We discussed in the first section of this chapter some of Meinong's problems in regard to the apprehension of factuality. Meinong had asserted in the second edition of *Über Annahmen* that the factuality of an objective is presented to the mind whenever that objective is before the mind through an evident judgment. Evidence, as a 'content-like' feature of judgments, was supposed to bring factuality before the mind. One of the objections we raised against this view was the following. According to Meinong, when someone judges with evidence that the earth is round, the objective which he apprehends, *as he apprehends it*, has the modal property of factuality. This is to say that there is before the person's mind an objective to the effect that the objective that the earth is round, again according to Meinong's theory, is factual. But it is also possible for someone to believe mistakenly that an objective is factual. Thus there seems to be no difference between the objective which is before the mind of the person who judges with evidence and the objective which is before the mind of the person who believes something mistakenly.

Meinong discusses this difficulty at some length in *Über Möglichkeit und Wahrscheinlichkeit*.[32] To see clearly how it arises, recall a similar problem in regard to existence. If the round square is really round, Russell argued against Meinong, then the existing round square must exist. But it does, of course, not exist. Hence the round square is also not really round. Meinong, we remember, introduced a distinction, in rebuttal, between existence and existing and claimed that the existing round square does indeed have the determination of existing, but does not exist. Why did Meinong not simply claim, in answer to Russell, that existence is so different from ordinary properties that Russell's argument breaks down on this account alone? Meinong subscribed also to the principle of unlimited freedom of assumption, so he had to admit that one can indeed conceive of an existing round square just as well as of a round square. He held, furthermore, that whatever one thus conceives of has all the features which it is conceived to have.

The situation is quite analogous in regard to factuality as a modal property of objectives. If one assumes, even mistakenly, that a certain objective O is factual, then there is a second-level objective before the mind to the effect that O is factual. But this shows that an objective cannot be said to be factual merely because it is before a mind as being factual. What kind of objective, then, must be before the mind if we are to be sure that it is factual? As in the case of existence, Meinong simply invents a new modal property – super-factuality, so to speak – which he calls the modal feature. Just as the existing round square is said to be existing without having existence, so the objective O *is factual* is said to attribute factuality to O, even if O is not really factual, that is, even if O does not really have the modal feature. But it is immediately clear that this second modal property does not remove Meinong's difficulty; it merely pushes it one step back. When someone judges with evidence that the earth is round, according to this new analysis, the objective before his mind, *as it is before his mind*, does not only include factuality, it even includes the modal feature. Presumably, this is what distinguishes it from the objective that O is factual; this latter objective can even be before the mind of someone who does not judge with evidence. But we can raise the same objection as before: Can one not mistakenly believe, not only that a certain objective is factual, but also that it has the modal feature? And if one can believe this, then there is again no difference in kind between the objective judged with evidence and the objective mistakenly believed. As soon as Meinong realizes that the introduction of the modal feature does not save his view, he adds a new dogma: While it is possible to believe that an objective is factual when it is not, it is not possible to believe that it has the modal feature, when it does not have this feature:[33]

> My solution is based on the presupposition that our contemplative
> apprehension of objects is limited insofar as, in particular, the
> apprehension of the modal feature is reserved for penetration
> [evident judgment]. This contradicts somewhat the opinion of
> ordinary life which finds its theoretic expression in the principle
> of unlimited freedom of assumption, and according to which,
> unless accidental limitations come into play, one can assume
> anything, one is able to think of anything. This principle, if I see
> correctly, does indeed require a restriction in regard to the modal
> feature.

Meinong, it is clear, can solve the problem more easily, on the level of existence and factuality, if he is willing to restrict the principle of unlimited freedom of assumption. He could have decreed that one cannot assume that an object exists, unless it does in fact exist; and that one cannot assume that an objective is factual unless it is indeed factual. Needless to say, this decree would hardly have inspired consent; for nothing is easier than to assume that things exist when they do not and that states of affairs are the case when they are not. Moreover, if it is impossible to believe that an objective has the modal feature unless it really has it, how can one ever be mistaken in such matters?

This objection puts Meinong's predicament in a glaring light. Meinong is searching for a feature of objectives which must fulfill two conditions. First, it must belong only to factual objectives. Second, and more importantly, it must appear before the mind as belonging to an objective if and only if it does indeed belong to the objective. This second requirement is necessary because otherwise no inspection of any objectives could ever tell us whether or not that objective is factual. But this second condition invites the objection just outlined by Meinong. Assume that I believe that objective O is factual when it is not. Now, if I cannot really have the objective *O is factual* before my mind by believing it, but must have some other objective before my mind which somehow does not really amount to *O is factual*, how could I then ever be mistaken about matters of truth and falsehood? On the other hand, for my belief to be false, I must indeed have been able to believe that *O* is factual. But then this very objective must be able to appear before my mind, and this means that *O* can appear before my mind as being factual when it is not. Since we accept this second alternative, we cannot deny that any objective can appear before the mind as being factual. We must, therefore, acknowledge that the second condition mentioned above cannot be met. And this means that we have to face up to the fact which Meinong cannot bring himself to accept, namely, that objectives do not exhibit a feature which guarantees their factuality. There simply is no such characteristic of objectives and, hence, no such refutation of the skeptic. [34]

Appendix I

Meinong's Ontology[1]

I   We must turn, in the first place, to a philosophical discipline which is not as yet part of the tradition, which is therefore in a certain sense new, and about which I have said some things which were intended to be of a fundamental nature. To begin with, it is impossible to give a regular definition of entity [*Gegenstand*]; for genus and differentia are lacking, since everything is an entity. However, the etymology of the word 'gegenstehen' yields at least an indirect characteristic, since it points to the experiences which apprehend entities; but these experiences must not be thought of as somehow constituting the entities. Every inner experience, at least every sufficiently elementary one, has such an entity; and insofar as the experience finds an *expression* – hence first of all in the words and sentences of language – this expression has a *meaning* [*Bedeutung*], and this meaning is always an entity. All knowledge, too, deals therefore with entities.

But large and important groups of entities have found no home in the traditional sciences; these sciences, moreover, are for the most part exclusively concerned with a knowledge of reality [*Wirklichen*], while even unreal things with being, things without being, possibilities, and even impossibilities can be objects of knowledge, namely, of a knowledge which is of interest to the as yet theoretically naive person only, as it were, when it promises to serve as a means for knowledge of reality. In contrast to such a preference for reality, which, in fact, has been overcome so far in no science, there exists the obvious need for a science which deals with entities without any restriction, especially without restriction to the special case of existence, so that it can be called *existence-free* [*daseinsfrei*]. This science about entities as such, or about pure entities, I have called the *theory of entities*.

Much of what belongs to this theory has already been studied under the title 'Logic' (especially: 'Pure Logic'); and that modern mathematical logic belongs completely to the realm of the theory of entities is only concealed by its goal of being a calculus, which seems to favor an extensive externalization [*Veräusserlichung*] in the sense of the logic of extensions, while it is just a complete internalization [*Verinnerlichung*] which the theory of entities strives for and makes possible. People have dealt with topics from the theory of entities since antiquity under the heading of 'Metaphysics,' and, especially, under the heading of 'Ontology' as a part of metaphysics; and they have not always failed to recognize the characteristic feature of freedom from existence. But as a goal in itself, the concept of a theory of what is free from existence has, so far as I can see, never been espoused. According to this concept, there belongs to the theory of entities everything that can be made out about entities irrespective of their existence (for example, whatever it is that holds for the class of all colors which make up the 'color space,' as distinguished from the 'color body' which is restricted to the psychologically given); hence, everything that is a matter of *a priori* knowledge, so that the *a priori* can be treated as a defining characteristic of the kind of knowledge of which the theory of entities consists.

What belongs to the theory of entities is thus what is rational. Insofar [as it is that], it is therefore anything but a newly discovered country, but rather, in regard to one of its most important parts, mathematics, the justly admired standard of scientific precision. What is new is, perhaps, an insight into the peculiarity of this country and into the nature of its boundaries – unless one should rather speak of its boundlessness. In this respect, it is a kind of companion piece to metaphysics which tries to comprehend the totality of reality, while the theory of entities, because of its freedom from existence, tries to encompass also everything that is not real. Naturally, this freedom from existence does not mean that entities as such cannot have existence in the true sense. The fact that the kind of consideration and knowledge peculiar to the theory of entities therefore also appears where it can be applied to existents, constitutes one of the main values of the postulation of the new science.

Just as the concept of an entity in general is to be determined, at least *cum grano salis*, with an eye on *apprehension*, so are the main groups of entities characterized in regard to the main groups of apprehending experiences; and apprehensions are, as mentioned, all elementary experiences. Corresponding to the four main groups of the latter – to presentation [*Vorstellen*], thought [*Denken*], emotion [*Fühlen*], and desire [*Begehren*] – there are, therefore, four main groups of entities: objects [*Objekte*], objectives [*Objektive*], dignitatives [*Dignitative*], and desideratives [*Desiderative*]. However, the characteristics of the latter are not derived from the characteristics of the apprehending experiences. For this reason, nothing stands in the way of assigning to the immeasurable realm of objects, for example, also the inner experiences, even though these inner experiences cannot be given through presentations, but can only be apprehended through self-presentation or with the help of imagination.

II Among these four groups of entities, the just mentioned first group, that of *objects*, allows us, because of its variety, accessibility, and hence familiarity, to ascertain some characteristic contrasts, which can then also be extended to the other groups of entities. Above all, there are entities which are built, as it were, upon other entities and which, therefore, have to be called *entities of higher order* [*Gegenstände höherer Ordnung*] as compared with those entities of lower order on which they are based. For example, the relation of difference is a *superius* [*Superius*] relative to what is different, the respective *inferiora* [*Inferioren*]; similarly, the melody relative to the individual tones of which it is composed. In the first case, one deals with a *relat* [*Relat*] (one usually says, including an objective, 'relation' [*Relation*]); in the second case, with a complex [*Komplex*] (one says often, in analogy to 'relation', 'complexion' [*Komplexion*]). *Superiora* are always *inferiora* for even higher *superiora*. These *ordered series* [*Ordnungsreihen*] are always open at the top. However, in the opposite direction, they must always lead to *infima* [*Infima*]. A relat which is based exclusively on other relats and, equally, a multitude [(*Mehrheit*] which consisted only of multitudes, would form a faulty infinite series (the principle of the obligatory *infima*). The infinite divisibility of a straight line does not prove the contrary; for a straight line is not a multitude. Therefore, there can be no relations without non-relational, and hence in this sense absolute, terms: an absolute relativism, as it is called, is impossible.

Furthermore, objects are such that their nature either allows them, as it were, to exist and to be perceived or prohibits it, so that, if they have being at all, this being cannot be *existence*, but only *subsistence* [*Bestand*] in a sense which has to be explained further. For example, it cannot be doubted that the difference between red and green has being, but this difference does not exist, it merely subsists. Similarly, the number of books in a library does not exist in addition to the books; the number of diagonals of a polygon exists, if that is possible, even less. But we must acknowledge, surely, that each of these numbers subsists. I have called such relats and complexes *ideal* relats and *ideal* complexes in contrast to *real* relats and *real* complexes; the latter can be perceived, for example, between color and place, and reveal themselves to be real by being perceived. In this way, what is perceivable shows itself to depend on perception: only by means of perception can one know, in the last analysis, that a thing of a certain color is located at this particular place, that a colored surface has this or that shape, that it is large or small, etc. By contrast, one cannot see the difference between red and green in the same way as these colors themselves; nor does one need perception, since one can infer from the very nature of red and green that they are different. Here the *inferiora* yield the *superius* in a way which can be known a priori; the ideal relat and ideal complex, respectively, is *founded* [*fundiert*] by its *inferiora*.

Finally, objects are either completely or incompletely determined or, for short, they are either *complete* or *incomplete*. Every real thing is such that any determination whatsoever either belongs to it or does not belong to it (according to the Principle of the Excluded Middle), while, for example, every conceptual object [*Begriffsgegenstand*], say, 'the triangle,' is such that infinitely many determinations (like being equilateral, having a right angle) it neither has nor does not have (hence, it does not fall under the Principle of the Excluded Middle). Entities of the latter kind, that is, incomplete entities, are, unless they contain an inner contradiction, undetermined also in regard to their being, as long as we are talking about being in the usual sense. On the other hand, there exist or subsist in some cases complete objects which have such incomplete objects as determinations so that the latter are in this way 'involved' [*implektiert*] in the former. In regard to such 'involving objects' [*Implektenten*], incomplete objects have under favorable circumstances *pseudo*-being [*implexives Sein*] or *pseudo*-so-being [*implexives Sosein*], respectively. The relationship between such entities on the one hand and Platonic ideas and universals on the other is unmistakable.

III *Objectives*, whose peculiarity is reflected most directly by the fact that, under favorable circumstances, they do not only have being, but always also are being (in the wider sense) (R. Ameseder), are characterized, in contrast to all other entities, by the fact that they belong without exception to one of the two poles of the opposition between *position* [*Position*] and *negation* [*Negation*], which is completely unique and unbridgeable. What are called 'negative objects,' like non-smoker, uninvolved person, non-straight, etc., are not companion pieces to this contrast, but signify that an object is characterized by means of one pole of this contrast itself. Position and negation (not to be confused with affirmation and negation) is always a matter of the objective, but they have a part in the positum [*Positum*] and negatum [*Negatum*], which, as a rule, are objects. One must also avoid the misconception that non-being, because of its linguistic expression, is the negatum of the positum 'being,' which it is only in exceptional cases. As a rule, non-being is just as much a positum as being or, even more accurately (in case one wants to stress, by using the word 'positum,' the obligatory part which an explicitly taken position plays): 'non-being' is normally as positive as 'being,' namely, the counterpart [*Widerspiel*] which stands, so to speak, on the same level opposite to being.

If one takes the same point of view in regard to objectives which was advantageous above in regard to objects, then one recognizes that every objective is an ideal entity of higher order which, like an object, can be more or less determined. As in the case of objects, there are also ordered series of objectives, and these, too, are open at the top, while they are closed off at the bottom by an objective, in agreement with the law of the obligatory *infima*.

The much smaller qualitative diversity of objectives, compared with that of objects, allows us to make some survey of their kinds. *Being* in the widest sense, which we encounter in every objective, is either *being* in the narrower sense (paradigm: 'A is'), or *so-being* ('A is B'), or *conditional being* [*Mitsein*] ('If A, then B'). Traditional logic, which often speaks of 'judgments' when it means objectives, since it does not recognize objectives, and which, by the way, also speaks of concept instead of the entity which falls under the concept [*Begriffsgegenstand*], and which, in particular, often talks of 'objects,' this tradition distinguishes, accordingly, between the judgment of being (especially, the existential judgment), the categorical judgment, and the hypothetical judgment. That there is also a separate group of objectives corresponding to the disjunctive judgment appears dubious: one may surmise that the peculiarity of such judgments does not consist in a new kind of objective, but in special determinations of the complex of objectives which is always present in such cases, determinations which can also be present for objectives of so-being, conditional objectives, and even for objectives of being. The two groups of objectives with obligatory double *inferiora*, objectives of so-being and conditionals, show these *inferiora* as standing in characteristic relations: predicative connection for so-being, *implication* [*Implikation*] for conditionals. Implication occurs only between objectives, while predication is above all a matter of objects.

Being (in the narrower sense), as already mentioned, can be existence, but also subsistence: the sun exists, equality – and, similarly, any other ideal entity – cannot exist, but can only subsist. Existence itself, too, does not exist (and similarly, any other objective), but can only subsist. What exists, also subsists; what does not subsist, does not exist either. The difference between these two modes of being, which is in this way indirectly given, appears also when we compare them directly; and here, as little as in the case of ordinary empirical matters, should one object in principle against the legitimacy of appealing to ultimate data. But even what neither exists nor subsists, since it is prior to apprehension, has still a remnant of positional character [*Positionscharakter*], *Aussersein*, which, therefore, no entity seems to be lacking, with the exception, perhaps, of very special complicated cases.

So-being is either what-being [*Wassein*] ('The horse is a mammal') or how-being [*Wiesein*] ('Snow is white'); expressions like 'Birds have wings' and 'The hare runs' seem to be special cases of how-being. It is often advisable, when dealing with such objectives having two parts, to conjoin the second term of the material, the predicate, with the real core of the objective, while abstracting from the subject; hence to form, in regard to 'A is B,' the concept being-B. Such a *'predicative'* [*Prädikativ*] can then, again, be attributed to the subject. Conditionals seem to divide into cases where the objectives which occur as *inferiora* stand in the 'if'-relation and those where they stand in the 'because'-relation. It has as yet not been investigated in what way the above mentioned contrast between pseudo-being and pseudo-non-being [*ausserimplexivem Sein*] affects the various modes of being here listed.

The peculiarity of being in the widest sense, that is, of objectives, manifests itself perhaps most radically in those determinations of it which have always been called *'modal.'* Only the objective can, under favorable circumstances, be said to be *factual*; other entities, again, [can be said to be *factual*] at best through the objective, as it were. Factuality constitutes one end of a line of quantitatively variable data, the *possibilities*, the other end of which consists of the zero of possibility or unfactuality. Every greater possibility (including factuality) constitutes the *'potius'* [*Potius*] for every smaller possibility (with the exception of zero possibility) as a *'deterius'* [*Deterius*]. Every possibility coincides necessarily with the possibility of the opposite which completes it as a unit, if it does not have a *potius* above it, that is, in case it is a 'main possibility' [*Hauptmöglichkeit*]. *Necessity*, too, is a modal determination of some objectives; its nature seems at present to be describable only with the help of apprehension. It is not an increased factuality at all, but rather occurs even in connection with merely possible objectives.

IV Objects and objectives are not the only basic groups of entities. It has turned out that there are at least two more basic groups which I have called *'dignitatives'* and *'desideratives.'* They are more closely related to objectives than to objects in that they, too, are by their very nature entities of higher order, based on objects or, on occasion, on objectives, and governed by the law of the obligatory *infima*. Moreover, each one of these groups is determined by an opposition which is peculiar to it, which is obviously analogous to the opposition between position and negation, and which also cannot be reduced to an opposition between positum and negatum. To the dignitatives belongs the old triad: *true* (insofar as this is not exclusively a matter of apprehension), *beautiful*, and *good* – in addition, most likely, pleasant as well. *Ought* [*Sollen*] and *purpose* [*Zweck*] can be seen to be desideratives.

Appendix II

Meinong's Life and Work[1]

The choice of my vocation was determined neither by family tradition nor by environment. My father, who, according to well-authenticated tradition, is a member of the house of Handschuchsheim, belonged to the army of Austria, in deep loyalty to the Emperor, from the Wars of Liberation to the end of the Italian Campaign in 1859. But this did not prevent him from transmitting the Josephine spirit, which he had received from his father (who immigrated from Germany to Austria), to his family in such a way that we children never saw in our title, which we had hardly been aware of, any kind of privilege. For the rest of my life, this has remained the natural expression of a sentiment which does not claim privileges that are unjustified. I hope to have been faithful to this sentiment in spirit as well as in conduct; it determined the choice of my pen name. Concessions to slogans or party politics have always been alien to me in this matter.

That my cradle stood on Polish soil (Lemberg, 1853) was due to the occupational duties of my father; our family has always been German. I spent the years of my schooling exclusively in Vienna. Beginning with 1862, I was for six years a private student, then for two years a public student of the Vienna Academic Gymnasium. I have to thank the influences of those years, as they came, especially, from Professors Karl Greistorfer (German) and Leopold Konvalina (Philosophy), for the fact that, against the original plan of my family, which wanted me to be a lawyer, and in spite of the, at times, very strong wish of mine to study music, science became in the end my life's vocation.

I entered the University of Vienna in the fall of 1870; at first, with the intention of studying German Philology and history. After W. Scherer followed a call to Strassburg, my interests, mainly under the influence of O. Lorenz, Th. Sickel, and M. Büdinger, centered on history. I was graduated in the summer of 1874, with history as my major, with a dissertation about Arnold of Brescia. The philosophical interests, which I had brought with me from the gymnasium, receded into the background during the first years at the university and were awakened again only in connection with the purely external occasion of having to take the *Officium* of the philosophical

Nebenrigorosum. I had chosen for my preparation, with cavalier ignorance of the difficulties, Kant's *Critique of Pure Reason* and *Critique of Practical Reason.* I tried to do justice to the task before me without any professional or even literary help, in purely autodidactic fashion. And the results of my criticism of Kant, made with naive radicalism, must have been primitive, indeed. But without knowing it, I began with this study, which was anything but easy, my life's work.

I entered the law school of the University of Vienna in the Fall of 1874 as a regular student, still with the intention of deepening my historical knowledge. Earlier, I had attended there, for two semesters, lectures on economics by Carl Menger, perhaps his first; and this, no doubt, must have been of help to my later work in the theory of value. But my decision to turn to philosophy was firmly made even before the Winter semester 1874/75. Franz Brentano, whom I had met for the first time in connection with my *Nebenrigorosum* in philosophy, had nothing to do with this decision. But my acquaintance with Brentano was enough to give me confidence that my theoretical endeavors, which were still of an autodidactic nature, could be richly furthered by him. Therefore, I conveyed my decision to Brentano and asked for his guidance. Brentano, by fulfilling my request, gave lavishly from his riches; as an example, as a conscientious teacher and kind adviser, for what may stand the proof of my own academic career. If I, nevertheless, at no time had so close a relationship with Brentano as, according to C. Stumpf's respectful memorial notes, others were fortunate to have, the still living younger man must undoubtedly shoulder the blame for this, although his own memory does not help him here. I have often experienced in the meantime how students, who have just become independent of their teacher, jealously guard their independence, especially from their teacher, even though it was this very independence which he had unceasingly tried to instill. Such worries may have been caused with special ease by a forceful personality like Brentano; and they may then have become the origin of misunderstandings whose consequences have been with me deep into my later work. But what in life could not be layed to rest, in death it has been reconciled; and before the inner eye of my memory, there stands, once again, as a treasure I shall never lose my admired teacher, a figure of spiritual beauty, bathed in the golden sunshine of the summer of his own and my youth.

It agrees with my historical past, but contrasts strangely with the kind of research I later settled on, that I turned in philosophy, too, at the beginning to historical tasks. Such a task was the investigation – suggested to me, I believe, by Brentano – of the significance of the two editions of Hume's main work. This investigation was before my mind as a more distant goal when I wrote the *Hume Studies* I, which was submitted to the Vienna philosophical faculty as a *Habilitationsschrift.* While even in this work problems of the theory of abstraction and the theory of concepts played a larger role than may be desirable in an historical book, the *Hume Studies* II are already dedicated in the subtitle to the theory of relations, a theory of whose connection with the later theory of entities I had then, of course, not the faintest idea. *Hume Studies* I and II indicate through the dates of their publication in the *Sitzungsberichte der Wiener Akadamie der Wissenschaften* the tenure of my activity as a *Privatdozent* of philosophy at the University of Vienna from the summer of 1878 to and including the summer of 1882. During that time, A. Höfler, Chr. v. Ehrenfels, and A. Oelzelt-Newin were my students.

The completely unexpected appointment as *Extraordinarius* of philosophy at Graz took me in the late fall of 1882 to the place which has become the arena of my life's work. Quite naturally, it was at first still my connection with Vienna which extended now across the Semering; for example, Chr. v. Ehrenfels completed his philosophical studies and graduated from the University of Graz in 1885; A. Höfler supported the defense of the then threatened education in logic and psychology in the Austrian middle schools in the book *Über philosophische Wissenschaft und ihre Propädeutik* (1885), he was graduated from Graz in 1886, and he stayed in Graz during the Winter of 1886/87, during which time he started on his textbooks in logic and psychology; finally, A. Oelzelt-Newin was graduated in philosophy in 1888, but this graduation was only for formal reasons not confirmed by the education office. But many other things, too, which only later came to full fruition, had their beginning during those years of being *Extraordinarius* in Graz. The seminar exercises, which were always important to me and which I had supervised already in Vienna from the very first semester on as a *Dozent* under the title 'Philosophische Sozietät,' these exercises were continued in Graz under the same title, until they were replaced by a formal philosophical seminar in the fall of 1897. Beginning with the Winter semester of 1886/87, I organized the first experimental psychological demonstrations in Austria, using for this purpose equipment which had been acquired through private channels. I had already given the first psychology course with demonstrations (of a very modest sort) in Vienna around 1880. The experimental demonstrations had to be interrupted in 1889 because of insufficient space in the old building of the university and because the equipment was in the long run not adequate. But these demonstrations have to be viewed as a preparation for the founding of the psychological laboratory of the University of Graz, which has existed since 1894 (as the first experimental psychological institute in Austria), and whose collection of equipment includes now as gifts the pieces which I contributed earlier as well as a valuable collection contributed by A. Oelzelt-Newin in 1893. The publications of this time, not as yet mentioned, are mainly sketches; but the paper 'Zur erkenntnistheoretischen Würdigung des Gedächtnisses' was my first attempt to include among epistemological investigations surmises and, hence, intellectual activities other than perfectly ideal ones. During this period, the most enjoyable successes of my teaching are connected with the names K. Zindler and E. Martinak, even though the former solved the conflict between philosophy and mathematics as vocations later in favor of mathematics.

The accomplishments of the period of thirty years which passed since my appointment as *Ordinarius* of philosophy in Graz in the Spring of 1889 and my marriage in the Fall of the same year, can be outlined with larger strokes. At the beginning of this period, I took part in the work of my chosen field of inquiry in three areas – namely, in epistemology, beginning with my first philosophical steps; in psychology, especially after the need for an experimental approach in this science at universities had dawned on me and, later on, when this approach itself had become more familiar; finally, in ethics, especially in its foundation in the theory of value. I had occasion to investigate these foundations because of the course on 'Practical Philosophy' which I had to give every year even during the first few years after I had become *Ordinarius*. It had been clear to me for some time that history, with which I had once started, was farthest removed from my talents. One of the most important but rather late (hardly before 1900) achievements of these years is the insight that I had worked, from the very beginning of my philosophizing, in a certain area and in that area more than in any other. Of course, the importance of this insight does not consist in the fact that it concerns me personally, but in the fact that the nature of this area of inquiry has so far not been recognized, even though it is of the greatest importance to the whole of philosophy and even beyond. I am talking about the theory of entities, which was anticipated as a special science in 1903 [Meinong is here referring to the article 'Bemerkungen über den Farbenkörper und das Mischungsgesetz,' *Zeitschrift für Psychologie*, 33 (1903), 1–80], but was explicitly postulated in the *Untersuchungen zur Gegenstandstheorie und Psychologie*, which was published in honor of the tenth anniversary of the founding of the psychological laboratory in Graz. Almost all of my earlier publications, even though that was not then clear to me, had dealt more or less explicitly with this new science, especially the pieces 'Zur Psychologie der Komplexionen und Relationen,' 'Über die Bedeutung des Weberschen Gesetzes,' further 'Über Gegenstände höherer Ordnung,' but also the book *Über Annahmen*, to which I shall have to return, especially chapter 7 of its first edition, and, finally, 'Bemerkungen über den Farbenkörper und das Mischungsgesetz.' Later, I dedicated a special publication to the defense of the new science, namely, the paper 'Über die Stellung der Gegenstandstheorie im System der Wissenschaften.' Furthermore, the second edition of *Über Annahmen* is in many parts explicitly based on investigations in the theory of entities, and the book *Über Möglichkeit und Wahrscheinlichkeit* has, especially in its first main part, which deals with possibility, the character of a study in the theory of entities. It became one of the most important endeavors of my life to secure its rightful place for the theory of entities, once I had recognized its legitimacy.

Hopefully, the newer discipline has not been emphasized at the expense of the older, the theory of entities at the expense of the theory of knowledge. As far as epistemology is the theory of *a priori* knowledge, it is directly affected by developments in the theory of entities. The theory of empirical knowledge, on the other hand, is treated in the work *Über die Erfahrungsgrundlagen unseres Wissens* (1906) and the last chapters of the book *Über Möglichkeit und Wahrscheinlichkeit*, which deal with memory and induction. The earlier (1886) attempted 'Erkenntnistheoretische Würdigung des Gedächtnisses' led to a thorough investigation of surmise, a topic that had been completely neglected by the tradition in logic and epistemology. A study of the elements of the theory of probability, [a study] which is based on that part of the theory of entities which deals with possibility, is also a study of the role which the *a priori* plays in surmise. Traditional theory of knowledge has been concerned with vagueness even less than with uncertainty; I have tried to take a first step in the direction of removing this neglect [Meinong refers in a footnote to the article 'Abstrahieren und Vergleichen' and to the *Erfahrungsgrundlagen*]. I thought that the results of certain investigations in the theory of entities and the theory of knowledge could be used to defend an old inductive argument for a general causal law as well as to give a new proof for it [Meinong is here referring to his *Zum Erweise des allgemeinen Kausalgesetzes*, which appeared in the *Sitzungsberichte der kais. Akad. d. Wiss. Phil.-hist. Kl.*, CLXXXIX (1918)].

I hope to have opened new ways for psychological research, especially in my book *Über Annahmen* (Leipzig, 1902; second, revised and expanded, edition in 1910), by pointing out an additional kind of experience which, as it were, lies between presentation and judgment, which has an analogue in the presentations of imagination, and which, in turn, points to analogous cases in the area of emotions and desire, thus suggesting an extention of the concept of imagination from the intellectual area to the emotional one, and hence to all the basic classes of inner experiences. More specific problems of psychology are treated in 'Über die Bedeutung des Weberschen Gesetzes' (1896), 'Zur experimentellen Bestimmung der Tonverschmelzungsgrade' (1897; together with St. Witasek), 'Über Raddrehung, Rollung, und Aberration' (1898), and in 'Bemerkungen über den Farbenkörper und das Mischungsgesetz' (1903). Questions from non-experimental psychology are discussed in 'Beiträge zur Theorie der psychischen Analyse' (1893) and in 'Abstrahieren und Vergleichen' (1900). Results concerning the psychology of apprehension, and hence the psychology of knowledge, which were first published in the second edition of the *Annahmen*, have been developed during the relatively recent past into the views of *Über emotionale Präsentation* (1917); these views, I think, show how the psychologism of my earlier position on the theory of values can be overcome.

For my theory of values, the early discovery was fundamental that value feelings, if they are not represented by surrogates, are judgmental feelings. Judgmental feelings form a class of experiences which were defended in the monograph 'Über Urteilsgefühle, was sie sind und was sie nicht sind.' However, the first ideas concerning this topic can be found in the *Psychologisch-ethischen Untersuchungen zur Werttheorie* (1894), which, together with the appendix 'Über Werthaltung und Wert,' constitute the beginnings of a general theory of value, and which have thus become the origin of or point of contact with all the works which I have since then published in this field. The fact that Chr. v. Ehrenfels published similar views in a series of articles which started to appear already a year earlier (1893) in the *Vierteljahrsschrift für wissenschaftliche Philosophie* (and then later in his *System der Werttheorie*), is due to my teaching a course in ethics in 1884/85. The main content of this course, clarified during the intervening years, was published in the *Psychologisch-ethischen Untersuchungen*. Since important parts of this work have unavoidably become antiquated by the investigations of the last twenty-five years, it needed a new treatment. The main results of this new treatment are contained, in a very compact form, in the talk before the congress at Bologna entitled 'Für die Psychologie und gegen den Psychologismus in der allgemeinen Werttheorie' (1911). More detailed expositions, which are in part already finished, are supposed to be included in the third volume of my *Gesammelte Abhandlungen* (perhaps, under the headings 'Zur Grundlegung der allgemeinen Werttheorie' and 'Ethische Bausteine').

I can hardly think of these *Abhandlungen* as my own publication. They were prepared for the occasion of my sixtieth birthday by my older students under the leadership of A. Höfler. Volume 1 contains psychological works; volume 2, works from the theory of knowledge and the theory of entities; the third volume, which is still projected, will be dedicated to value theory. The editors have brought these works, which are partially rather old, up to date by making careful and knowledgeable additions; they have thus made these pieces useful for contemporary investigations.

There are two further respects, which give me as much honor as pleasure, in which the sixty-first year of my life has once again brought me in touch with my earliest scientific activity. During the first half of 1914, I was first called to the university of my youth and then elected as a full member (I had been a corresponding member since 1906) of the *Akademie der Wissenschaften*, under whose auspices I had once published my first independent studies. But even though I had to sacrifice the attractive prospect of teaching at the Vienna *alma mater* to the hope for an assured continuity of the work that may be left to me, I have very gratefully used the opportunity, which the membership offers to me, to publish in the volumes of the Vienna *Akademie* the two already mentioned works: *Über emotionale Präsentation* and *Zum Erweise des allgemeinen Kausalgesetzes*.

As the most important academic achievements during the time of my *Ordinariat*, I have to note the already mentioned creation of the psychological laboratory in 1894 and of the philosophical seminar in 1897, as well as the healthy development of these two institutions. Their financial endowment could later be enlarged because there was the possibility of a position at Kiel (1898, in place of A. Riehl). The productivity of these institutions is amply demonstrated by the number and the names of the authors who, as my students, were a part of them (including the members of the *Philosophische Sozietät*): R. Ameseder, V. Benussi, W. Benussi-Liel, A. Faist, A. Fischer, W. A. Frankl, E. Mally, E. Martinak, R. Saxinger, E. Schwartz, O. Tumlirz, F. Weber, F. Weinhandl, St. Witasek, K. Zindler), as well as by the publications of these authors. Moreover, among those just mentioned, E. Martinak acquired the *Venia legendi* for philosophy at Graz in 1895; St. Witasek, in 1899; V. Benussi, in 1905; E. Mally, in 1913; and O. Tumlirz, that for pedagogic, in 1919. In addition, philosophy at Graz acquired a welcome additonal teacher in 1913 through the *Habilitation* of H. Pichler, who, coming from the school of W. Windelband, participates most laudibly in the investigations which are done at Graz in the theory of entities. Science, no doubt, has already profited from the work of so many young, and for the most part, uncommonly gifted scientists, a work which aims at similar goals, even though it is done independently. The very least one can say is that the progress of the work on problems in which I am particularly interested would have been much slower without this collaboration.

As the years have passed, the extent of my scientific activity has been somewhat curtailed, since I could leave the work in experimental psychology more and more in the hands of my students Witasek and Benussi. In the fall of 1914, at my request, the leadership of the psychological laboratory was transferred to Professor Witasek. But a malignant illness of the stomach, which already seemed to have yielded to medical attention, took him, after only half a year, away from his family, his friends, and from his science, a science in which, as an acknowledged researcher and highly admired teacher, he had such a great success. For me, the loss of this most faithful friend and forever helpful companion of twenty years of work, in whose hands I had long ago decided to put my life's work as a legacy – for me, this loss has been and remains to be the most painful blow of my personal and academic life. The task of having to replace the irreplaceable in the psychological laboratory has fallen to V. Benussi. He admirably fulfilled this task until the change in the world situation in the fall of 1918 took him back to his home in the south and, hence, away from the institute in Graz which he had adorned for nearly twenty years.

Thus the fate of humanity, the fleetingness of life, has already more than once knocked loudly on the portals of the house on which I have worked for a life time. It will not be long now, and the same fate will ask of me a very personal tribute. I hope that my endeavors will then have been successful, that they will have permanently enriched future generations, even if only by a modest increase in knowledge or in the hope for knowledge.

Notes

Preface

1 J. N. Findlay, *Meinong's Theory of Objects and Values*, 2nd ed. (Oxford, 1963), p. 348.
2 This phrase is from Gilbert Ryle's article in the *Oxford Magazine* 26 October 1933.

Chapter I   Individuals and Properties

1 See *Hume Studien I: Zur Geschichte und Kritik des modernen Nominalismus*, 1877, reprinted in *Gesammelte Abhandlungen*, vol. 1 (Leipzig, 1914); I shall refer to the pages in this reprint. There is a translation of both *Hume Studies* by K. Barber: *Meinong's Hume Studies: Translation and Commentary* (University Microfilms, Ann Arbor, Michigan, 1966). Barber discusses the *Hume Studies* in two articles in *Philosophy and Phenomenological Research*, 30, (1970), pp. 550–67, and 31 (1971), pp. 564–84.
2 These two views are thoroughly discussed in G. Bergmann, *Realism. A Critique of Brentano and Meinong* (Madison, Milwaukee, and London, 1967).
3 For Brentano's ontology see, especially, *Kategorienlehre* (Leipzig, 1933). Compare also K. Twardowski, *Zur Lehre vom Inhalt und Gegenstand der Vorstellungen* (Vienna, 1894); and E. Husserl, *Logical Investigations*, translated by J. N. Findlay (New York, 1970).
4 *Gesammelte Abhandlungen*, vol. 1, p. 19.
5 *Ibid.*, vol. 2, p. 81.
6 See *Three Dialogues* (vol. 2, pp. 231–2 of the A. A. Luce and T. E. Jessop edition of *The Works of George Berkeley*) (London, 1948–57)); and also *Principles*, sec. 49.
7 *Gesammelte Abhandlungen*, vol. 2, p. 134.
8 John Locke, *An Essay Concerning Human Understanding*, book II, xxiii, sec. 2. Compare also E. Allaire, 'The Attack on Substance: Descartes to Hume,' *Dialogue*, 3 (1965), pp. 284–7.
9 Compare the chapter on structures in my *Ontological Reduction* (Bloomington and London, 1973).

10 See, for example, Husserl's *Logical Investigations*, vol. 1, pp. 337–50.

11 *Gesammelte Abhandlungen*, vol. 1, p. 22.

12 Compare Barber's 'Meinong's Hume Studies, Part I,' *Philosophy and Phenomenological Research*, 30 (1970), 550–67, pp. 555–8.

13 *Gesammelte Abhandlungen*, vol. 1, p. 75, n. 19.

14 A version of this argument appears also in a recent book on universals. See N. P. Wolterstorff, *On Universals* (Chicago, 1970), p. 139.

15 F. Brentano, *Psychologie vom empirischen Standpunkt*, edition of the *Philosophische Bibliothek* (Hamburg, 1955 and 1959), vol. 2, pp. 202–3, p. 212; and *Kategorienlehre*, p. 20.

16 Compare G. E. Moore, 'Are the Characteristics of Particular Things Universal or Particular?', reprinted in *Philosophical Papers* (London, 1959), pp. 17–31. Moore's early ontology was very similar to Meinong's. See, for example, G. Bergmann, 'Inclusion, Exemplification, and Inherence in G. E. Moore,' reprinted in *Studies in the Philosophy of G. E. Moore* (Chicago, 1969), pp. 81–94; and H. Hochberg, 'Moore's Ontology and Nonnatural Properties,' *ibid.*, pp. 95–127.

17 See G. F. Stout, 'The Nature of Universals and Propositions,' in *Proceedings of the British Academy*, 10 (1921–2), pp. 157–72; 'Are the Characteristics of Particular Things Universal or Particular?', in *Proceedings of the Aristotelian Society*, supp. vol. 3 (1923), pp. 114–22; 'Universals Again,' *ibid.*, 15 (1936), pp. 1–15; and 'Things, Predicates and Relations,' *Australasian Journal of Psychology and Philosophy*, 18 (1940), pp. 117–30.

18 'The Nature of Universals and Propositions,' pp. 8–9.

19 See my 'Sensory Intuition and the Dogma of Localization,' *Inquiry*, 5 (1962), pp. 238–51.

20 See, for example, *Gesammelte Abhandlungen*, vol. 1, pp. 18–20; and also vol. 2, pp. 47–50.

21 Compare Barber's 'Meinong's Hume Studies; Part I: Meinong's Nominalism,' *Philosophy and Phenomenological Research*, 30 (1970), p. 561.

22 See 'Über die Erfahrungsgrundlagen unseres Wissens,' in *Abhandlungen zur Didaktik und der Philosophie der Naturwissenschaften*, vol. 1 (Berlin, 1906), 379–491, p. 405.

23 This distinction plays a crucial role in Brentano's and his students' philosophies. Compare, for example, the long – not to say tedious – discussions of this distinction in Twardowski's *Zur Lehre vom Inhalt und Gegenstand der Vorstellungen* and Husserl's *Logical Investigations*. In the background stands C. Stumpf's *Über den psychologischen Ursprung der Raumvorstellung* (Leipzig, 1873).

24 Compare Barber's discussion of Meinong's remark in his 'Meinong's Hume Studies; Part I,' pp. 562–4.

25 *Principles*, sec. 12 of the Introduction.

26 *Ibid.*, sec. 16 of the Introduction.

27 *Gesammelte Abhandlungen*, vol. 1, pp. 10–11. Meinong speaks actually about abstracting from a complex presentation (*Vorstellung*), but for the sake of simplicity of exposition I shall continue to overlook Meinong's identification of a presentation with its intention.

28 *Logical Investigations*, vol. 1, p. 374.

29 *Ibid.*, pp. 376, 379–81.
30 '*Abstrahieren und Vergleichen*,' reprinted in *Gesammelte Abhandlungen*, vol. 1, 445–92.
31 See *Gesammelte Abhandlungen*, vol. 1, pp. 484–91.
32 *Ibid.*, p. 490.
33 See G. Frege, *The Foundations of Arithmetic*, German text and English translation by J. L. Austin, 2nd rev. ed. (Evanston, 1968), sec. 53.
34 Compare, for example, 'On Concept and Object,' in *Translations from the Philosophical Writings of Gottlob Frege*, edited by Peter Geach and Max Black (Oxford, 1952).
35 *Gesammelte Abhandlungen*, vol. 1, p. 16.

Chapter II Ideal and Real Relations

1 Compare, for example, J. Weinberg, *Abstraction, Relation, and Induction* (Madison and Milwaukee, 1965).
2 See, for example, G. Bergmann, 'The Problem of Relations in Classical Psychology,' reprinted in his *The Metaphysics of Logical Positivism* (New York, 1954).
3 For a recent example of a straightforward 'reduction' of relations see M. Fisk, 'Relatedness without Relations,' *Noûs*, 6 (1972), 139–51.
4 *An Essay Concerning Human Understanding*, book II, chapter xii, sec. 1.
5 *Hume Studien II: Zur Relationstheorie*, 1882, in *Gesammelte Abhandlungen*, vol. 2 (Leipzig, 1913).
6 This is the relation which I called *similarity* in the last chapter, because that is what it is usually called. But from now on, I shall generally use Meinong's term 'equality' (*Gleichheit*).
7 *Gesammelte Abhandlungen*, vol. 2, p. 38.
8 *Ibid.*, pp. 42–3.
9 *Ibid.*, p. 43.
10 *Ibid.*
11 We must keep in mind that, strictly speaking, the relation here mentioned is just a particular instance of the inequality relation.
12 *Gesammelte Abhandlungen*, vol. 2, p. 44.
13 *Ibid.*, pp. 46–8. (Compare also Christian Sigwart's letter to Meinong in *Philosophenbriefe. Aus der wissenschaftlichen Korrespondenz von Alexius Meinong* (Graz, 1965), pp. 83–4.)
14 On this issue see K. Barber, 'Meinong's *Hume Studies*. Part II: Meinong's Analysis of Relations,' *Philosophy and Phenomenological Research*, 31 (1971) pp. 564–84.
15 *Gesammelte Abhandlungen*, vol. 2, p. 76.
16 Meinong touches upon this issue in two later articles. *See* 'Abstrahieren und Vergleichen' (1900), and 'Bemerkungen über den Farbenkörper und das Mischungsgesetz' (1903), both in *Gesammelte Abhandlungen*, vol. 1.
17 On the ontological significance of equivalence relations and so-called definitions by abstraction see my *Ontological Reduction* (Bloomington and London, 1973), chapter 8.
18 See B. Russell, *The Principles of Mathematics*, 2nd ed. (London, 1937),

p. 51. See also his *An Inquiry into Meaning and Truth* (Baltimore, 1962), p. 325.

19 *Gesammelte Abhandlungen*, vol. 2, p. 87.

20 Of course, a law (a certain kind of quantified state of affairs) may also be *derived* from other laws.

21 For a defense of such relations see, for example, R. M. Chisholm, *Theory of Knowledge* (Englewood Cliffs, 1966), chapter 5.

22 *Gesammelte Abhandlungen*, vol. 2, p. 88.

23 *Über Annahmen*, 2nd ed. (Leipzig, 1910), pp. 215–16.

24 Compare my *Ontological Reduction*, chapter 10.

25 See G. Frege, *Begriffsschrift* (Halle, 1879), p. 4, translated in *From Frege to Gödel*, edited by Jean van Heijenoort (Cambridge, Massachusetts, 1967).

26 See, for example, G. Bergmann, 'Comments on Professor Hempel's "The Concept of Cognitive Significance," ' reprinted in Bergmann's *The Metaphysics of Logical Positivism* (New York, 1954), and W. V. Quine, 'Necessary Truth,' in *The Ways of Paradox* (New York, 1966).

27 *Gesammelte Abhandlungen*, vol. 2, p. 107.

28 What we can and cannot imagine must be distinguished from what we can and cannot conceive of. Although we cannot imagine the state of affairs that, say, a surface is both red and green all over at the same time, we can easily conceive of such a state of affairs. How, otherwise, could we believe that *it* does not obtain?

29 Compare G. Bergmann, 'Synthetic a priori,' reprinted in *Logic and Reality* (Madison, 1964).

30 *Gesammelte Abhandlungen*, vol. 2, p. 108. (Compare Husserl's reference to Descartes' 'chilagon' in a similar context in the *Logical Investigations*, translated by J. N. Findlay (New York, 1970), vol. 1, pp. 301–2.)

31 *Ibid.*, p. 118.

32 *Ibid.*, p. 123.

33 *Ibid.*, p. 122.

34 See, for example, *Über Annahmen*, 2nd ed., pp. 90–2.

35 *Gesammelte Abhandlungen*, vol. 2, p. 130.

36 *Ibid.*, p. 131.

37 *Ibid.*, p. 132.

38 See his *The Principles of Mathematics*, p. 63.

39 *Ibid.*, p. 64.

40 Nor should one argue from the fact that every relation has at least two *terms* that it must hold between at least two *existents*. It is, indeed, of the essence of certain relations that they can hold between an entity that exists and an entity that does not exist. The intentional relation, as we shall see, is of this kind.

41 L. Wittgenstein, *Tractatus Logico-Philosophicus* (London and New York, 1961), p. 105, (5.5303).

42 See Frege's 'On Sense and Reference,' in *Translations from the Philosophical Writings of Gottlob Frege* (Oxford, 1960), pp. 56–7.

43 This possibility is in the spirit of Wittgenstein's 5.53 of the *Tractatus*: 'Identity of object I express by identity of sign, and not by using a sign for identity. Difference of objects I express by difference of signs.'

44 This idea goes back to Russell's 'On Denoting' and is elaborated in F. B. Fitch, 'The Problem of the Morning Star and the Evening Star,' *Philosophy of Science*, 16 (1949), pp. 137-41; and in A. F. Smullyan, 'Modality and Description,' *Journal of Symbolic Logic*, 13 (1948), pp. 31-7.

45 *Gesammelte Abhandlungen*, vol. 2, pp. 132-3.

46 The referents of such expressions as 'all fish,' 'some fish,' and 'a fish' play an important role in Meinong's later philosophy. See below, in chapter X, the section on incomplete objects.

47 See my 'Common names,' reprinted in *Essays in Ontology* (The Hague, 1963).

48 *Gesammelte Abhandlungen*, vol. 2, p. 138.

49 *Ibid.*, pp. 138-9.

50 *Ibid.*, p. 140.

51 *Ibid.*, p. 141.

52 With the introduction of real relations, Meinong must distinguish between foundations and terms; for foundations are all there really is in the case of ideal relations, but not in the case of real relations. Compare his 'Über Gegenstände höherer Ordnung und ihr Verhältnis zur inneren Wahrnehmung,' *Gesammelte Abhandlungen*, vol. 2, pp. 396-401.

53 *Gesammelte Abhandlungen*, vol. 2, pp. 144-5.

54 *Ibid.*, pp. 154-5.

Chapter III Ideas and their Intentions

1 K. Twardowski, *Zur Lehre vom Inhalt und Gegenstand der Vorstellungen* (Wien, 1894). I have prepared a translation of this work and hope that it will be published soon.

2 *Ibid.*, chapter 1.

3 *Ibid.*, chapter 6.

4 Compare, for example, the excerpts from the *Psychologie vom empirischen Standpunkt* in *Realism and the Background of Phenomenology*, edited by R. M. Chisholm (New York and London, 1960).

5 For a detailed discussion of this view see Husserl's *Logical Investigations*, vol. 2, pp. 597-631.

6 See below chapter VIII, sec. 2.

7 *Op. cit.*, pp. 31-2.

8 It is therefore tempting to identify Twardowski's *contents* with Frege's *senses*, and the former's *objects* with the latter's *referents*. But this would be a mistake; for we must keep in mind that while contents are mental entities, senses are nonmental.

9 See Twardowski, *op. cit.*, pp. 105-9; and also Husserl's criticism of Twardowski in the *Logical Investigations*, vol. 1, pp. 360-1.

10 This paper first appeared in the *Zeitschrift für Psychologie und Physiologie der Sinnesorgane*, 21 (1899), pp. 181-271. It is reprinted in *Gesammelte Abhandlungen*, vol. 2. Page references are to the *Gesammelte Abhandlungen*.

11 *Ibid.*, p. 381.

12 *Ibid.*, p. 383.

13 *Ibid.*, p. 384.

14 *Ibid.*, p. 384.

15 See G. E. Moore's review of A. Messer's *Empfindung und Denken* in *Mind*, 19 (1910), 403–4; and also his 'The Refutation of Idealism,' reprinted in *Philosophical Studies* (London, 1922).

16 We must note that matters are complicated in the 'Refutation of Idealism' by the fact that Moore there talks only about sensations and their objects.

17 *Gesammelte Abhandlungen*, vol. 2, p. 385.

18 Moore claims the same transparency, not for the content, but for the act: 'And, in general, that which makes the sensation of blue a mental fact seems to escape us: it seems, if I may use a metaphor, to be transparent – we look through it and see nothing but the blue; we may be convinced that there *is something* but *what* it is no philosopher, I think, has yet clearly recognized.' ('The Refutation of Idealism,' *Philosophical Studies*, p. 20.)

19 That the intention is a part of the mental act is, of course, one of the views which, according to Moore, leads to idealism. See his explication and criticism of this view in 'The Refutation of Idealism.'

Chapter IV Objects of Higher Order

1 I shall refer, as usual, to the reprint in the *Gesammelte Abhandlungen*, vol. 2.

2 *Zeitschrift für Psychologie und Physiologie der Sinnesorgane*, 2 (1891), pp. 245–65; also contained in the *Gesammelte Abhandlungen*, vol. 1.

3 For details see my *Ontological Reduction*.

4 The simplest example of a structure is an ordered pair. The characteristic relation is in this case isomorphic, as one usually says, to the predecessor relation between natural numbers.

5 *Gesammelte Abhandlungen*, vol. 1, pp. 281–2. (Ehrenfels remarks, in a letter to Meinong, that Mach had already presented this argument in 1865. See *Philosophenbriefe* [Graz, 1965], pp. 74–5.)

6 *Ibid.*, pp. 283–4.

7 Of course, by 'similar' we do not mean here 'the same number of members.'

8 Nor, we should add, does Wertheimer: '. . . other explanations were also proposed. One maintained that in addition to the six tones there were intervals – relations – and that *these* were what remained constant. In other words we were asked to assume not only elements but "relations-between-elements" as additional components of the total complex. But this view failed to account for the phenomenon because in some cases the relations *too* may be altered without destroying the original melody.' (Willis D. Ellis, *A Source Book of Gestalt Psychology* [New York, 1950], p. 4.) We do not hold, of course, that the characteristic relations of two structures must be the *same* in order for the structures to be 'similar.' It suffices that they are similar to each other. Recall, for that matter, the traditional notion of isomorphic structures.

9 *Gesammelte Abhandlungen*, vol. 1, p. 284.

10 The fact that one usually says of relations (and properties) rather than of structures that they are isomorphic to each other could signify a pervasive blindness to the ontological category of structure. This blindness is not

surprising if we recall the traditional attempts to reduce even classes to other kinds of entities. On such attempts in general see my *Ontological Reduction*.

11 *Gesammelte Abhandlungen*, vol. 1, p. 285.

12 *Ibid.*, pp. 289-90.

13 I do not wish to imply here that there always exists a certain relation which 'connects' a relation with its terms. It is precisely the lesson of Bradley's 'paradox' that, while non-relational entities cannot be connected with each other without a relation, a relation does not require a further relation in order to be connected with its terms.

14 See, for example, K. Grelling and P. Oppenheim, 'Der Gestaltbegriff im Lichte der neuen Logik,' in *Erkenntnis*, 7 (1937-1938), pp. 211-25, 357-9; and C. G. Hempel and P. Oppenheim, 'The Logic of Explanation,' reprinted in *Readings in the Philosophy of Science*, edited by H. Feigl and M. Brodbeck, (New York, 1953).

15 See my paper 'Perceptual Objects, Elementary Particles, and Emergent Properties,' in *Action, Perception, Reality, and Theory* (Indianapolis, to appear). This is a *Festschrift* for Wilfrid Sellars.

16 *Gesammelte Abhandlungen*, vol. 2, p. 386.

17 Hochberg has given an ingenious explication of Moore's notion of a non-natural property in terms of this asymmetry. A non-natural property, in a nutshell, is a property *of* a complex of properties (or instances). Such a property is quite obviously not a part of the complex of which it is a property. See H. Hochberg, 'Moore's Ontology and Nonnatural Properties,' reprinted in *Studies in the Philosophy of G. E. Moore*, edited by E. D. Klemke (Chicago, 1969).

18 I am excluding here so-called complex properties. I have argued elsewhere that there are no complex properties. See my *Ontological Reduction* and also 'Russell's Paradox and Complex Properties,' *Noûs*, 6 (1972), 153-64.

19 *Gesammelte Abhandlungen*, vol. 2, p. 388.

20 This does not really tell us what numbers are. Meinong does not seem to distinguish between, say, the number *four* and the object *four nuts*. But he claims a few pages later that the number is also an object of higher order.

21 *Gesammelte Abhandlungen*, vol. 2, pp. 389-90.

22 *Ibid.*, pp. 390-91.

23 *Ibid.*, footnote 26 on p. 474.

24 *Über Annahmen*, 2nd ed., pp. 268-78.

25 *Gesammelte Abhandlungen*, vol. 2, p. 392.

26 *Ibid.*, p. 395.

27 *Ibid.*, p. 397.

28 *Ibid.*, p. 398.

29 It is also Schumann's objection in the article 'Zur Psychologie der Zeitanschauung,' *Zeitschrift für Psychologie und Physiologie der Sinnesorgane*, 17 (1898), 106-48. Meinong's paper is a reply to this article.

30 *Gesammelte Abhandlungen*, vol. 2, p. 423. Compare also Husserl's discussion of the same problem in *Logical Investigations*, vol. 1, pp. 416-19.

31 *Ibid.*, p. 424.
32 *See* 'Abstrahieren und Vergleichen,' in *Gesammelte Abhandlungen*, vol. 1, pp. 443–92.
33 *Gesammelte Abhandlungen*, vol. 2, pp. 426–7.
34 *Ibid.*, pp. 445–6.
35 Compare also Meinong's later remarks on this point (*Ibid.*, pp. 455–61) in which he claims, among other things, that to speak of past, present, and future is to speak about relations between intentions and their mental acts. It is Meinong's view that past, present, and future are just as little mind-independent features of objects as their being thought of is.
36 *Ibid.*, pp. 447–8.
37 *Ibid.*, p. 448.
38 *Ibid.*, p. 449.
39 *Ibid.*, p. 451.

Chapter V   Assumptions and Objectives

1 *Über Annahmen* (Leipzig, 1902). There is also a revised edition of this book which appeared in 1910. In this chapter, I talk only about the first edition; chapter 9 is about the second edition. I shall refer to the two editions as *Über Annahmen* I and *Über Annahmen* II, respectively.
2 In the second edition, they play a dominant role and occur already in the third chapter.
3 The view of Brentano's which is here discussed is his earlier view as formulated, for example, in his *Psychologie vom empirischen Standpunkt*, in the edition of the *Philosophische Bibliothek* (Hamburg, 1955 and 1959). See also D. B. Terrell's translation of parts of this work in *Realism and the Background of Phenomenology*, edited by R. M. Chisholm (New York and London, 1960). Meinong discusses Brentano's view in an article in the *Göttinger Gelehrte Anzeigen* of 1892, pp. 443–66.
4 *Über Annahmen* I, pp. 2–3.
5 Russell, in his review of Meinong's book, sees this very clearly. Compare his 'Meinong's Theory of Complexes and Assumptions (II.),' *Mind* 13 (1904), 33–54; pp. 338–9 and pp. 351–2. Compare also Meinong's later remark about this topic in *Über Annahmen* II, p. 72.
6 *Über Annahmen* I, pp. 6–13.
7 See G. Frege, 'Die Verneinung,' translated in *Translations from the Philosophical Writings of Gottlob Frege* (Oxford, 1960).
8 Compare my *Ontological Reduction*, chapter 1.
9 See Twardowski, *op. cit.*, chapter 3.
10 *Über Annahmen* I, pp. 19–20.
11 *Ibid.*, pp. 24–5.
12 *Ibid.*, pp. 26–31.
13 *Ibid.*, p. 95.
14 *Ibid.*, p. 99.
15 *Ibid.*, pp. 99–101.
16 *Ibid.*, pp. 101–4.
17 *Ibid.*, p. 103.

18 *Über Annahmen* II, p. 234.
19 *Über Annahmen* I, p. 105.
20 See 'Phantasievorstellung und Phantasie' in *Gesammelte Abhandlungen*, vol. 1.
21 *Über Annahmen* I, pp. 113–18.
22 *Ibid.*, pp. 118–19.
23 *Ibid.*, p. 119.
24 *Ibid.*, pp. 121–2.
25 *Ibid.*, pp. 123–4.
26 *Ibid.*, pp. 126–7.
27 *Ibid.*, pp. 128–9.
28 Russell comes very close to advocating this solution to the problem of how complex entities are presented to the mind. See his 'Meinong's Theory of Complexes and Assumptions (II),' *Mind*, 13 (1904), pp. 350–1; and also the third article by the same title, *ibid.*, pp. 517–19.
29 *Über Annahmen* I, p. 130.
30 *Ibid.*, pp. 132–3.
31 *Ibid.*, p. 135.
32 On this point, compare also Twardowski, *op. cit.*, p. 93 and Findlay's *Meinong's Theory of Objects and Values*, 2nd ed. (Oxford, 1963), pp. 16–17.
33 See my *The Structure of Mind* (Madison and Milwaukee, 1965), pp. 114–118.
34 *Über Annahmen* I, p. 143.
35 Russell criticizes this view in his review of Meinong's book. See Russell's 'Meinong's Theory of Complexes and Assumptions (II),' p. 345.
36 This relation, of course, would have to be some kind of part-whole relation rather than exemplification.
37 *Über Annahmen* I, p. 145.
38 *Ibid.*, p. 147.
39 *Ibid.*, pp. 150–5.
40 Meinong notices the ambiguity in the word 'object' later and makes the appropriate distinction.
41 *Über Annahmen* I, p. 154.
42 *Ibid.*, pp. 156–7.
43 *Ibid.*, p. 159.
44 *Ibid.*, p. 163–4.
45 *Ibid.*, p. 164.
46 *Ibid.*, p. 177.
47 *Ibid.*, pp. 178–9.
48 Those who argue for instances of relations, as we saw earlier, do not understand that (2) is a description of a relation.
49 *Über Annahmen* I, pp. 179–80.
50 *Ibid.*, p. 180.
51 *Ibid.*, p. 187.
52 *Über Annahmen* II, pp. 65–9.
53 *Über Annahmen* I, p. 189.
54 *Ibid.*, pp. 193–4.

Chapter VI Being and Aussersein

1 'Über Gegenstandstheorie,' in *Gesammelte Abhandlungen*, vol. 2, pp. 483–530. This paper has been translated into English by Issac Levi, D. B. Terrell, and Roderick M. Chisholm and appears in *Realism and the Background of Phenomenology* (New York and London, 1960).

2 See Bolzano's *Wissenschaftslehre*, new edition, 4 vols. (Leipzig, 1929), vol. 1, paragraph 67.

3 See B. Kerry, 'Über Anschauung und ihre psychische Verarbeitung,' *Vierteljahrsschrift für wissenschaftliche Philosophie*, 10 (1886), pp. 428, 444.

4 K. Twardowski, *Zur Lehre vom Inhalt und Gegenstand der Vorstellungen*, pp. 23–4.

5 *Ibid.*, p. 24.

6 Since I hold that all mental acts intend states of affairs, there are in my view no presentations. But it is nevertheless true that every act has an intention, namely, a state of affairs. Compare my *The Structure of Mind*, pp. 76–82.

7 We shall see that there are really several relations of this kind.

8 *Gesammelte Abhandlungen*, vol. 2, p. 486.

9 *Ibid.*, p. 519.

10 *Ibid.*, pp. 520–1.

11 *Ibid.*, pp. 489–90.

12 *Ibid.*, p. 491.

13 *Ibid.*, pp. 491–2.

14 See, for example, Russell's review of the *Untersuchungen zur Gegenstandstheorie und Psychologie* in *Mind*, 14 (1905), 530–8, pp. 532–3; and also his 'On Denoting,' *Mind*, 14 (1905), pp. 479–93.

15 For our purposes, it makes no difference whether we consider the definite description expression itself or Russell's 'definition' of it in terms of the so-called existential quantifier and the uniqueness clause.

16 Compare my *Ontological Reduction*, chapter 6.

17 Russell is well aware of this fact. He tries to avoid our view about the peculiarity of the part-whole relation by adopting his so-called multiple relation theory of belief. See, for example, his 'On the Nature of Truth,' *Proceedings of the Aristotelian Society* (1906–7), 28–49, pp. 46–7.

18 The quantifiers range, in Russell's theory, over existents only. There are, of course, systems in which there are also quantifiers for merely possible entities.

19 See Meinong's *Über die Stellung der Gegenstandstheorie im System der Wissenschaften* (Leipzig, 1907), p. 39. This work appeared first in the form of three articles in the *Zeitschrift für Philosophie und philosophische Kritik*, vols 129, 130 (1906 and 1907).

20 Thus I reject (like Frege) the view that 'men' in 'All men are mortal' 'supposites' for a number of individual men. 'Men,' as Frege pointed out, represents here, as everywhere else, the property of being a man.

21 We would make a similar reply to Findlay's version of Meinong's argument. See Findlay's *Meinong's Theory of Objects and Values*, 2nd ed. (Oxford, 1963), p. 53.

22 *Gesammelte Abhandlungen*, vol. 2, p. 492.
23 *Ibid.*, p. 493.
24 *Ibid.*, pp. 493–4.
25 In his book *Über die Erfahrungsgrundlagen unseres Wissens* (Berlin, 1906), p. 22, Meinong remarks: 'But existential assertions also, as language has them at its disposal, can easily cloud the issue rather than throw light on it; especially, when they occur in a form like "Water exists" and thus create the impression, by means of a superficial analogy to judgments of so-being like "The water murmurs," that existence is, as it were, a piece of an object like murmurs; but existence is nothing more than the objective.'
26 See *Über die Stellung der Gegenstandstheorie im System der Wissenschaften*, p. 20. Ameseder's article is the second one of the collection of essays called *Untersuchungen zur Gegenstandstheorie und Psychologie* (Leipzig, 1904).
27 He used to call the third mode of being 'Quasi-being.' On this matter see also *Über Annahmen* II, pp. 79–80.

Chapter VII Empirical Knowledge: Perception and Introspection

1 *Über die Erfahrungsgrundlagen unseres Wissens* (Berlin, 1906). I shall abbreviate this title by '*Erfahrungsgrundlagen*.'
2 *Gesammelte Abhandlungen*, vol. 2, p. 123.
3 *Erfahrungsgrundlagen*, pp. 8–9.
4 *Ibid.*, pp. 15–16. Meinong talks about 'inner' as well as 'outer' perception.
5 *Ibid.*, pp. 17–18.
6 This is not quite correct, as we shall see in a moment. The characteristic of evidence distinguishes perception from hallucination and illusion.
7 *Ibid.*, p. 20.
8 *Ibid.*, pp. 20–1.
9 *Ibid.*, p. 21.
10 Husserl, for example, holds this view, too. See his *Logical Investigations*, vol. 2, p. 458.
11 *Erfahrungsgrundlagen*, p. 21.
12 *Ibid.*, pp. 21–2.
13 When I say '*A* is green,' the listener does not know what state of affairs I mean, unless he knows what '*A*' is a label of. When I say 'The book on my desk is green,' on the other hand, the listener knows what state of affairs I have in mind, even if he does not know what entity the expression 'the book on my desk' describes. This shows how labels differ from descriptions for the purposes of communication.
14 *Erfahrungsgrundlagen*, pp. 24–5.
15 For details, see my *The Structure of Mind*, chapter 1.
16 I hold that, as a matter of fact, all mental acts are propositional. There simply are no such acts as presentations. As Meinong's philosophy of mind develops, we notice how presentations become less and less important in that theory.
17 *Erfahrungsgrundlagen*, p. 25.

18 Meinong even allows here for the possibility that an ordinary perceptual object may not be a complex at all, but a 'substance' with many properties. *Ibid.*, p. 27.

19 *Ibid.*, p. 30.

20 What he sees, though, is not a pink rat or any other existing perceptual object. Compare my *The Structure of Mind*, chapter 6, and also G. Bergmann's 'Realistic Postcript,' in his *Logic and Reality* (Madison, 1964).

21 *Erfahrungsgrundlagen*, p. 31.

22 Evidence, of course, plays a large role in the views of most of Brentano's students. Compare, for example, Husserl's *Logical Investigations*, especially, vol. 1, pp. 187–96.

23 *Erfahrungsgrundlagen*, pp. 31–2.

24 *Ibid.*, p. 32.

25 Compare also *Über Möglichkeit und Wahrscheinlichkeit* (Leipzig, 1915), p. 440.

26 Compare on this point Frege's argument against any attempt to define truth in terms of a characteristic of judgments in his 'Der Gedanke, eine logische Untersuchung,' *Beiträge zur Philosophie des deutschen Idealismus*, 1 (1918), pp. 58–77; this paper is translated as 'The Thought' and appears in *Mind*, 65 (1965), pp. 289–311.

27 *Erfahrungsgrundlagen*, p. 33.

28 See *Philosophenbriefe* (Graz, 1965), p. 165.

29 *Ibid.*, p. 167, pp. 171–2, p. 175, p. 179.

30 *Ibid.*, p. 171.

31 *Erfahrungsgrundlagen*, p. 34.

32 See my *The Structure of Mind*, chapter 6.

33 Is awareness, so understood, a genus? I am inclined to believe that one can distinguish between sensing and awareness proper. Awareness proper is of mental acts and mental acts only, while one senses sense-impressions and other sensations.

34 We shall see in a moment that this kind of evidence is not evidence for certainty, but a different kind of evidence.

35 *Erfahrungsgrundlagen*, pp. 39–40.

36 From *The Assayer*. See *The Philosophy of the 16th and 17th Centuries*, edited by R. Popkin (New York, 1966), p. 65.

37 *Erfahrungsgrundlagen*, p. 40.

38 Berkeley, for example, does realize, though, that these qualities 'are in the mind only as they are perceived by it—that is, not by way of *mode* or *attribute* but only by way of idea.' (*A Treatise Concerning the Principles of Human Knowledge*, paragraph 49). But Berkeley does not explicate this way of being in the mind.

39 The confusion between identity and 'logical' equivalence seems not to be eradicable in contemporary philosophy.

40 A. Eddington, *The Nature of the Physical World* (Cambridge, 1928), pp. xi–xii.

41 See, for example, M. Brodbeck, 'Mental and Physical: Identity vs. Sameness,' in *Mind, Matter, and Method*, edited by P. K. Feyerabend and G. Maxwell (Minneapolis, 1966), pp. 40–58.

42 For a more detailed discussion of this matter see my article 'Perceptual Objects, Elementary Particles, and Emergent Properties,' in *Action, Perception, Reality, and Theory, a Festschrift for Wilfrid Sellars*, edited by Hector-Neri Castañeda (Indianapolis, forthcoming).

43 This does not mean, though, that the properties of structures may not be 'reducible' in an entirely different way; a way which has nothing to do with what there is and, therefore, should not be called reduction at all. See, for example, the following definition of emergence by Hempel and Oppenheim: 'The occurrence of a characteristic W in an object w is emergent relatively to a theory T, a part relation Pt, and a class G of attributes if that occurrence cannot be deduced by means of T from a characterization of the Pt-parts of w with respect to all the attributes in G.' (C. G. Hempel and P. Oppenheim, 'The Logic of Explanation,' in *Readings in the Philosophy of Science*, edited by H. Feigl and M. Brodbeck, [New York, 1953], p. 336.)

44 *Erfahrungsgrundlagen*, p. 43.

45 *Ibid.*, p. 89.

46 Notice that while it makes sense to think of certainty as a property of judgments, it makes no sense to think of surmise as a property of judgments. This suggests that surmises form a kind of mental act rather than constitute a property of judgments. However, Meinong quite clearly thinks of evidence for certainty and evidence for surmise as two properties of judgments.

47 *Ibid.*, p. 94.

48 *Ibid.*, pp. 96–7.

49 *Ibid.*, pp. 99–100.

50 *Ibid.*, pp. 102–3.

51 *Ibid.*, p. 103.

52 *Ibid.*, p. 55.

53 For greater details, see my *The Structure of Mind*, chapter 1.

54 *Erfahrungsgrundlagen*, p. 57.

55 See, for example, Brentano's *Psychologie vom empirischen Standpunkt*, vol. 1, pp. 169–70.

56 See, for example, Aristotle's *De Anima*, III, 2, 425b, 10–20; Brentano's *Psychologie vom empirischen Standpunkt*, vol. 1, pp. 159–60; and Husserl's *Logical Investigations*, vol. 2, p. 543.

57 See Brentano's *Psychologie vom empirischen Standpunkt*, vol. 1, pp. 131–59.

58 *Ibid.*, vol. 1, pp. 166–7, 173–4, and p. 202.

59 *Erfahrungsgrundlagen*, p. 58.

60 *Ibid.*, pp. 59–60.

Chapter VIII   Rational Knowledge: The Theory of Entities

1 'Über die Stellung der Gegenstandstheorie im System der Wissenschaften,' *Zeitschrift für Philosophie und philosophische Kritik*, 129 (1906), pp. 48–94, 155–207; *ibid.*, 130 (1907), pp. 1–46. I shall quote from the special edition in book form with the same title (Leipzig 1907) and call it *'Stellung.'*

2 See, e.g., R. M. Chisholm, *Perceiving* (New York, 1957), pp. 115–25.

3 *Stellung*, p. 8.

4 See, for example, Bergmann's description of Brentano's view in his *Realism*, pp. 242–6.

5 Husserl, for example, shares this view. See his *Logical Investigations*, vol. 2, pp. 552–3.

6 *Stellung*, pp. 14–20.

7 See Russell's review of the *Untersuchungen zur Gegenstandstheorie und Psychologie* (Leipzig, 1904) in *Mind*, 14 (1905), pp. 530–8.

8 *Stellung*, pp. 17–18.

9 *Ibid.*, p. 17.

10 In a letter to Meinong, dated 5. xi. 1906. See *Philosophenbriefe*, pp. 151–2.

11 The golden mountain which is now located at the end of the rainbow over there is, therefore, a complex object – a nature, to be more precise – which contains some kind of spatial 'determination' and some kind of temporal 'determination,' but, of course, no place and no moment.

12 *Über Möglichkeit und Wahrscheinlichkeit* (Leipzig, 1915), p. 282.

13 *Stellung*, pp. 20–7.

14 I am convinced, for a number of reasons, that there are no complex properties. But this is a different story altogether. See my 'Russell's Paradox and Complex Properties,' *Noûs*, 6 (1972), 153–64.

15 *Stellung*, pp. 40–1.

16 Whether or not there are 'perfect' circles is one question, whether or not we are ever presented with the property (*perfect*) *roundness* is quite another question. Even if the answer to the first question is negative, the answer to the second need not be negative, too.

17 See E. Mach, *Erkenntnis und Irrtum* (Leipzig, 1905), pp. 359, 365, 402, 410.

18 *Stellung*, p. 42.

19 *Ibid.*, p. 45.

20 *Ibid.*

21 See my article 'Russell's Paradox and Complex Properties,' mentioned in footnote 14.

22 *Stellung*, p. 46.

23 There is a problem here: If we restrict the properties of an object to those that are actually before the mind when we conceive of the object, then it turns out that the round square is not really a contradictory object; for the properties of being round and being square are not contradictories.

24 However, we cannot really conclude, Meinong is going to say, that the desk does not have these other properties. In regard to any one of these properties, the desk is simply *indeterminate*.

25 Of course, we hold that to be imagined by someone is not really a property of anything.

26 In this paper, reprinted in the *Gesammelte Abhandlungen*, vol. 1, Meinong discusses the interesting problem of what works of art are; for example, the question of what a symphony is.

27 *Gesammelte Abhandlungen*, vol. 1, p. 599. (The quotation is from page 487 of an article by Lipps 'Weiteres zur "Einfühlung",' which appeared in the *Archiv für die gesamte Psychologie*, 4 [1903].)

28 *Ibid.*, p. 603.

29 I here leave out all complications arising from negation.

30 This is not quite accurate for at least two reasons. First, while the nature consists of properties, the billiard ball consists of instances. Second, as will appear presently, while the billiard ball either has or does not have any given property *F*, this is not true of the round square.

31 There is a problem though, as we noted in the last chapter. Meinong talked there as if there is a difference between the two objectives: (1) *A* is round and (2) <Round, Square > is round, even if *A* is the same entity as < Round, Square >. But he never explains what this difference is.

32 See Russell's article in *Mind*, 13 (1904), pp. 204–19, 336–54, and 509–24.

33 See Moore's 'Necessity,' *Mind*, 9 (1900), pp. 289–304.

34 *Stellung*, p. 53.

35 *Ibid.*, p. 54.

36 *Ibid.*, footnote 1.

37 *Ibid.*, p. 63.

38 *Ibid.*, p. 65.

39 *Ibid.*, p. 66.

40 See pp. 27-9 above.

41 This does not exclude the possibility, though, that there are other arithmetic statements which may be known by induction.

42 For details, see the first three chapters of my *Ontological Reduction*.

43 Compare, for example, Russell's description of the situation in his *Principles of Mathematics*, pp. 373–4.

44 Compare, in this connection, Frege's disagreements with Hilbert in the articles and letters published as *On the Foundations of Geometry and Formal Theories of Arithmetic*, translated by Eike-Henner W. Kluge (New Haven, 1971).

45 *Stellung*, p. 78.

46 *Ibid.*, p. 80.

47 *Ibid.*, pp. 127–30.

48 This article is reprinted in the *Gesammelte Abhandlungen*, vol. 1.

49 *Gesammelte Abhandlungen*, vol. 1, pp. 465–75.

50 *Stellung*, p. 121.

51 We must keep in mind that, in regard to description expressions, we must always distinguish between what they describe and what they represent. The indefinite description 'a man' describes, in my opinion, an individual thing, but it represents a complex part of certain states of affairs, for example, of the state of affairs represented by 'A man entered the room.'

52 And Meinong also seems to identify *a horse* with *some horse*. Thus 'the horse,' 'a horse,' and 'some horse' all represent the same entity, namely, what I have called the nature *horse*.

Chapter IX   The Apprehension of Objects

1 *Über Annahmen*, 2nd ed. (Leipzig, 1910). I shall refer to this edition by 'Über Annahmen II.'

2 *Über Annahmen*, II, p. 234.

3 Compare Husserl's characterization of apprehension: 'Apperception is, according to us, the surplus, which is found in experience itself, in its descriptive content as opposed to the raw existence of sense, and is in essence such as to make us perceive this or that object, see this tree, e.g., hear this ringing, smell this scent of flowers etc. etc.' (*Logical Investigations*, vol. 2, p. 567).

4 *Über Annahmen* II, p. 236.

5 *Ibid.*, pp. 237–8.

6 *Ibid.*, p. 238.

7 Meinong thus establishes a connection between his theory of apprehension and the theory of meaning as outlined by Husserl in the first investigation of the *Logical Investigations*.

8 *Über Annahmen* II, p. 239–40.

9 Since Meinong claims that even judgments rest somehow on assumptions, he says on page 241 of *Über Annahmen* II that apprehension is ultimately always a matter of assumptions.

10 *Über Annahmen* II, p. 243.

11 *Ibid.*, pp. 245–6.

12 *Ibid.*, p. 269.

13 We shall see in a moment that a description expression, according to Meinong, is really associated with three rather than just two entities.

14 See my *Reflections on Frege's Philosophy*, pp. 167–74, and also my forthcoming article 'Definite Descriptions.'

15 *Über Annahmen* II, p. 270.

16 *Ibid.*, p. 271.

17 *Ibid.*, p. 273.

18 *Ibid.*, pp. 275–6.

19 See Husserl's *Ideas. General Introduction to Pure Phenomenology* (London, 1931).

20 G. E. Moore, 'Some Judgments of Perception,' in *Philosophical Studies* (London, 1922), p. 230; my italics.

21 *Über Annahmen* II, p. 276.

22 *Ibid.*, p. 277.

23 See the *Logical Investigations*, vol. 2, pp. 578–80.

24 *Über Annahmen* II, p. 86, pp. 341–2.

25 *Logical Investigations*, vol. 2, pp. 597–659.

26 *Über Annahmen* II, p. 279.

27 *Ibid.*, p. 280.

Chapter X   Modalities

1 *Über Möglichkeit und Wahrscheinlichkeit* (Leipzig, 1915). I shall abbreviate this title to '*Möglichkeit.*'

2 See *Über Annahmen* II, pp. 80–3.

3 *Ibid.*, p. 85.

4 *Ibid.*, p. 86.

5 *Ibid.*, p. 87.

6 *Ibid.*, p. 88.

7 *Ibid.*, pp. 89–91.

8 *Ibid.*, p. 90.

9 *Ibid.*, pp. 91–2.

10 Thus Meinong, like many philosophers before and after him, is led to reject the Principle of the Excluded Middle in view of what is now often called the problem of future contingents. For some papers on this problem see *The Philosophy of Time*, edited by R. Gale (New York, 1967).

11 *Möglichkeit*, pp. 165–7.

12 *Ibid.*, pp. 168–9.

13 *Ibid.*, p. 169.

14 *Ibid.*, p. 171–3.

15 *Ibid.*, p. 179. I assume that Meinong has such complete objects as *a particular golden mountain* and *a particular round square* in mind. On this matter see our discussion of the apprehension of complete objects by means of incomplete ones a few pages from now.

16 *Ibid.*, p. 184.

17 Findlay, too, seems to be surprised about Meinong's inclusion of Brown among the incomplete objects. See the footnote on page 173 of his *Meinong's Theory of Objects and Values* (Oxford, 1963).

18 But Brown is, of course, identical with itself.

19 However, Meinong claims in a footnote that even though Brown is not brown, it may be, say, light. He admits, though, that this fact belongs to that unclarified chapter of the theory of entities which deals with properties of properties (*Möglichkeit*, p. 185, footnote).

20 *Möglichkeit*, pp. 185–6.

21 *Ibid.*, p. 188.

22 *Ibid.*, p. 189; my italics.

23 *Ibid.*, p. 194–201.

24 *Ibid.*, p. 204–5.

25 *Ibid.*, p. 207.

26 *Ibid.*, p. 210.

27 *Ibid.*, pp. 211–12.

28 Originally, we introduced the notation '<. . .>' in order to represent complexes of instances and of properties. $<F>$, of course, is not a complex in this original sense. Yet, it is an 'individual' rather than a relation, a property, or an objective, namely, an individual which *has* the property F. For this reason, I keep using the original notation, even though it is not, strictly speaking, correct in this case.

29 *Möglichkeit*, p. 213.

30 *Ibid.*, p. 216.

31 It should be noted that Meinong's view on possibility yields an explication of dispositions as 'permanent possibilities.' See, for example, *Möglichkeit*, p. 226.

32 *Ibid.*, pp. 263–8 and 276–85.

33 *Ibid.*, p. 283.

34 Nor is there a similar feature corresponding to existence (or any other mode of being). One can inspect a thing in order to find out whether

or not it has the property of being olive green, but one cannot inspect it in order to find out whether or not it has the characteristic of existence.

Appendix I

1 This is a translation of a part of Meinong's contribution to the book *Die Philosophie der Gegenwart in Selbstdarstellungen* (Leipzig, 1923). The part is entitled 'Zur Gegenstandstheorie.' Meinong's contribution to the book was written at the beginning of 1920, shortly before his death on November 27, 1920.

Meinong's terminology is at times rather idiosyncratic. I have, therefore, sometimes used his own Latin terms.

Appendix II

1 This is a translation of another part of Meinong's contribution to the *Philosophie der Gegenwart in Selbstdarstellungen*.

Index

Abstraction: and attention, 13 f; and color, 15 f; and concepts, 16; and incomplete objects, 175 ff; and the nominalism-realism issue, 13 ff; and predication, 125; and properties, 131; and properties of properties, 17 f; as source of universality, 13 f

Acts of comparison, and similarity between structures, 60

Allaire, E., 237

Ameseder, R., 235, 247; on being, 118 f, 227

Analytic judgments, and completed objects, 211 f

A posteriori knowledge, and real objects, 70 f

Apprehension: and assumptions, 186; and *Aussersein*, 182 ff, 186; and incomplete objects, 207 ff; and intentionality, 182 ff; and knowledge by description, 188; and main categories, 225 f; and meaning, 184; and non-existent objects, 185 f; and perception, 188 f; and predicative judgments, 187 f; and presentations, 183 f; and sense-impressions, 183; compared with knowledge, 182; four kinds of, 225; nature of, 184 f; of complete objects, 193, 210; of complexes, 197 f; of complex objects, 89 ff, 191 ff; of factuality, 200 ff; of objects in objectives, 102 f; of possibility, 204 f; of relations, 99 f, 197 f

A priori knowledge: and ideal relations, 46 f; and identity, 126 f; and mathematics, 171 f; and non-Euclidian geometry, 173 f; and predicative judgments, 125 ff; and relations, 23; and the theory of entities, 111, 225;

defined, 169; nature of, 122; of ideal objects, 70 f; of part-whole relation, 125 f

Aristotle, 249

Arithmetic, and experience, 171 ff

Association, 4, 22; as a real relation, 47; contrasted with conjunction, 17 f; contrasted with exemplification, 64 f

Assumptions: and apprehension, 186; and apprehension of complex objects, 92 f; and apprehension of relations, 68; and argument from negation, 79 ff; and conviction, 80; and dependent clauses, 85; and hypothetical judgments, 85; and meaning of sentences, 83 ff; and negative judgments, 88; and non-existent objects, 86 ff; and questions, 84; as expressed by sentences, 83 f; as source of intentionality, 86 f; involved in all conceptions, 89; stand between judgments and presentations, 79 f; unlimited freedom of, 160, 221

Attention: and abstraction, 13 f, 131; and apprehension of ideal objects, 71

Aussersein: and apprehension, 182 ff, 186; and fictional characters, 166; and the pure objects, 117 ff, 167; as a third mode of being, 106 f, 112 ff; explicated, 117 ff; of intentions, 56

Austin, J. L., 239

Auxiliary objects, 211 f

Barber, K., 237, 238, 239

Being: Ameseder on, 118 f; and incomplete objects, 214; as a matter of objectives, 118 f; as a third mode, 112; kinds of, 69 f, 227 f; not an object, 118 f; of incomplete objects,

255

General ideas: and common names, 41 f; and natures, 42 f; as indeterminate, 177

Geometry: and nonexistent objects, 162 ff; as knowledge *a priori*, 173 f

Gestalt theory, and complexes, 57 f

Greistorfer, K., 230

Grelling, K., 243

Hallucination, contrasted with perception, 123, 131 ff

Heijenoort, J. v., 240

Hempel, C. G., 243, 249

Hilbert, D., 251

Hochberg, H., 238, 243

Höfler, A., 232, 235

Hume, 231; and causality, 35; and relational view of space and time, 25

Husserl, E., 237, 238, 240, 241, 243, 247, 248, 249, 250, 252; and complete objects, 213; and distinction between act, content, and object, 47; and existence of contents, 55; and idealism, 216; and instances of properties, 6; and theory of entities, 106; on abstraction, 14; on apprehension of complexes, 191 f; on descriptions, 196; on presentations, 197

Ideal objects: apprehension of, 70 f; are known *a priori*, 70 f; are not perceivable, 70 f, 129 f; subsist, 69

Ideal relations, are known *a priori*, 46 f

Ideas: and descriptions, 51 f; and other contents, 197; as contents of presentations, 55; general *vs* abstract, 13 f; identified with concepts, 16; of complex entities, 75 f, 197 f; of instances, 14; of relations, 47; properties of, 54; relations between them, 23 f

Identity: and *a priori* knowledge, 126 f; and descriptions, 38 ff; and substitutivity, 39 f; arguments against, 36 ff; contrasted with equality, 25; distinguished from equivalence, 140; Frege on, 38 f; of intentions, 40 f; Russell on, 37; Wittgenstein on, 38

Imagination: and different kinds of laws, 33 ff; and fictional characters, 165 f; and necessity, 33 ff; and synthetic *a priori*, 33 f

Immanent object, Brentano's notion of, 53

Impossibility, two kinds of, 204

Impossible entities, as homeless entities, 158, 174

Incompatibility: and causality, 35; as ideal relation, 27 ff, 46; as relation between objectives, 30

Incomplete objectives, and incomplete objects, 206

Incomplete objects: and abstraction, 175; and concepts, 175 ff; and contents, 196 f; and descriptions, 195 f; and incomplete objectives, 206; and indefinite descriptions, 177 f; and individual things, 180; and natures, 177 f; and nominalism, 180 f; and pseudo-being, 214 f; and pseudo-so-being, 217 f; and representationalism, 215 f; as involved in complete objects, 214 f; as natures, 43; being of, 206 ff; compared with properties, 179 f; contrasted with complete objects, 226; contrasted with individual things, 220; contrasted with properties, 220; their role in apprehension, 193, 207 ff

Indefinite descriptions, and incomplete objects, 177 f

Independence: and thinghood, 11 f; of being from so-being, 159 ff

Indeterminate object, *see* incomplete object

Individual things: and incomplete objects, 180; and relations, 25; as extensions of concepts, 18 f; as independent entities, 11 f; contrasted with complexes, 168, 194; contrasted with incomplete objects, 220; form a category, 4

Individuation: and natures, 42 f; and places and moments, 11 ff; of mental entities, 13, 44; problem of, 8 f

Induction: and mathematical knowledge, 171; and synthetic *a priori* knowledge, 28 ff

Instances: and abstraction, 13 f; and intuitions, 10; and nominalism, 5 f; and predicative judgments, 94 f; and the dogma of localization, 10; as a category, 10, 57; as complete objects, 206; as foundations of relations, 24 f; as independent entities, 11 f; compared with places and moments, 12; contrasted with properties, 130 f, 206; ideas of, 14; Meinong's argument for, 6; of colors, 139 f; of properties, 5; of relations, 100 f

Intentionality: and dispositions, 86; and apprehension of wholes, 193 f; as characteristic of the mental, 157 f; as pertaining to the content, 93; based on assumptions, 86 f; expli-

Intentionality—*cont.*
cated in terms of apprehension, 182 ff
Intentional relation: and contents, 55 f;
and non-existent objects, 85 f; and
objectless ideas, 108 f; as similar
to the part-whole relation, 113;
contrasted with part-whole relation,
43 f; existence of its terms, 109 f;
is an ideal relation, 90 f; nature of,
109
Intentions: and affirmative, evident
judgments, 85; and contents, 197;
and descriptions, 51 f; distinguished
from contents, 48 ff; identity of,
40 f; of complex ideas, 75 f, 90 f; of
general ideas, 41 f; of ideas, 17; of
mental acts, 18; primary *vs* secondary,
92; theory of, 107, 111
Introspection, of presentations, 151 ff
Intuitions: and instances, 10 f; and
negation, 89; contrasted with concepts, 18, 88 ff; *see also* presentations

Jessop, T. E., 237
Judgments: as expressed by sentences,
84; based on presentations, 86;
Brentano on, 49, 94; consist of affirmation or denial, 79; distinguished
from perception, 129; distinguished
from presentations, 79; hypothetical,
85; intend objectives, 95 f; involve
conviction, 79 f; Kant on, 78; not
based on presentations, 97; of different levels, 97; of perception, 123 ff;
of second level, 202 f; position of,
79 f; their intentions, 78 f

Kant, 231; and instances, 10 f; and
intuitions, 10 f; and judgments, 78
Kerry, B., 246; and the distinction
between content and object, 52, 54;
on object-less ideas, 107
Klemke, E. D., 243
Kluge, W., 251
Knowledge: about entities without
being, 156; and empirical concepts,
170 f; and induction, 171; and non-
Euclidian geometry, 173 f; and
representationalism, 136 f; by
acquaintance and by description,
188; characterized by evidence, 134 f;
contrasted with direct acquaintance,
136 f; deals with entities in general,
224; objects of, 224; of external
world, 121
Konvalina, L., 230

Labels, contrasted with descriptions,
38 f, 127 f

Landmann-Kalischer, E., on evidence,
134 f
Laws: and accidental generalities, 32;
and imagination, 33 ff; and necessity,
30; as the basis for necessity, 31 ff
Leibniz, and relations, 21; his principle,
52
Levi, I., 246
Lipps, Th., 250; on fictional characters,
165
Localization: and perception, 130 f;
dogma of, 10 f
Locke, 2, 237; and relational view of
space and time, 25; and relations, 22;
and the indeterminate triangle, 73;
on primary and secondary qualities,
142 f
Logic: as part of the theory of entities,
224; nature of, 175
Lorenz, O., 230
Luce, A. A., 237

Mach, E., 242, 250; on the objects of
geometry, 162
Mally, E., 235
Many-valued logic, and possible objectives, 205 f
Martinak, E., 232, 235
Marty, A., on the temporal status of
objectives, 103 f
Maxwell, G., 248
Meaning: and apprehension, 184; and
assumptions, 83 ff; and entities, 224;
as the object of presentations, 56;
of words, 56, 83; Twardowski on,
83
Menger, C., 231
Mental activity: and apprehension of
ideal objects, 70 f; and ideal relations,
45; and ideas of relations, 47; and
relations, 22 f; as source of ideas,
97; in introspection, 154
Mental acts: and intentionality, 157 f;
argument against, 152 f; as complexes, 56; different kinds of, 84;
introspection of, 152 f; of perception,
129
Messer, A., 242
Metaphysics, part of the theory of
entities, 225
Modal feature, and factuality, 221 f
Modalities: and objectives, 105; kinds
of, 228; ontological status of, 31 ff
Moore, G. E., ix, 238, 242, 243, 251,
252; and complete objects, 213; on
existence of contents, 55; on necessity, 169; on perception of complex
objects, 191 f

INDEX

Natures: and *a priori* knowledge, 122; and complexes, 167; and individuation, 42 f; as incomplete objects, 43, 177 f; as intentions of general ideas, 42 f; *see also* incomplete objects

Necessity: and causality, 35 f; and certainty, 32 ff; and entailment, 170; and evidence, 30; and imagination, 33 ff; and different kinds of laws, 30; and negation, 81; and rational evidence, 204; and sense-dimensions, 33 f; as feature of objectives, 35; as relation between objectives, 169 f; explicated, 31 ff; Frege's explication, 31; kinds of, 31; of objectives, 105

Negation: and argument for assumptions, 79 ff; and complexes, 81 f; and conception, 89; and exemplification, 82; and necessity, 81; and objectives, 227; as constituent of state of affairs, 80; different views on, 81 f; Frege on, 81; its ontological status, 81 f; not a matter of intuition, 89; not a matter of presentation, 80 f

Negative judgments, and assumptions, 88

Negative properties, 81 f

Nominalism: and abstraction, 13 ff; and incomplete objects, 180 f; and instances, 5 f; contrasted with realism, 1 ff

Non-being, as a positive entity, 227

Non-Euclidian geometry, and rational knowledge, 173 f

Non-existent objects: and apprehension, 185 f; and assumptions, 86 ff; and factual objectives, 168 f; and intentional relation, 85 f; and predicative judgments, 161 ff; and presentations, 53 f; as intentions, 107 ff; properties of, 50, 107 ff, 164 ff; Russell on, 114 ff

Noumenal properties: as isomorphic to phenomenal ones, 146 f; their apprehension, 146

Numbers: and theory of entities, 111; as objects of higher order, 65 f; as projectible to noumenal world, 148

Objectives: and incompatibility, 30; and necessity, 169 f; and Principle of Excluded Middle, 205 ff; as homeless entities, 160; as indirectly presented, 137; as presented by judgments, 97; as represented by sentences, 103; as subsistents, 96 f, 103; as timeless, 103 f; distinguished from objects, 96; form category, 98; identified with relations, 99; kinds of, 105, 113, 227 f;

modal properties of, 105; nature of their being, 120; of being, 189; relations between them, 105

Objects: as constituents of objectives, 102; as the meaning of words, 56; contrasted with concepts, 18; distinguished from contents, 48 ff; distinguished from objectives, 96; kinds of, 225 f; no negative ones, 80 ff; properties of, 54; real *vs* ideal, 69 ff; *see also* intentions

Oelzelt-Newin, A., 232

Oppenheim, P., 243, 249

Part-whole relation: and argument for instances, 6 f; as a founding relation, 62 f; compared with intentional relation, 113; contrasted with exemplification, 2, 62 f, 161 f; knowledge of, 125 f

Perception: analysis of, 149 f; and apprehension, 188 f; and hallucination, 123; and ideal objects, 129 f; and properties, 130 f; and sense-impressions, 129 f; and verbal expressions, 127; as *a posteriori* knowledge, 122; as irreducible, 129; causes of, 132; contains existential judgment, 123 ff; definition of, 138; distinguished from judgment, 129; does not involve predication, 123 ff; nature of, 123 ff; of colors, 139 ff; of real objects, 70 f, 226; of wholes, 191 f

Perceptual judgments, and non-existent objects, 128 f

Perceptual objects: and places, 12 f; as complexes, 4; as complexes of properties, 2 ff; as individuals, 2; as structures of particles, 141 f

Phenomenology, compared with the theory of entities, 47, 106

Pichler, H., 235

Places: as parts of complexes, 72 ff; compared with spatial points, 73

Popkin, R., 248

Possibility: and factuality, 203 f; and incomplete objectives, 206; and Principle of Excluded Middle, 205 ff; and pseudo-being, 216 f; and pseudo-so-being, 217 f; and surmise, 204; apprehension of, 204; as the basis of probability, 220; explicated, 31 ff, 218 f

Possible objectives, and many-valued logic, 205 f

Predicative judgments: about non-existent objects, 156, 161 ff; analysis of, 94 f; 125 ff; and apprehension,

260